*5 Steps to ALTERing Your Attitude
About Health, Money, and Relationships*

REAL LIFE
MANAGEMENT

REAL LIFE

WAYNE E. NANCE
with WILLIAM HENDRICKS and J. KEET LEWIS

Originally published as *Thin, Rich, and Happy*

A Fireside Book
Published by Simon & Schuster
New York   London   Toronto   Sydney

FIRESIDE
A Division of Simon & Schuster, Inc.
1230 Avenue of the Americas
New York, NY 10020

First Fireside trade paperback edition January 2008

FIRESIDE and colophon are registered trademarks of Simon and Schuster, Inc.

For information regarding special discounts for bulk purchases, please contact
Simon & Schuster Special Sales at 1-800-456-6798 or business@simonandschuster.com.

Designed by William Ruoto

Manufactured in the United States of America

10 9 8 7 6 5 4 3 2 1

The Library of Congress has cataloged the hardcover edition as follows:
    Nance, Wayne E.
        Thin, rich, and happy : take 3 minutes to start your new life / Wayne E. Nance
with William Hendricks & J. Keet Lewis.
            p.   cm.
        "A Fireside book."
        Includes bibliographical references and index.
        1. Conduct of life 2. Weight loss. 3. Finance, Personal. 4. Happiness.
I. Hendricks, William. II. Lewis, J. Keet. III. Title.
BF637.C5 N36 2007   2006052133
158.1—dc22

ISBN-13: 978-0-7432-8937-5
ISBN-10:   0-7432-8937-4
ISBN-13: 978-0-7432-8939-9 (pbk)
ISBN-10:   0-7432-8939-0 (pbk)

Originally published as *Thin, Rich, and Happy* in 2007 by Fireside

This book is dedicated to all the people who are struggling with weight, money, and/or relationship issues. I have lived with all three of these challenges at one time or another in my life, and I know all too well the loneliness—even hopelessness—that one can feel in the midst of these battles. This book is meant to bring good news and hope to anyone fighting the good fight.

CONTENTS

INTRODUCTION A Crisis in America

I want you to let your mind indulge in a little bit of fantasy for a moment. Imagine yourself in a very successful career. You're making quite a bit of money—well into six figures. You've got a gorgeous 6,000-square-foot home with a fancy pool and a waterfall in the backyard. Parked in your three-car garage is an imposing Mercedes-Benz sedan. On your wrist is an enormous Rolex watch, the one with all the diamonds on it that dazzles everyone who sees it. Sound like a life you'd care to have?

It did to me. It's the American Dream, after all. And in 1984, I had that dream and more. I was the kid from the poor side of the tracks who had raised himself up by his bootstraps, got a good education, went to the big city, worked hard, and eventually met with success.

And you know what? There's not a thing wrong with that. If that picture is similar to a dream you've always had, or a dream you've actually attained, I say, "Great! Don't give up on that dream. Keep that dream alive."

But know this: if you had seen me living that dream in 1984, you'd have said, "Wayne Nance has the perfect life." But you'd have been dead wrong! Because the truth is, my life was out of control. Meaning that I was making bad decisions that created serious long-term consequences for my happiness, health, wealth, and family.

Do you ever feel as if your world is spinning out of control? A lot of us do in the post-9/11 world, with the economic downturn that followed, the disaster of the stock market and the loss of many people's retirement funds, the ever-present threat of terrorist attacks, the downsizing of companies and the offshoring of American jobs, the erosion of values as corporate scandals have come to light, and so many other things that make us worry about the future.

Those are serious matters, for sure. But did you know that there's a crisis in America that actually affects more people on a practical, daily basis than any of those "world-class" headline-grabbers? It's a crisis that shows up all over the place but can be seen most graphically in three areas that all of us deal with every day: the lifestyle issues of food, money, and relationships. To put it bluntly, way too many Americans are fat, broke, and unhappy at home and at work. Consider:

- 67 percent of Americans are estimated to be overweight or obese by Centers for Disease Control (CDC) standards.
- 85 percent of Americans will retire with Social Security benefits as their only means of support. In other words, they're *broke*.
- 51 percent of Americans are *divorced*. Many others remain in marriages that might be called "psychological divorce."

Clearly, something's wrong in America! Especially if you overlay those numbers on top of each other. Just imagine three pie charts showing the 67 percent of Americans who are overweight, the 85 percent who will retire virtually broke, and the 51 percent who are divorced. Stack them on top of one another, and what do you see? That a lot of Americans are all three—fat, broke, *and* unhappy in their relationships. But that's not the worst of it. The saddest thing is that many people struggling with one, two, or even all three of these problems don't even think they have a problem! Take obesity, for example. A 2004 Associated Press poll found that six people out of ten who qualified as overweight by government standards said their weight was just fine—healthy, even.

Or consider this observation from the national sales manager of a company that helps small businesses and individuals facing bankruptcy work out settlements with their creditors: "From personal experience, I see that as people get further into debt . . . they start making short-term decisions and don't prioritize their debt correctly. Eventually, they start feeling overwhelmed, give up and go into denial."[1]

What happens when someone goes into denial about their debt? They go deeper in debt. They may also start eating. Indeed, *The Toque,* a satirical Canadian website, imagines a VISA card issued by McDonald's called (you guessed it) the McVISA. The idea is that people will be more likely to eat at McDonald's if they can charge their Big Macs.

With that premise, the site invents twenty-two-year-old Josie Amblin, a student who uses her McVISA card *at least ten times a week*! "I can't stop," she confesses to a fictitious reporter. "It's just so easy to purchase a burger and fries with credit. I know I can't afford to eat at McDonald's this often, but I can't help myself!"

Amblin racks up $2,100 on her McVISA card, even though it only has a $1,500 credit limit.[2]

The whole story is a spoof, of course. But it hits the nail on the head. "I can't stop! I can't help myself!" That's the cry of someone whose lifestyle is out of control. Someone who is making bad choices that will create serious long-term consequences for their happiness, health, wealth, and family.

In 1978, I was a poster child for being out of control in all three of the lifestyle areas I've mentioned. I weighed 315 pounds (that's fat, by the way, even if you're six feet, one inch tall). I was a financial advisor, but I had five credit cards maxed out. And at home, my wife, Shannon, wasn't exactly happy with me because she and my daughter never saw me because I was too busy making money for the family. At least that's what I always told them (and myself): "I have to work this hard to provide for our family." Yeah, right!

I was in total denial. I was caught up in a crisis that I didn't even see. I was succeeding and making lots of money, and by society's standards I was doing just fine. Only I wasn't doing fine. You're not doing fine when you can't bend over and tie your shoes without being out of breath. You're not doing fine if you're giving great financial advice to other people, but your own financial condition is a house of cards just waiting to collapse. You're not doing fine if you never spend time with your family because you've got to keep one step ahead of the hounds that are chasing you.

Because I didn't have any boundaries, I let other people's opinions determine my opinion of myself. I looked fine to them, so I thought everything about me was fine, too. But it wasn't. My life was out of control.

Some people hit bottom and then finally wake up. I had to hit bottom *three times* before I woke up! (I've always known I was a slow learner.) The first wake-up call came in 1978, when I was twenty-eight years old, with a beautiful wife, a one-year-old daughter, and another baby on the way. I was just at the point when a young man should be enjoying life to the full. Instead, my doctor was warning me that if I didn't stop eating, I'd never see my fortieth birthday. Was that what caused me to change my ways? No! Guess what I did when I left his office? I headed straight across the street to a pancake house. I'm not kidding! And I charged the meal on a credit card. (You see, I *do* understand someone like Amblin!)

So what was my first wake-up call? It happened during my annual visit to the "Big Men's" store. I was packing on so much weight that every year I needed new clothes—in the next larger size. You can imagine how embarrassing it was to make that trip. So it became my style to shift attention (and blame) away from myself by complaining about the clothing manufacturers in Asia and how they were cutting their styles too small, or to joke that my wife was shrinking my clothes in the washer.

But on one trip, when I started mouthing off, the old tailor spoke up. For ten years he had listened to my bull and said nothing. This time around he had had enough. He was getting ready to retire, so what did he care? Right there in front of my wife, he turned to me and said, "It's not your wife or the Taiwanese, pal. If you weren't such a fat slob, you wouldn't have a problem!"

I was stunned. I'd never been so insulted in my life. How dare he! Boy, was I ever mad! So I showed him. Why, I walked right out of that store without buying so much as a dime of new clothing!

But in truth, that guy did me a favor. Because what he said was true. And it hit home. I was fat. Overweight. Obese. Whatever you want to call it, it doesn't matter. What matters is that I finally faced up to a cold, hard reality: my weight was out of control.

At some level I'd known that for years. But I had been in denial about it for years, too, really since I was a boy. You see, I come from a dysfunctional family on the outskirts of Houston, Texas ("dysfunctional" means you can get away with anything if you'll just deny reality). Our family was the kind where Momma cooked everything in bacon grease. And if somebody didn't have a third helping of pie for dessert, she'd feel totally offended. But guess what? In spite of Momma's cooking there wasn't a single "fat" person in the family. No, sir! We weren't fat, we were just "big-boned." That extra 50 or 60 or 90 or 100 pounds everyone was carrying was just the result of a "slow metabolism." Just a "large thyroid." And so Momma always told me that being fat just runs in our family. We had that "fat gene" going, don't you know? (You see how denial starts early?)

With a background like that, it's no surprise that early on I became the fat kid. Eventually, the fat kid grew up to be the fat man. Only I wouldn't admit that I was a fat man. I had all kinds of excuses to say I wasn't. I was in total denial. "Justifiable denialism" is what I call it. I lied to myself to justify my poor decisions. But the scales don't lie, and your waist doesn't lie, and your health doesn't lie. And by the time I was twenty-eight I was getting sick and feeling tired. And to be honest, I was sick and tired of being sick and tired.

So I did what almost everyone does when they finally accept the truth that they're carrying too much weight: I went on a diet. In fact, I went on lots of diets. The grapefruit diet. The water diet. The low-carb diet. The six-meals-a-day diet. You name it, I tried it.

Sure enough, I lost weight. And gained it back. So I'd go on another diet, and lose weight. And then after I'd lost the weight, I'd quit the diet and I'd gain the weight back. Plus a little bit more. So I'd go on another diet, and lose the weight again. And then . . . well, you get the picture.

One diet I followed was Dr. Atkins's first diet. He had two of them over the years. I tried the first one. He said if you ate about as much cheese and eggs and red meat as there are in the state of Texas, you'll lose weight. I tried that and I did lose weight. I lost about forty or fifty pounds, and pretty quickly. But then I was diagnosed with a fissure tear in my colon, because I wasn't eating any fiber or carbohydrates.

Surgery laid me up for a month. And while I lay in that bed, I said to myself, "If I ever stop bleeding and get out of this bed, I'm going to learn something about nutrition," because I had never learned anything about it in school. I had been an athlete, but in my day the people in charge just said, "Eat chicken-fried steak, Wayne. You need something that'll stick to your ribs. Don't worry about the gravy. You'll run it off." I knew nothing about nutrition, food supplements, or how to balance my diet.

So when I got well, a friend told me about a book by Covert Bailey titled, *Fit or Fat?* Boy, was that a lucky break! Bailey had a great concept: fat makes you fat. That was in 1979. Amazing, isn't it? Fat makes you fat. When I read that, I realized that about 98 percent of what I was eating contained fat. I also discovered that when I wasn't eating fatty foods, I was eating Oreos and chocolate milk and stuff that was loaded with sugar.

Bailey opened my eyes to a lot, and I was shocked to learn how much I didn't know about nutrition. After that, I couldn't learn enough about it. I got really serious about what I ate, and I lost more than a hundred pounds over a two-and-a-half-year period. All of a sudden I was the new thin guy. The 205-pound guy instead of the 315-pound guy.

So I'd gotten my life under control, right? Not exactly. I was only focusing on my weight. My spending was still out of control. Which means my work habits were out of control. At 205 pounds I wasn't spending any more time with my family than when I'd weighed 315. I'd gone from being a big, fat, broke man with a lot of stress and an unhappy family to a thinner broke man with a lot of stress and an unhappy family.

Fast forward to 1984. By then, as I've said, I was making quite a bit of money. I had the house, the car, the watch, the American Dream. I sincerely thought I had it made. And I was thinner, too.

And yet . . . what difference does it make if you live to be one hundred if you're miserable? I was miserable. I went through tremendous mood swings and depression. I thought, "How can I be depressed when I've got it all?"

About that time I went on a trip to Philadelphia. I was now in insurance, and a very large insurance company wanted to honor me as one of its top ten salespeople in the country. Quite an honor! As I was riding on the bus from the airport to the hotel, we stopped at a red light downtown. I looked over and saw a big Catholic church. Suddenly tears started coming down my cheeks. I felt terribly sad. "I really don't want to go to that hotel," I was thinking. "I just don't want to go. I don't want to be honored. I don't want anybody giving me an award for being a guy that's a workaholic who never sees his family, who just focuses on his money, his Mercedes, and himself. I feel very fake. I don't feel good about this at all."

But soon I was dropped off at the hotel. Sure enough, I had my big private suite, all decked out with a complimentary fruit basket and a bottle of champagne. That was kind of cruel in a way, because I didn't have Shannon there to enjoy it with me. The fact is, she had declined to come to the convention. She didn't like being with me at that point in my life, because I was pretty much a jerk.

So there I was, the big shot in his big fancy room—all by his lonesome for a whole week. And boy, was I lonesome! So one day, right in the middle of the convention, I walked out of that hotel and went and found that Catholic church. I'm not Catholic, but I went inside and ducked into a pew and got down on my knees, and I cried out to God: "Help me understand why I'm so miserable!"

I didn't really know what to expect. Nothing happened right away. I finished the convention, collected my award, and went home. About a week later, Shannon told me that our girls' elementary school was having an open house, and she wanted me to go and meet their teachers. I was still feeling kind of depressed, so I said I didn't want to meet any teachers. But for some reason I relented and went anyway.

My older daughter's fourth-grade teacher had asked the students to make posters in answer to the question, "If you could have three things in your life, what would you want?" I looked carefully at the artwork arrayed on the bulletin board. Of the thirty-two kids in that class, twenty-six of them had drawn as the top three things they wanted out of life: more money, a sports car, and a big house.

Suddenly a light went off in my head. It was my second wake-up call. I thought about those posters all the way home—driving in our Mercedes-Benz to our six-thousand-square-foot home, driving past the other six-thousand-square-foot homes in our subdivision, each with a Mercedes-Benz or sports car in its three-car garage. By the time we arrived I had clarified my thinking. "You know what?" I told Shannon. "I'm miserable. I'm miserable because I'm trying to keep up with the Joneses, and I never wanted to be a Jones to start with. The worst of it is that we're sending that message to our kids, and it's the wrong message."

Within a year of that night, we sold the house, got a smaller house in a different neighborhood, I traded in the Mercedes for a pickup, started wearing cutoffs, and got a Mickey Mouse watch made of plastic. I said to myself, "I don't know where I'm going from here, but I'm going to refocus." And in that way I came to grips with the fact that my financial lifestyle was out of control, and I needed to start dealing with the money issue, just as I'd worked on the weight issue.

But I wasn't out of the woods yet. Far from it. In 1992 Shannon and I hit rock bottom in our marriage. Remember, I'd been in denial for years thinking that if I just provided a nice lifestyle for my family, they'd think I was great. Sure, we'd downscaled to a more modest home and all, but I was still providing well for my family.

But one day Shannon finally decided to cut to the truth. "Wayne, you're basically a jerk," she said. You can see that people sometimes have to shoot pretty straight in order for me to "get" what they're saying.

At first I felt terribly defensive. "Look at all I've done for you!" I thought to myself. "Look at all I've provided for us! Just look at all I've managed to accomplish in my life! Why, don't you realize you're talking to Wayne Nance here?"

But she was firm and clear: "I hate to tell you, Wayne, but you're just a jerk. I don't like you. And I hate to tell you the truth, but your kids don't like you very much, either."

That was yet a third wake-up call. Somehow the thought that the four people I cared about most in this world didn't like me very much got my attention. "This isn't working well," I thought. "I started out fat, and I fixed some of that. Then I started chasing money, and I fixed some of that. Yet now my family doesn't like me very much. I think I better take a long, hard look at myself."

So I did. I went for counseling and had a lot of discussions over a long period of time. I came to grips with the fact that life is complicated. You can fix one thing about yourself, but that may only lead to problems with other things. The real question is, *what's driving your behavior?* What's the underlying thing that's creating all the surface problems you're trying to fix? That core thing is what you've got to go after.

It was at that point that I encountered a powerful truth: there is more to managing one's lifestyle than merely making "right" choices. You see, almost all the diets, budgets, relationship books, and other lifestyle advice I had gotten said that if I just made the "right" choices, everything would work out. Just eat less fat. Just stay within a budget. Just tell your wife you love her more. Just show up at your kid's soccer game. Just count to five when the annoying person at the office pushes your buttons. Those were all the "right" choices. Do those and you'll get your life under control.

Problem is, I'd made a lot of those "right" choices. But my life still was not working. Worse yet, I was having to put enormous energy into making "right" choices. So much energy, in fact, that if I let my guard down for an instant, or if I felt tired or down or angry or whatever, I'd just blow off my resolve and do it the old way— order that extra meat patty and the double fries, buy that tie that cost twice what I intended to pay, take on that extra speaking engagement even though I'd promised Shannon I'd be home that weekend. Clearly, something else was contributing to my behavior besides making "right" choices, important as those were.

That's when I encountered this breakthrough truth, the truth that allowed me to start getting my life under control: *most of what causes us to make the lifestyle decisions we make is not our choices, but our attitude and our beliefs.* By *attitude* I mean the inborn "wiring" that we brought with us into the world. Our attitude has to do with our basic outlook or orientation toward life, what we focus on, what matters to us, what we put our energy into. Attitude makes the biggest difference in our behavior. Later in the book I'll take you through a simple 3-Minute Survey that will show you your attitude, and I'll tell you where you can get more information about your "hardwiring."

When I learned that the core of my lifestyle problems was my attitude, I started on a journey that continues to this day. I wondered, "Am I the only person in America who is struggling with food, money, and relationships?" What I discovered shocked me.

I began going to health spas and fitness centers, where I traded speaking and training for the opportunity to interview spa participants. That gave me lots of firsthand data about the issues people really struggle with.

I found that *millions* of Americans are in crisis in those three areas. In addition, I discovered that there is a link among those three issues—obesity, debt, and divorce. The link is people's underlying attitudes. I discovered that *certain attitudes are especially at-risk for obesity, debt, and divorce.* In other words, many of the same people who struggle with their weight and other health issues struggle with their money and related financial issues, and also struggle with their relationships, both at home and at work. They struggle because of their attitudes. And sadly, they don't even realize that their attitudes are leading to self-defeating and self-destructive behaviors!

Would you like to know whether you (or someone you care about) are one of those people? Better yet, would you like to know how you can regain control over your lifestyle, no matter what your wiring may be? This book will help you do that.

First it will help you understand your attitude and how it affects everything you do and every decision you make. Then it will take you through the same five-step plan that helped me lose more than a hundred pounds and keep the weight off for more than fifteen years. The same plan that helped me pay off my five credit cards, so that today Shannon and I live debt-free. The same plan that has allowed Shannon and me to stay married—and increasingly happy—for thirty-one years.

Now let me point out that I have not written this book on my own. This is a joint venture between me and my co-authors, Bill

Hendricks and Keet Lewis. We decided that we would write the book from my perspective, using the first-person singular ("I," "me," "my"). But rest assured that this book expresses a common understanding among three partners. Indeed, Bill and Keet will tell you that they, too, have felt out of control at various times in their lives. They use this program daily to better manage their lives and businesses.

Bill understands the challenge of keeping life in balance, having lost his wife to breast cancer several years ago, and single-parenting his three daughters in their adolescent and teen years. Meanwhile he has headed a consulting practice that uses the phenomenon of giftedness to work with businesses, nonprofits, and churches to manage their strategic "people issues," and with individuals seeking career guidance.

Keet has an extensive background in managing companies spanning several industries. Today he is a busy entrepreneur with a variety of business and charitable activities. He teaches the concepts in this book in his consulting work with companies, schools, and religious organizations. Like me, he has struggled at times with his weight and finances, and he has personally witnessed the success of our program.

Others have also contributed to the ideas presented in this book. I've mentioned Covert Bailey's influence on me. Keet first learned about attitudes from his friend, Zig Ziglar, who taught him that attitude is everything. As Zig so aptly puts it in his foundational work, *See You At the Top* "Your attitude determines your altitude," and that "we can Alter our lives by Altering our Attitudes."

Keet began his personal dedication to understanding behavioral science when, as the CEO of a manufacturing company, he studied and applied the principles relating to temperament as explained by bestselling author Dr. Tim LaHaye in his classic work, *Why You Act the Way You Do*. Dr. LaHaye wrote many other books on temperament, and they are a must read for any serious student of the subject. Additionally, Dr. James Dobson, Dr. John C. Maxwell, Dr. Steve Farrar, Dr. Howard Hendricks, Dr. Bill Bright, Josh McDowell, Dennis and Barbara Rainey, Dr. Tony Evans, Rich DeVos, and Dr. Ron Jenson have all contributed much to our understanding of lifestyle issues like parenting, personal responsibility, and leadership through their very insightful writings. All of them have helped to lay a foundation for our work at Real Life Management.

Keet, Bill, and I hope that this book will be a helpful complement to the work of people like Bailey, Ziglar, LaHaye, Dobson, Maxwell, Rainey Jenson, and others who have pioneered in the field of attitude and lifestyle management. Above all, we want this book to offer hope.

If I was able to regain some control of my life, you can do the same, no matter how desperate you feel your life has become. I've helped countless people just like you over the years through my training workshops and seminars at corporations, health spas, financial planning firms, universities, churches, and many other settings. Almost all of the folks I've met have tried way too many of the quick-fix diet, budget, and relationship gimmicks on the market. Most of them were discouraged. A lot of them were desperate. Some had even given up. "I'll never change!" they said. If that's how you feel, I implore you to keep reading. Because I'm not going to ask you to change.

You read that right. I'm not going to ask you to change. The word "change" implies that you need to make a 180-degree turnaround and basically become someone other than who you are. I'll never ask you to do that. God wired you the way you are, and I'm fine with that. I want you to be fine with that, too. *You are just fine the way you are!* But I know you're not happy with the way you *live.* So come on inside this book with me, because I've got a proven strategy to help you turn your life around.

CHAPTER 1 # Why Quick-Fix Schemes Never Work

I was speaking to a group of women at a wellness spa near Nashville, Tennessee. The spa had asked me to present a seminar on "foodaholism," the idea that food has become one of the worst addictions in the United States today.

"Any of ya'll struggle with that?" I asked.

A wave of nervous snickers rippled across the room and finally broke into open laughter as the women turned to each other with looks that seemed to say things like, "Oh, yeah!" and, "I can't believe he asked that!"

It *was* a rather pointed question, since not one of those women weighed less than two hundred pounds, and a few weighed considerably more. That wouldn't have been a problem necessarily, except that a number of them couldn't have been more than 5'2" or 5'4" tall.

Aware that their laughter was really a sign of embarrassment, I eased the tension the way I often do, by poking some fun at myself and letting them know I could personally relate to their situation.

"When I was growing up I was always known as the fat kid. You know how that works. Somebody would ask who Wayne Nance was, and people would say, 'Oh, he's the fat kid,' and the person would immediately nod, because then he'd know exactly whom they were talking about.

"I was the fat kid, but I didn't think anything of it because Momma kept telling me I wasn't fat, I was just 'big-boned.' Years later, I learned a lot about the physiology of the human body, especially as it relates to weight control. And you know what I discovered? Bones don't weigh 315 pounds. If you stacked all the bones in my body on a scale—just the bones, without the rest of me—they'd probably add up to about 30 pounds. That's it! Which means if I weighed 315 pounds (which I did at one point in my life), 285 pounds of that must be something besides bones."

A number of the women laughed and rolled their eyes at that point. Clearly they had heard similar excuses from their mothers.

Next, I tackled my Momma's argument that my thyroid was underactive. Maybe that's why I carried so much weight. I could tell that the women listening had heard that line before, too. "The truth," I explained, "is that folks who have hypothyroidism—a genetic malfunction that causes the thyroid gland to not produce enough hormones, thereby slowing down one's metabolism—make up less than 1 percent of the population."

"Less than 1 percent," I emphasized, "and yet 67 percent of adults in America are overweight. As a recovering fat man, I can assure you that I didn't have a slow metabolism. I mean, I could eat two double cheeseburgers with the super fries and milk shake, and I'd be hungry again in just a couple of hours. My body would burn right through those calories! Yes, sir, there were a lot of things slow about me in those days, but my metabolism wasn't one of them."

The point of my self-directed humor was not to be cruel, but to be honest. I wanted to help those women take a candid look at a problem they had struggled with their whole lives—the problem of their weight. Specifically, the problem of too much weight.

Now I realize that for some readers, weight may not be your issue. But if not, there's a good chance that debt and/or problems in your relationships are. So as you read this chapter, don't think that it doesn't apply to you just because it's an illustration about obesity. I could just as easily have told a story about people struggling with their finances or their relationships. All three areas—

weight, money, relationships—are profoundly affected by a person's underlying attitudes.

For instance, just as too much weight was killing those women at the health spa, too much debt could be killing you. Are you aware of that? According to Dr. Edward Charlesworth, an expert on stress, money is the leading cause of stress in America. No surprise there. Recall that in the Introduction I pointed out that 85 percent of Americans will retire broke. How much stress do you suppose that creates, and will create? In turn, stress is a leading factor for cancer, heart disease, and many other illnesses. Indeed, many experts believe that stress is the number one cause of death in the United States today. Money issues (especially debt) are the leading cause of that stress. Bottom line: debt is every bit as deadly as obesity.

Let's go back to the ladies at the health spa. As I got into the main content of what I had to tell them, they were listening carefully and asking great questions. I was so encouraged! They seemed grateful that someone was finally shooting straight with them. And they were really starting to "get" what I was saying about how quick-fix diets and rapid-loss weight programs are not the way to lose weight and stay healthy because . . .

Suddenly, right in the middle of my talk, one lady whose name tag read "Ginny" shot up her hand and blurted out, "Mr. Nance, look, I've tried everything you're talking about and then some. I've tried every single diet you've mentioned, and even a few you haven't. I've bought no end of fitness equipment off the TV. I've joined a different health club every January for the past seven years. None of it has worked for me!" Ginny had a surly look on her face, and I could tell she wasn't buying a word of what I was saying.

Actually, that had been apparent from the get-go. During the entire first thirty minutes of my presentation, Ginny had sat stone-faced, slumped in her chair, arms folded tight. She looked as if she were daring me to make her smile. Believe me, I tried! But it was like blasting granite. Her whole body language—all 5'3" and 230 pounds of it—sort of taunted me to prove something to her. But nothing I said seemed to reach her. So I wasn't surprised when she challenged me. Clearly, Ginny wasn't enjoying the afternoon. Clearly, she was not a very happy person.

In fact, Ginny struck me as a defeated person—like so many overweight people I've met (as well as broke and divorced people, and unhappily married people). They've heard it all. The pitch for the nutritional supplement that will cut their weight by two-thirds, give them the energy of a triathlete, and make them irresistibly attractive again to their spouse. The fancy belly bumper that will shrink the blubber on their abs to a sixpack of steel-tight muscle—in just ten days! The juice extractor that will suck those magic nutrients out of carrots and broccoli and serve them up in a liquid brew that tastes better than any milk shake they've ever had—only $149.95, shipping and handling *free,* if you order right away!

Yes, they've heard it all. But none of it has worked. They're still fat. Worse, they're utterly defeated.

Ginny had the look that says, "Wayne, save your concern. Maybe you genuinely want to help me get my life together. That's great. But you just don't understand. This time, you've met your match. It's never going to happen for me. I just don't have what it takes. I'll never change."

To be honest, when Ginny interrupted my talk to vent her frustration, I felt frustrated with Ginny. But I also felt a lot of compassion. Because Ginny reminded me of me. There was a time in my life when I was just as certain that my life would never be altered. I, too, had tried the quick fixes she'd mentioned. I, too, had made those endless New Year's resolutions. I, too had attended all those self-help seminars and read all those books and pursued all those other schemes for lifestyle management. But they hadn't worked for me, just like they hadn't worked for Ginny, nor will they work for you. And here's why: almost all of those approaches are based on a number of terribly flawed assumptions, specifically:

1. *"People are all pretty much the same."* Have you ever noticed how books on lifestyle management make sweeping generalizations about human beings as they dispense advice? For example, most of them assume that all of us are motivated by goals, plans, rewards, success, money, prestige, self-interest, saving time, having more/bigger/better things, having people think well of us, making our lives easier, and on and on. But for every statement that begins, "Everyone needs," or "Everyone believes," or "People always," or "It's just human nature," there's almost a 100 percent certainty that someone somewhere is an exception to whatever follows. Actually, *lots* of "someones somewhere."

Take goals. Almost every prescription for self-improvement that I've ever come across says something like, "If you want to succeed at this, you've got to have a goal." Now I believe strongly in goals. In fact, later in this book I'll talk about setting some goals. But what if you're one of the *millions* of people in this world who doesn't do life by goals? It's not that you *can't* set a goal, it's that goal-setting is not how you're *wired*. It's not part of your makeup. God didn't design you that way. You use other means for moving ahead—perhaps a picture or vision in your mind, perhaps a blueprint or model or set of instructions that you follow, perhaps a leader or coach or friend whom you trust.

Goals work great for people who are naturally motivated to set goals. They don't work so well for people who are wired in other ways. The point is that every human being is unique. Each of us has a unique "hardwiring" that doesn't fundamentally change throughout our life. Any scheme for lifestyle improvement that fails to take into account how *you* are naturally wired is ultimately doomed to failure. That's why in the next chapter I'm going to take you through an exercise that reveals a lot of how *you* are motivated to function.

2. *"The same prescriptions will work for everyone."* This assumption goes hand-in-hand with the previous one. In fact, it is based on the previous idea that everyone is the same. If everyone is the same, then universal, one-size-fits-all solutions will work for everyone.

For example, how many times have you heard "experts" say, "Americans should be saving 10 percent of their gross income." Is that true? Well, 10 percent may be an *average* of what all Americans, taken together, should be saving. But some of us need to be saving quite a bit more than that because of where we are in life and what our income level is and other factors. For others, such as retirees who have a handsome nest egg stashed away, 10 percent may be too aggressive. So how much should an *individual* household be saving? The most accurate answer is, "It all depends."

I could apply the same logic to almost every other area of lifestyle management: diets, working out, nutrition, vitamin supplements, budgets, insurance, 401(k) deductions, family schedules, times away with your spouse, vacations, Christmas shopping, you name it. There is no single prescription that fits every person, every family, every circumstance. We always must remember: one size does not fit all!

"That's depressing," I hear someone saying. "How can I know what to do?" The answer is: discover how *you* are wired (I'll help you do that in the next chapter) and customize the advice you get to your wiring—to who *you* are and how *you* do life. This is another way of saying, *take responsibility for how you live*. Don't just let someone else tell you how to run your life. They can tell you what has worked for them. But don't assume that their approach will work for you, since they are wired differently than you.

That's the approach I've taken with almost 100,000 individuals over the past seventeen years. First I've helped them discover their inborn, underlying attitudes, using the simple 3-Minute Survey. Then I've helped them customize a plan for working on their lifestyle issues according to their unique approach to life. My model has worked for people in corporations, health spas, colleges and universities, churches, and many other venues. It works because it takes into account individual differences.

3. *"Change is basically a matter of making the right choices."* Pick up any book on diet and nutrition, money management, or relationships, and you'll inevitably find that success depends on a set of choices you need to be making. "Eat this much of this." "Don't eat any of that." "Spend only this much." "Buy that kind of insurance." "Say these things." "Avoid that situation." It's as if life is a paint-by-numbers picture that you fill in with the right choices. Get those choices right, and everything will work out great.

The problem is, life doesn't work that way. The half-truth is that managing your lifestyle *does* involve making good choices. But where does the decision to make these choices come from? Most traditional approaches ignore the extent to which that inborn hardwiring that I will talk more about drives your decisions and behaviors.

Take Charlie as a case in point. Goodtime Charlie, his friends call him. It's an appropriate name, because Charlie is nothing if not friendly. He never met a person he didn't instantly like. For that matter, he never met a person who didn't instantly like him. Charlie's just got appeal oozing out of him. Not surprisingly, he spends all of his time in the company of others.

Now Charlie has *always* been that way, from the time he was a little baby. He's always gravitated to people. Indeed, everything he's ever achieved in his life he's done together with other people. And for good reason: the satisfaction that Charlie takes from being with other people is a function of his attitude, his hardwiring. In other words, Charlie doesn't have to *try* to like people, he just likes them. He cannot *not* like them. That's how he's wired.

Did I mention that Charlie is eighty-five pounds overweight and maxed out on two of his three credit cards? Charlie's wife got him to go to a seminar that their church sponsored on financial planning. The speaker had very good material. She talked about setting up a budget and paying off credit card purchases every month. Charlie listened carefully and even took notes. Why, he even went up to the speaker afterwards and told her she was the best seminar presenter he'd ever heard. She seemed flattered.

So guess what happened on the way home from the seminar. Charlie was so excited about what he'd heard that he invited another couple to join him and his wife for a snack at a nearby restaurant, so they could talk about it. When the waitress came, Charlie blared out, "Hey, I know! Let's get that fried onion they serve here for an appetizer. It's great!"

So the deep fried onion with the creamy dip soon arrived. Charlie was so animated that he ended up eating most of it while he chatted away with his friends.

Later, the waitress brought their meals—light sandwiches for the other three, but a huge double pastrami with cheese and chips for Charlie.

When the waitress brought the check, the husband of the other couple began to pull out his wallet. But Charlie waved him off and grabbed the bill. "This is ours," he said emphatically. When his friend began to protest, Charlie became adamant. "I won't hear of it. We invited you, and I've thoroughly enjoyed listening to your perspectives on the seminar. You've made this the perfect ending to a wonderful day." And with that, Charlie handed the waitress his credit card.

Now Charlie has broken almost every piece of advice that he's ever read or heard about sticking to a diet and keeping his spending under control. Why? Does he not *want* to make the right choices? In truth, he does. He's talked about that many times with his wife. So why does he keep making bad choices? Because Charlie is unaware that his inborn *attitude* predisposes him to order more food, to pay for the meal, and to pay for it on a credit card when he's already got two credit cards that are maxed out. For that matter, his attitude predisposes him to ask his friends out for a snack in the first place.

Charlie doesn't know anything about his attitude. He's just being Charlie. That's how it is with most people. They pay no attention to their particular wiring because they don't even know what it is. Their wiring is so natural to them that they don't even recognize how much it affects their decisions and behavior. They just do the things they do because, well, that's how they do life. They wouldn't think of doing it any other way.

So telling people to just make the right choices is a bit misguided. Better to show them how their attitudes affect their decisions, so that they can understand why they keep making bad decisions, and how they can start making good decisions—informed, intelligent decisions based on who they actually are.

4. *"People can change and 'become' whatever they want to be if they'll just put their mind to it."* This may be the most flawed assumption of all. But it is very common in our society. "Whatever the mind can conceive, the will can achieve." Have you ever heard something like that? Sure you have. In fact, you may have said something similar to your kids in an effort to inspire them to set their sights high: "Honey, you can become anything you want to be. You just need to decide what you want and then work hard to achieve it."

Now I would never want to discourage anyone from aiming high. In fact, I think one of the main problems folks have in managing their lifestyle is that they are settling for too little. They have no vision for their lives, nothing to shoot for, nothing to aspire to. As a result, they don't care about themselves nearly enough, and so they allow their habits to defeat them. Having a lofty dream to pursue is vital to self-enhancement.

But having said that, I must be clear: it is simply not true that you can become *anything* you want to be. For instance, I now weigh 228 pounds (a *trim* 228 pounds, I might point out). At one time in my life, I may have wanted to become an astronaut. But I weigh more than is acceptable to be an astronaut (not to mention that I'm scared of heights). So that option is off the table for me. I can't become an astronaut. Nor can I become a jockey. Given my size, I'd slow the horse down (or break his back).

The same principle applies to you, not just physically, but in terms of your hardwiring. Certain things fit you because of how you're wired, and other things don't. One person is great with math and numbers, but not so good with his hands. Another person can plan and organize a dinner party like nobody's business, but don't ask her to bake the cake. Every one of us has a particular way in which we're made, and that design fits us perfectly for some task or role in this world (by the way, it's important that we find what that task or role is, and go do it).

But that means we can't "become" just anything we want to be. In fact, the truth is that we can't become anything other than what we were made to be. That hardwiring is permanent. It doesn't fundamentally change over the course of our life. Charlie, whom I mentioned a moment ago, is always going to love being with people. That's never going to change. He's never going to "become" a recluse. Even if he tried, even if for some reason he built a cabin in the woods to live by himself as a hermit, he might survive all by himself. But he'll never *love* being by himself, because *he wasn't made that way*. He was made to love being with people.

The same is true for you. Who you fundamentally are will never change. Your values may change, your beliefs may change, your opinions may change, your relationships may change, your circumstances will almost certainly change. But your personhood—who you are—will never fundamentally change.

And that's a good thing! Because we *need* you to be who you are, so that you can make the contribution to this world that we need you to make. The contribution that you are uniquely designed to make.

And I hope hearing that removes a fear that may be lurking inside you as you read this book. Maybe you've read other books on lifestyle management, and you've discovered that all of them hope to produce *change* in your lifestyle. And that scares you to death! Because you're afraid that changing your lifestyle means you'll have to change who you are. You'll have to become someone else. You'll have to become like the person who wrote the book!

Not that that's all bad. You'd certainly like to have the physique of that fitness trainer with the snappy exercise book. You'd love to have the millions that the financial guru has who wrote *How to Get Rich As a Mattress Tester*. You'd be thrilled to have the marriage that the cute couple on the jacket of the relationship book has—and don't they look like a couple of models from Madison Avenue?

Sure, it's fun to imagine yourself as someone who is thin, rich, happy, or whatever. That's great! But deep down you don't *want* to "become" someone else. Do you? You want to solve your problems, you want to experience happiness, you want to feel better about your life. But do you really want to "become" an entirely different human being than you are? I've never met anyone who did.

Which is why *I will never ask you to change who you are*. Instead, I'll ask you to *come to terms with who you are*—with your inborn attitude—and then use your awareness of your attitude to make better choices that are customized to you and are in your best interest.

• • •

Thanks to flawed ideas like the ones I've just mentioned, a majority of Americans are now mired in a raging crisis of obesity, debt, and broken relationships. Most of us long for our lives to be different. But that will never happen unless each individual's process for making things different takes into account who you are and how you are wired.

And also takes into account one other thing: *nothing good happens fast*. Note that I'm not saying that good things have to take forever. I'm just saying that there are no quick fixes. Sorry if that disappoints you. But then, haven't you already been disappointed by all those quick fixes you've tried already?

The fact is, we live in a quick-fix society, and it's those quick fixes that have gotten us into so much trouble. Take food, for example. We've got "fast food," which can be bought with a fast and easy method called a credit card.

But say you're a little too quick with those credit cards and rack up too much debt. There are quick-fix solutions for that, too: debt consolidation, or, if that's not fast enough, bankruptcy. Many Americans file for bankruptcy two, three, even four times!

And how about marriage? If things aren't working out, it's become easier than ever with "no fault" divorce to "streamline" a divorce. In fact, all you need to get unhitched in most states is just cause, especially if you have a prenuptial agreement in place. All the paperwork's been done. Call it a "quick unfix." It's a boon to divorce lawyers and a tragedy for the family.

Quick fixes get us into trouble. But quick fixes can't get us out of trouble. Why? Because quick-fix, easy-answer, temporary solutions are no match for what turn out to be permanent, life-long issues. That's what weight is—a lifelong issue. That's what money is—a lifelong issue. That's what relationships are—a lifelong issue. Those issues are never going to go away. And the way each of us instinctively deals with those issues is never going to go away because our inborn attitude is never going to go away, nor will it fundamentally change. Our underlying attitude, whatever it is, will drive our approach to lifestyle issues for as long as we're alive.

So quick fixes won't work. Instead, the question we need to ask of any program for getting our lives under control is: *Is it a program we can do for a lifetime?* If it is, that's the one we want. If not, forget it.

So which program will last a lifetime? The answer is: only the one we can customize to fit our individual needs and attitudes.

This book lays out such a plan. It's a customized plan for taking control of your life—a plan that will last a lifetime, because it fits *you*. It's designed for *you*. We call this five-step plan the ALTER model.

The word "ALTER" is chosen on purpose. I've already said that I will never ask you to change who you are. The same is true for your lifestyle. I will never ask you to change your lifestyle. Most people think of "change" as a radical, 180-degree turnaround. "Change" implies that you are going in the wrong direction, or that you have already failed. For that reason, I avoid the word "change." It's asking too much. It's unrealistic. No matter how sincere I may be—or you may be—you're not going to do a 180-degree turnaround in your lifestyle. Not overnight, anyway.

But suppose I show you how to "ALTER" your lifestyle? In other words, how to make a less traumatic adjustment—more like a 5- or 10-degree course correction. Can you do that? Sure you can! Not that I'm stopping anyone from trying a sharper turn. You can attempt whatever degree of course correction you are willing to try. But in my experience, simple alterations prove much more manageable, and much more realistic. And for that reason, they yield much better results over time. Repeat: *over time.*

So here's a summary of the ALTER model. ALTER is an acrostic, as follows:

A = Awareness. The first step to managing your lifestyle is to understand the natural, inborn, hardwired attitude that drives your behavior. I'll help you do that in the next two chapters.

L = Learn. Getting serious about your lifestyle requires that you learn as much information as possible about the issue you want to work on. Chapters 4 and 5 will help you figure out what information you need, where to find it, and what to do with it.

T = Tactical plan. In this book I'm addressing the three lifestyle issues that are causing the biggest problems in our society—wellness, personal finances, and relationships, both at home and at work. Chapters 6, 7, and 8 cover these issues in detail. For each issue, I'll show you a ten-item checklist to help you create definable, realistic, and personally meaningful goals or outcomes, and then take steps toward those results.

E = Execute the plan. Good intentions have to translate into actual action. So in chapter 9 I'll offer you encouragement, tips, and techniques for working your personalized plan and learning to "walk your talk."

R = Re-evaluate. As you take action toward getting your lifestyle under control, you need to periodically evaluate your progress, looking at what has gone right, what has gone wrong, what you can do differently, and what your next plan of action should be. I'll show you how to do that in Chapters 10, 11, and 12.

"Well, that's all well and good," I can hear someone saying, "but you don't know me. Remember me? I'm that person you described earlier. I'm the person who will just never change. Because I *can't* change. You can't fix me! I'm hopeless."

Okay then, let's go back to Ginny, the lady I mentioned earlier. The one who said, "I've tried everything, and none of it worked." The one who wanted to prove me wrong. What did I tell Ginny? The same thing I'll say to you if you're thinking what she was thinking: "You're right. You can leave."

You could have heard a pin drop as all the other women in the room that day turned around to stare at Ginny—and at me. You could tell they were thinking, "Did he really just say what I think he said? Did he really tell her he can't help her, and she should just leave?"

They expected me to say the same thing everyone else had said to Ginny countless times before when she had said, in effect, "I'll never change." Maybe it's the same thing you're expecting me to say. Something sweet and kind and nice (and patronizing), like, "Oh, Ginny, trust me. You're gonna be fine. It's gonna be okay. You just hang in there and let me get through my information, and you'll be all right. This time will be different."

I didn't say that. I didn't say it to Ginny, and I won't say it to you if you're like Ginny. Because the truth is, Ginny wasn't ready to confront her issues. Remember, I said that food is an *addiction* (so is money). Ginny was addicted to food—just like I was. And it's a fundamental principle of working with addicts that you can't help an addict recover from her habit until she is ready to recover. Ginny wasn't ready. She didn't *want* to "get" what I had to say. She didn't *want* to be there with those other women, and work on her life in a relaxed, accepting environment the way they did.

And so I couldn't help her. I surely wanted to see Ginny find a way to make changes, but I couldn't want that change *for* Ginny. She had to want it for herself. I couldn't give her reasons for seeking change. She had to determine reasons of her own. And apparently she wasn't ready to do that. So I told her the truth.

When I told Ginny that, she immediately unfolded her arms, sat up on the front of her chair, glared at me, and said, "Do you mean you can't help me?"

"No ma'am, I can't help you." Pause. "I can't fix you. It's not my job to fix you. It's not my job to make your life work the way you want it to." Pause. I wanted that to sink in. And it did. I could tell she had been stopped in her tracks. She looked as if she didn't know whether to cuss me out, get up and walk out, or break down in tears. But she wasn't leaving, so I could tell she was holding out hope that maybe, just maybe, she'd encountered someone who might have some answers.

Finally I continued. "But if you're willing to acknowledge that you've got a problem, and that it's out of control, and that you want to regain control, and that you want to learn what you need to learn in order to regain control; and if you're willing to develop a plan of action that's just right for you, so that you can go to work on that problem; and if you're willing to work on that plan over time and take small but certain steps forward, and not let mistakes and failures and disappointments defeat you and get you off the track—then yeah, I can give you that direction. That's why I'm here today."

Perhaps you've picked up this book with thoughts similar to Ginny's. You've tried it all. None of it has worked. You've given up hope. You'll never change. And as if to prove that, you've picked up this book with the attitude, "Oh, here's another one. Let's see what this guy has. Let me go ahead and try his deal and see if I fail."

If that's what you're thinking, you're right. My colleagues and I can't help you. You can set the book aside. For the same reasons I gave Ginny.

But before you bail out, let me tell you the rest of Ginny's story. Ginny decided to stay put and finish the seminar. She paid a *lot* more attention after our tense exchange. I even saw her take a few notes and talk to some of the other participants at the breaks, asking questions and soliciting input.

Finally, at the end of the day she came up to me and stuck out her hand. "Wayne, I want to thank you for talking to me the way you did," she told me. I thought she was going to cry. I almost wanted to cry myself when she continued, "You know, you're the only person in my life who's ever been that honest. My mother always told me that same excuse you were talking about. She used to say, 'Ginny, it doesn't matter what you eat or don't eat, because slow metabolism just runs in our family.'"

Like so many people, Ginny had lived her whole life attributing her problems with weight to her DNA and the way her family had raised her. The result was one giant chip on her shoulder. But the reality was that she wasn't angry with me—she was angry with herself. Until that day, she hadn't wanted to deal with the truth. The truth was that her problems were not the result of any program, product, or process that had let her down. Her problems were the result of her own poor decisions. In other words, the problems were not something else; *she* was the problem. She was the source of her own troubles.

Do you know where those poor decisions were coming from? Ginny didn't. Most people don't. It was a breakthrough discovery for Ginny that day when she learned that her decisions about food, money, and relationships were being driven by her *attitude*—the inborn and instilled ways in which she was "wired" to do life. Ginny's hardwiring, her attitude, was dramatically affecting her behaviors. Like most people, Ginny was unaware of what her underlying attitude was all about.

So I had her do what this book is about to have you do. I had her take the Real Life Management 3-Minute Survey, which reveals the core attitudes that drive a person's choices. The 3-Minute Survey was like holding up a mirror to Ginny and saying, "Ginny, here's how *you* do life." She discovered that her unique approach to life actually predisposed her to some self-defeating patterns that accounted for her problems. By paying attention to those patterns, she was in a position to start making better decisions for herself and develop better habits.

The same holds true for you. You have a unique way of approaching life. A unique attitude. Unless you take that attitude into account, you'll probably never succeed long-term in gaining control of your lifestyle. Unless you pay attention to your attitude, you're liable to stay stuck in the conviction, "I'll never change!"

Would you like to break out of that mind-set, once and for all, the way Ginny did? And I did? And thousands of others I've worked with have? In the next chapter, I'll show you how.

CHAPTER 2

Can You Give Me 3 Minutes?

et me begin this chapter by stating something up front: I don't like personality tests. They're complicated. They take too long to fill out. They ask dumb questions that have nothing to do with me. Worst of all, they end up putting me in a box and assigning me a label that I can't shake.

So imagine my reaction in 1996, when I was speaking at an exclusive health spa near Phoenix, and the staff psychologist remarked, "Wayne, I love what you're saying about food and money, but you're missing it. You're not saying anything about the underlying emotions that cause people to act the way they do. Why don't you start using a personality test in your system? That way you can show people how their emotions and personalities affect their eating and spending habits."

"No, I don't like personality tests," I replied. "They take too long to fill out, they're complicated . . ." and so on. I gave her an earful. Then I said, "The only way I'd use a test is if it were quick, easy, and fun. It would have to be something that takes about three minutes to complete. The results would have to be so simple that even I could understand them. And the information from it would have to be something a person could actually use in their day-to-day life in a practical way."

The psychologist said she didn't know of any test like that. But she offered to show me some examples of what was out there, and maybe I'd see something that would work.

I was highly skeptical. But over the next few months we had a lot of discussions and engaged in some joint research. I experimented with a few tests with various audiences.

I didn't want a test to identify personality, which was not my focus. Personality isn't all that helpful in trying to understand why people spend too much, or overeat, or allow their spouse to dominate them, or struggle in personal relationships with family, supervisors, or coworkers. I've met fat people, broke people, and divorced people with every kind of personality you can imagine: outgoing and shy, funny and boring, organized and messy, persuasive and persuadable, friendly and standoffish, alert and asleep, smart and dumb. Personality doesn't make any difference. Something else accounts for the lifestyle decisions people make.

I call that core drive our *attitude*—attitude in the sense of how we are oriented toward someone or something else. When I played football in college, the coach put me at nose guard. I was 6'1" and weighed 230. When the other team had the ball, my job was to line up across from some guy who was maybe 6'6" and weighed 300, and create a pile that would allow our linebacker to tackle the opponent's running back. So everything I did during the week was to prepare myself for that moment. I studied that guy's game films. I practiced drills to get ready for his moves. I ate, slept, and dreamed about that offensive lineman. In short, my *attitude* for that week was more or less determined by that guy. I oriented my life around him. He became my sole focus, my sole preoccupation, essentially the sole priority of my life.

In a similar way, each of us is born with an *attitude* that heavily determines what we focus on in life.[1] That attitude affects what we pay attention to, what holds our interest, and what we consider priorities. Our attitude is inborn and remains substantially unchanged throughout life. Along with our beliefs (the primitive, emotional convictions about the world that we gain at a very early age), I believe that attitude accounts for 80 percent of any decision we make about a lifestyle issue.

Combining various elements from the tests that the psychologist showed me, I developed a tool to identify a person's core attitude. Eventually it was perfected into the Real Life Management 3-Minute Attitude Survey. Or, to keep things simple, the 3-Minute Survey.

The 3-Minute Survey is provided below. I want you to take a moment to fill it out. That's the first step in helping you devise a plan for gaining control of your lifestyle—a plan you can use the rest of your life. Remember the ALTER model that I mentioned in the previous chapter? "A" stands for Awareness. The first thing you need to do is to become *aware of your attitude,* because that's the ultimate driver behind your lifestyle decisions.

Instructions for Taking the 3-Minute Survey

Note: You should fill out the survey by yourself. This is not a group exercise.

1   The survey has four columns of words, labeled, "T," "R," "I," and "M," respectively. Go through each column and circle any words that you feel describe you. Circle as many words as you'd like. Don't over-analyze whether you should circle a word. Just go with your first reaction for whether the word describes you or not. Also, don't circle words that you think "should" describe you, or that your spouse or kids or parents or friends think should describe you. Just circle words that you think describe you. By all means, have fun with this and be as honest as you can. Remember, this is your chance to be *you*!

2   When you are finished circling words, count the number of words you have circled in each column and

REAL  LIFE
3-MINUTE SURVEY™

Name: _____

☐ ☐ ☐ ☐

Results - Letters (highest to lowest)

E-mail: _____ Date: _____

Instructions: Circle every word in the columns below that describes you, the more the better. After finishing, total the number of words in each column and place the total on the line located at the bottom of each column. You cannot have a tie in any two columns. If the totals in any column are the same, you must break the tie by either choosing another word in one column or omitting a word already circled in the other column. **You MUST finish with a different number in each column.**

T	R	I	M
organized	rational	independent	agreeable
determined	reserved	impulsive	peaceful
practical	visionary	creative	spiritual
decisive	logical	playful	trusting
fair	objective	daring	kind
stable	skeptical	restless	caring
sensible	analytical	outgoing	genuine
detailed	intelligent	energetic	romantic
realistic	controlling	passionate	optimistic
responsible	opinionated	humorous	cooperative
_____	_____	_____	_____
"T" Total	"R" Total	"I" Total	"M" Total

_____   _____
Composite T + R   Composite I + M

For your FREE summary report: Go to www.3MSurvey.com and follow the instructions.

You will need to enter your column totals T = _____ R = _____ I = _____ and M = _____.

and the Report Code: ThinRichHappy-Report

© 2007 Real Life Management, Inc.

write that number in the blank at the bottom of each column.

3   Look at the totals you've recorded in the blanks at the bottom of each column. Are any of the scores tied? If so, go through those tied columns again and break the tie by either circling an additional word in one of the columns or omitting a circled word in one of the columns. If this process creates another tie among the column totals, use the same process to break that tie. *You must finish with four different column totals—no ties allowed.* Don't get frustrated over the ties, just eliminate them. By all means don't ask someone else to help you break the ties. *You* know who you are.

4   Determine the composite T + R score by adding the two T and R column totals together. Then determine the composite I + M score by adding the two I and M column scores together. Write the composite scores in the two blank areas. Here, tied scores are allowed.

5   Determine your attitude scoring pattern: Which column has the highest number of words circled (look at the column totals). Write the letter at the top of that column in the first box of the four "Results" boxes to the right of your name (on the top right-hand side of the page). Which column has the second-highest number of words circled? Write the letter at the top of that column in the second box. Which column has the third-highest number of words circled? Write the letter at the top of that column in the third box. Which column has the least number of words circled? Write the letter at the top of that column in the fourth box. The four scores in the boxes create a scoring pattern, which we will discuss throughout this book.

6   At the bottom of the survey are instructions for how
         you can obtain a free summary report about your scor-
         ing pattern, as well as a significant discount on a
         larger, twelve-page report.

Congratulations! You have now completed the 3-Minute Survey.
Let's talk about what the scoring pattern means. That's what I'll do
in the rest of this chapter and the next chapter. At the end of this
chapter you will find an additional blank 3-Minute Survey that you
may copy and give to your family, friends, and co-workers.

The four letters in the scoring pattern are in order, from highest score to lowest score. The order of those letters forms a pattern.
Given that there are four letters, there are 24 possible combinations; however, when we account for intensity as you will learn in
Chapter 3, we arrive at 32 total scoring patterns.

The pattern of your 3-Minute Survey tells you what your core
attitude is. It's not absolute, but it does reveal a *great* deal about
the way you live your life and communicate on a daily basis—the
way you make health and wellness decisions, money and spending
decisions, relationship decisions, and many other decisions affecting your lifestyle. It also reveals a range of priorities.

Let's talk about the first letter in your pattern. There are four
possibilities, T, R, I, or M as follows:

- *If you lead with a T:* "T" stands for "tactical." I chose that
  term because T's tend to be planners. They pay attention to
  deadlines and are painstaking with details. They set goals
  and are very reliable. They focus on efficiency, are highly
  organized, and tend to remain stable no matter what the
  circumstances.
- *If you lead with an R:* "R" stands for "rational," because
  R's are the great logical thinkers of the world. R's focus on

issues and ideas. They are quite discriminating, and they don't mind challenging other people's opinions. They also will defend their position quite strongly. They pay a lot of attention to facts, and when it comes to money they tend to pay special attention to the bottom line. R's are often strategic in their thinking in that they see the "big picture" quickly.

- *If you lead with an I:* "I" stands for "impulsive" or "independent," because I's are playful and willing to have fun on the spur of the moment. They tend to be extravagant and generous. They are creative and like to do a lot of things at once. They have an infectious optimism and are invariably cheerful. They take great pride in their accomplishments and don't mind telling others about them.

- *If you lead with an M:* "M" stands for "mellow," because M's tend to be laid-back and easy to get along with. They see the best in others and like to give people a chance. They are usually sensitive and eager to please. They seek harmony in relationships, and they are prone to trust others. They are idealistic in the sense that they see people in terms of ideals to pursue, whether or not those ideals can ultimately be realized. Some people like the word "ministry" to describe the "M" attitude, and you are welcome to use it if it suits you.

Now as you read those descriptions, you may be thinking, "That doesn't describe me very well. I'm sort of like that, but not all the time. Sometimes I'm quite different from that." Okay, okay, hold on. Remember that there are *three other letters in the pattern.* The first letter is like the outer layer of an onion. It's the first thing we see you doing, your first priority, as it were. But if that first priority is satisfied, you then begin to pursue other priorities that are hidden at deeper levels, deeper layers of the onion. That's what the other three letters are all about. So it's not just the first letter that's important, *it's the overall pattern that's important.*

Let's take an example to illustrate. Suppose your scoring pattern is MRIT. Notice that M is in the first position. That means that in most situations in life, your first and foremost priority is reflected by your concern about people. You focus a lot on other people. You pay attention to what they need, how they feel, what they believe, what's going on with them, what's going on with their family, and so forth. People are your primary focus, your number one priority.

So now suppose I come to you and say, "Hey, I've written a book on lifestyle issues. Would you like to read it?" Your answer, as an M, will most likely depend on whether you feel my book will benefit the other people in your life. For instance, you might be thinking, "Will Wayne's book help me be a better partner to my spouse? A better parent to my kids? A better employee for my boss? Would this be a book my friends would read? Will it help me build my relationship skills to better serve my clients and business associates? Does Wayne seem friendly? Does he seem like someone I'd like to get to know? Does Wayne seem to care about people? Can he relate to where people really live?"

Now let's say that you are satisfied that I'm safe and approachable and empathetic and concerned. You've got an R in the second position, the second layer of the onion. Remember, R stands for "rational." So once I've satisfied the people-priority of your M, I now encounter your logical, analytical side. And so when I tell you about my book, the next thing you want to know is: What sort of authority and credentials do I have? What's the argument of the book? Who has endorsed it, and what are their credentials? Why should you believe anything I have to say? How will this book compare to other things you've read on the same topic? Does Wayne seem like someone you should pay any attention to? The R may be in the second position, but it plays a very important role in how you make decisions, as it is your second priority.

Well, let's say I somehow satisfy your M's concern or priority about people, as well as your R's interest in logic and reason. The third letter in your pattern is an I. I love I's, because I'm an I. My first letter is an I. However, your first letter is an M. Your *third* letter is an I. Which means I've got my work cut out for me. Only after I've assured you that I'm both trustworthy and respectable do I get to have some fun with you. But by then, you're more than willing to have some fun. That's what your I in the third position means: "Wayne, your book better be helpful for all the people I care about. And it better make sense and be based on rock-solid facts. But don't bore me with it, either. Keep it interesting. Use some humor. Tell some jokes. Keep me awake. 'Cause if you don't, I'll set it aside." That's what your I means for my book.

In last place you have a T. T stands for "tactical," meaning responsible, ordered, stable, and precise. The fact that T is the last letter in your pattern means that you probably are none of those things, at least not very much and not most of the time. If anything, you find people who are like that to be among your *least* favorite (even though you are an M and love most people). So let's say that my book had a few typos, or that the notes were not in perfect stylebook format, or that a minor detail mentioned on page 23 was slightly contradicted by a detail on page 148. You probably wouldn't even notice such things, and if you did, they probably wouldn't matter to you. (By the way, you needn't worry about gaffes like that in this book, because the publisher has employed lots of T's to make sure those kinds of mistakes don't happen.)

Do you see how a scoring pattern helps reveal the priorities in the way a person approaches life? We call that approach one's *attitude*. Every human being has a particular attitude, and that attitude affects how each person does life. We've looked at *one* scoring pattern. There are 31 others. Every one of them deals with life differently.[2]

Later we'll see how your scoring pattern affects your lifestyle decisions. You may be interested to know that your pattern predicts whether you are at risk for obesity, debt, or troubled relationships. For instance, if the first two letters in your scoring pattern are IM or MI, you are at risk for obesity and debt because your attitude predisposes you to be impulsive and/or not to set boundaries. If your first two letters are TR or RT, you are at risk for troubled relationships because your priority on structure and/or reason predisposes you to overlook the emotional and relational needs of the people in your life.

For now, though, I want to stay with the positive and point out that *your attitude, no matter what it is, is an inherently good thing.* If you believe, as I and my co-authors do, that your life is ultimately a gift from God, then it follows that your "wiring" is a gift from God, too. We call it your *giftedness.* It's the gift you've been given with which to make a contribution to the world. Think about that! You are equipped with a unique and special way of doing life, a way that fits you perfectly for certain tasks.

Take the T's, for instance. A moment ago I said that T's had worked on this book to make sure that every detail is buttoned down, every fact is checked, every "i" is dotted and every "t" is crossed (no pun intended). T's naturally do that, and for that reason they do it better than anyone. If I've got a set of numbers that needs checking, I want a T on the job. If I need to make plans for travel, I want a T to handle that. If I've got money that needs to be managed in a very prudent, conservative manner, I would do best to hire a T as the money manager.

T's are the stable, practical, principled people of the world. For that reason you'll find T's succeeding as accountants, money managers, chief financial officers, logistics supervisors, quality control managers, bank tellers, insurance claims processors, librarians, pilots, engineers, and administrative assistants (among many other occupations).[3] Wherever you need to be able to *count* on someone, you'll rarely go wrong with a T in the position.

Now I can almost hear a bunch of R's and even some I's and M's reacting to the last couple of paragraphs by saying, "Well, I can do that!" And perhaps you can, especially if you happen to have a T as your second letter. And you may be able to do "T work" rather well. But I'm not talking about what someone *can* do, rather what someone *most naturally* does. T's just *naturally* incline toward order, practicality, and a conservative, realistic approach. That's their great contribution to the rest of us. Without T's in the world, I's like me would run things recklessly. Without T's, R's would dream up great ideas but never see them implemented. Without T's, the M's would bankrupt us all by giving our money away to needy causes. Thank God for T's!

But thank God for R's, too. If you lead with an R, the rest of us count on you to think things through. In fact, we envy your smarts. Sometimes we find you hard to understand, but that doesn't mean we don't respect you. We've learned by experience that you weigh the facts and come to well-reasoned conclusions. I suspect that Thomas Jefferson was an R. Albert Einstein was probably an R. Carl Sagan was no doubt an R.

Those leading with an R bring intelligence to the affairs of humankind. For that reason we find R's succeeding as CEOs, college professors, research chemists, judges, editors, physicists, psychiatrists, credit analysts, general contractors, financial planners, software designers, orchestra conductors, film producers, police sergeants, weather forecasters, and high school principals (among many other occupations). Wherever you need someone to assess what is known and *think it through*, an R is the right person for the job.

Again, I'm not saying that T's, I's, and M's are not intelligent. They are, and they are especially intelligent in some ways that R's are not. But the point is that R's *naturally* make use of their brain first—and the human brain is a pretty powerful tool to put on any task! I've never encountered a situation where an R wasn't able to point out some critical factor that the rest of us were overlooking. Without R's in the world, the T's would keep us in the status quo forever. Without R's, the I's would have no one to tell them that despite their charm, the emperor has no clothes. Without R's, the M's would trust anyone and everyone—and follow them right over the cliff. Thank God for R's!

And thank God for those who lead with an I, too. The playful, endearing I's. I's bring fun into the world. They take risks. Relentlessly energetic, they boldly go where no one has gone before. They do so with a charm that the rest of us can't help but follow—or at least admire. We may shake our heads at their dramatic antics and their inflated pitches, but we instinctively know that without the I's there would be no Disney World, no *Peter Pan,* no rock music, and no iPods.

"I" might just as well stand for "inspiration," for I's are in love with life. For that reason you'll find I's succeeding as entrepreneurs, novelists, salespeople, art directors, preachers, insurance agents, actors, wide receivers, journalists, film directors, jazz musicians, helicopter pilots, tattoo artists, and poets (among many other occupations). I's communicate a compelling vision that cries out for response from others.

You can see where this is going. T's, R's, and M's can also be inspired and inspiring. But I's *naturally* live for the moment and experience things in the moment that elude the rest of us. Without I's in the world, the T's would have no one to disrupt their plans. Without I's, the R's would have no one to communicate their brilliant ideas to the rest of us. Without I's, the M's would have no one to lift their spirits and call them to action about the cares and concerns of humanity. Thank God for I's!

And finally, thank God for M's. No one is more loyal, more

compassionate, more empathetic, and more giving than an M. When things are at their worst and life has got us down, it's an M who will stand by us and give attention to our needs. Whereas others demand only answers from us, the M seeks understanding. And while others are trying to fit us into their agenda, the M is thinking about how they can serve our agenda. M's make great friends, trustworthy companions, and passionate lovers.

In short, those who lead with an M keep the vision of Mr. Rogers alive: they seek to make every day a beautiful day in the neighborhood. For that reason you'll find M's succeeding as social workers, customer service representatives, hospice workers, customer support VPs, industrial psychologists, chaplains, charity event sponsors, greeters at Wal-Mart, ambassadors and diplomats, ice cream vendors, bartenders, priests, small business owners, and professional Santa Clauses. M's provide the relational glue that binds communities together.

Am I saying that T's, R's, and I's are incapable of feeling any concern for others? Of course not. But M's *naturally* focus on other people. People are their first priority. It's the way they perceive life. Without M's in the world, the T's would grow cynical about human nature and quickly neglect human nurture. Without M's, the R's would turn life into a coldly analytical process of making one calculated decision after another. Without M's, the I's would push "fun" beyond acceptable limits, to the point of being downright offensive. Thank God for M's!

So are there any downsides to leading with a T, an R, an I, or an M? Absolutely! Every one of the lead letters has the potential to cause trouble for oneself and others. The very strengths that so naturally fit a person to certain tasks can also become weaknesses if used in inappropriate or extreme ways. They also can cause stress for others, especially those for whom your lead letter is the *last* letter in their scoring pattern. Consider:

- T's, with their practical bent and ability to handle details, can create stress for others if they become insufferably picky, stubborn, concerned only with their plan, insensitive to the legitimate needs and feelings of others, and boring as heck by focusing on irrelevant minutiae.
- R's, with their keen smarts and analytical minds, can create stress for others if they become arrogant know-it-alls, cynical, judgmental, greedy, stingy, lost in evaluation, coldly rational, emotionally inscrutable, and controlling.
- I's, with their charm and playfulness, can create stress for others if they become irresponsible, reckless, controlling, insensitive, unrealistic, unpredictable, undependable, and emotionally extreme (high or low).
- M's, with their benevolent nature, can create stress for others if they become too idealistic, naive, gullible, lacking in boundaries, overcommitted, vulnerable, easily broken-hearted, compromising, overly revealing, and always willing to take the blame.

This is so important that I encourage you to reread the above descriptions in light of your pattern. It may be a real wake-up call for you to realize how you may appear to people around you, and especially those for whom your lead letter is their *last* letter. That means your first priority is their last priority. Imagine how that affects your relationships at home, at work, and elsewhere!

Each of the lead letters has a "dark side" to it. And when you add the other three letters to form a pattern, you *multiply* the extent to which every person has a potential "dark side" to their makeup. Remember what I've been saying: our inborn attitude drives our lifestyle decisions. If we merely act instinctively, our attitude—as revealed by our scoring pattern—can blind us to what is truly in our best interest. We'll keep making unbalanced decisions about food, money, and relationships. It is that "dark side"—the abuse and misuse of core strengths—that accounts for why and how people get into trouble with their lifestyle. We'll see that more in the next chapter.

For now, though, I want you to grasp that your attitude, whatever it is, is a fundamentally positive thing. It represents strengths that you naturally possess. And those strengths endow you with unique capacity to make a significant contribution to the world.

So the question becomes: are you using *your* attitude to make *your* unique contribution, or are you allowing it to create a lifestyle issue—be it obesity, debt, or a troubled relationship—that is undermining your efforts? I want to help you be all that you were meant to be. In the next chapter, I'll show you more about your scoring pattern, so that you can use it to pursue a positive vision for your life.

REAL  LIFE
3-MINUTE SURVEY™

Name: _____

Results - Letters (highest to lowest)

E-mail: _____   Date: _____

Instructions: Circle every word in the columns below that describes you, the more the better. After finishing, total the number of words in each column and place the total on the line located at the bottom of each column. You cannot have a tie in any two columns. If the totals in any column are the same, you must break the tie by either choosing another word in one column or omitting a word already circled in the other column. **You MUST finish with a different number in each column.**

T	R	I	M
organized	rational	independent	agreeable
determined	reserved	impulsive	peaceful
practical	visionary	creative	spiritual
decisive	logical	playful	trusting
fair	objective	daring	kind
stable	skeptical	restless	caring
sensible	analytical	outgoing	genuine
detailed	intelligent	energetic	romantic
realistic	controlling	passionate	optimistic
responsible	opinionated	humorous	cooperative

_____	_____	_____	_____
"T" Total	"R" Total	"I" Total	"M" Total

_____   _____
Composite T + R   Composite I + M

For your FREE summary report: Go to www.3MSurvey.com and follow the instructions.

You will need to enter your column totals T = _____ R = _____ I = _____ and M = _____.

and the Report Code: **ThinRichHappy-Report**

CHAPTER 3　　**Your "Wiring" Floats Your Boat**

arry had struggled with his finances his entire life. Not that he was in debt. For the most part, he had tried very hard to keep his spending under control. But he knew there were many financial matters that he had allowed to fall by the wayside. For instance, he had very little in savings. He didn't have much life insurance, and he knew his family would be in trouble if something happened to him. He had no investments to speak of, except a few shares of stock that his grandparents had given him on his twenty-first birthday.

Larry was like so many people in that he spent most of his income on immediate needs: a mortgage, car payments, groceries, utilities, paying the bills, supporting his family. He'd read *The Millionaire Next Door* and other material about everyday people who live conservatively and save up a tidy nest egg. But he himself could never quite get there.

Then one day Larry's church announced that it was sponsoring a special seminar on financial planning. "That sounds like something I should do," he thought to himself. And so, on a cold, rainy Saturday in October, Larry and eight other people showed up at their church to attend the "Getting Your Financial House in Order" seminar.

The speaker was a very winsome and distinguished-looking Certified Financial Planner with many years of experience in helping couples evaluate their financial picture and set up a plan to accomplish their financial goals. The presenter furnished each participant with a thick three-ring binder filled with charts, graphs, tables, worksheets, spreadsheets, and lots of articles on topics like term insurance versus whole life, the time value of money, dollar cost averaging, tax-deferred annuities, the long-term performance of stocks versus real estate, and retirement planning.

A lot of the presentation went over Larry's head. But one thing he "got" was the presentation on budgeting. Larry had heard about budgets his whole life, but he had never kept one. He'd never really understood the purpose of a budget, nor had he seen its value. But for some reason, on that morning he woke up to the simple but powerful idea that a budget was a way for him to track his expenses and see where he stood, so that he could make wise spending choices.

The presenter gave the group a worksheet that showed how to set up a family budget. That was the biggest takeaway from the seminar for Larry. In fact, when he got home that afternoon, he went straight to the desk in his den where he kept the family's financial information, and he began working with a calculator to fill in the budgeting worksheet and create a spending plan for his family. By the time his wife was tucking their kids into bed, Larry had a finished budget.

Larry chose the next day after lunch to tell his family that they now had a budget. "Okay, everyone, I have an announcement to make," he began, his voice ringing with enthusiasm. His wife raised her eyebrows in surprise, and his two kids looked up from the Sunday comics they had been reading. "As you know, I went to the Getting Your Financial House in Order seminar yesterday. I learned a lot of things about money. But the most important thing was that our family needs to follow a budget. So I've worked up a budget for us, and I'd like to go over it with you now."

Three blank faces were now looking at Larry. There was a giant pause. Finally his fourteen-year-old daughter asked, "So does that mean I start getting an allowance again?"

"Well, ummm . . ." Larry began to respond. He realized he'd

forgotten to include allowances in the budget, and so he wasn't exactly sure how to answer her question.

"What's a budget?" eight-year-old Jonathan asked. He'd never heard the term.

"Dear, don't you think you and I should discuss this first, before we talk about it as a family?" his wife asked.

"Well, I thought we had talked about it," Larry replied, somewhat taken aback. He could remember lots of times when his wife had said they needed to come up with a budget so that she would know how much she had to spend on groceries and other purchases. "I mean, you're always saying we need a budget," he continued, mildly defensive in his tone.

"Well, of course we need a budget. It's just that this is so sudden. We need to talk about what our priorities are before we start putting figures on paper. Besides, I'm not sure you realize how much things cost."

Larry was feeling rather uneasy by now. He thought his wife would be happy that he had finally acted on her suggestion. Instead, she almost seemed to be opposing him. So he said, "Look, I gave up a whole day yesterday to try and figure out our money situation. You told me that was a good thing to do. Now I've done all this work, and you just want to pick it apart."

"No, honey, that's not what I'm saying."

"Well, it sounds that way to me. I spent a lot of time on trying to put figures to our family's spending, and all you're doing is . . ."

"Daddy, would you like Susan and me to go watch TV or something while you and Mommy talk?" Jonathan interrupted. He knew from experience when his folks were getting ready to have an argument.

Larry's faltering attempt to get his family started on a budget remind me a lot of what I used to do in the late 1980s and early 1990s when I decided to get serious about working on my lifestyle issues. I felt very convicted that I needed to turn things around. So I did what a lot of folks do when they realize something needs to change: I marched straight home to my wife and three daughters determined to get them straight. That's right! I thought *they* needed to get straightened out, not me.

You know why I thought that? Because they are wired much differently from me, and so they make different decisions than I do. And believe it or not, I thought that was the source of our family's problems.

A whole lot of people feel that way. It's just human nature, I guess. We assume that if someone is different from us, there's something wrong with them. Have you ever noticed that?

You see it all the time in marriages. Larry and his wife are a case in point. Larry's scoring pattern leads with an I. "I" stands for impulsive. I's make sudden, quick decisions that lead to sudden, quick commitments. That's what Larry does after the seminar. Impacted as he is by the concept of a budget, he decides out of the blue that his family needs a budget. So he instantly goes on a one-day frenzy to come up with one.

Larry's wife, meanwhile, is much more practical. She leads with a T. She *knows* how much things cost, because she does 90 percent of the buying for the family. She's also wired to pay more attention to money.

So how does Larry react when she points out that he hasn't consulted her on formulating the budget, and therefore his budget figures may be unrealistic? Does he say, "Gee, honey, I'm so thankful that your practical, T-oriented mind is assisting me in thinking through this budget. I'm sure it will be a much stronger piece of work because of your awareness of how much things cost"? No, he doesn't do that at all! Instead, rather than praise her for speaking out of her strength, he does what most of us do when confronted with someone who does life differently than we do: he blasts her. "I've done all this work, and you just want to pick it apart." In effect, Larry is saying, "What's wrong with you? How dare you see this differently than I do!"

You can observe the same dynamic between parents and their kids. Imagine a mother who leads with a T, who likes order, structure, and organization, and is a self-managed individual who is quite competent at coming up with a plan and then following through on that plan without anyone's supervision. Meanwhile, she's got a ten-year-old daughter who is a free-spirited I, and cares little for how things look or where they belong. Suppose that little girl needs clear, specific instructions and frequent feedback when asked to complete a task.

Given the way each is wired, you can almost see the conflict coming when the mother tells her daughter, "You need to get your room cleaned up today." The mother turns away to work on other chores. What's the little girl going to do? She might actually go in her room and start throwing the clothes off her bed. But then she spies a book she'd laid aside a couple of days before, and starts wondering how the story comes out. Next thing you know, she's deeply involved in reading the book.

Then her mother comes into the room. "I thought I told you to get this place cleaned up!" she says, obviously frustrated. The girl jumps up and begins to do things that look like "cleaning up." But after the mother leaves, it's just a matter of time before she's distracted again with a new interest—maybe a scrapbook she's been working on, or a toy she comes across, or an instant message that pops up on her computer screen.

Whatever takes the daughter off task, she's certain to hear her mother's stern voice when the mother comes by again: "Look, I've asked you twice now to work on this room. Now I'm not asking— I'm *telling*! I want it picked up! Why do I have to keep going over this?" That last question is the clincher. It's a version of, "What's wrong with you? How dare you approach this task differently than I would?"

This conversation ("What's the matter with you? How dare you do it differently than I do?") takes place every day in homes, schools, workplaces, houses of worship, soccer fields, basketball courts, highways, you name it. When someone behaves differently than we do, our first impulse is to assume that there must be something "wrong" with them. Our next impulse is to "fix them," to "straighten them out," which usually means to try and get them to do things the way *we* would do them. As if they had our wiring.

Can you see how the 3-Minute Survey speaks directly to this problem? The 3-Minute Survey shows that *every person is wired differently*. This means that every person approaches life differently. Every person acts differently. Every person makes different decisions based on their core, inborn attitude. That automatically means they'll deal with lifestyle decisions differently than we will.

But in that case, when it comes to altering our lifestyle and doing things differently, we don't need to worry about "straightening out" the people around us—our spouse, our kids, our co-workers, our friends, our customers. We should just assume they are wired differently, and so they will see things from a different perspective. That's a good thing, not a bad thing. It means they can help us with strengths that they have but we don't—and vice versa.

"Well, Wayne, that's all well and good," I hear someone saying. "I'm an R, and I can that see if my wife were an M, we'd clash on everything. But my wife's an R, just like me. According to your scheme, we should get along just fine. But we don't! We clash on everything, too. So what's up with that?"

What's "up" is two things. First, just because two people have the same lead letter doesn't mean they won't get into conflict. If anything, since both people in the situation mentioned are R's, they are *more* likely to get into conflict, because R's tend to be highly opinionated and controlling. R's are smart. R's like ideas. R's defend their ideas. R's assume they are right. Why, two R's might battle to the death, so to speak, just to prove to the other that they're right!

But there's a second, more important reason why two people with the same lead letter can clash. It's that they have three other letters in their patterns, and they will clash if the order of those three letters is quite different for the two of them. That difference accounts for a *lot* of the conflict people experience. The first two letters *in combination* are especially important for relationships. Let me show you why.

Go back to the 3-Minute Survey you filled out (page 36). I want you to draw a line down the center of the page between the R column and the I column. On the TR side of that division (the left-hand side) write the word "Head." On the IM side of that division (the right-hand side) write the word "Heart." What I want you to see is that T and R represent "head" letters, meaning that people who lead with a T or an R tend to approach life *first* through logic and reason based on hard information. I and M represent "heart" letters, meaning that people who lead with an I or an M tend to approach life *first* through intuition, relationships, and how they feel.

By the way, people sometimes ask me whether this distinction between "head" and "heart" is just another version of the popular left brain/right brain dichotomy. According to that scheme, people use the left side of their brain to be logical and practical, and they use the right side to be intuitive and emotional. Supposedly a person tends to favor using one side of the brain more than the other. Is that what I mean by "head" and "heart"? *The answer is no.* It's possible that there may be some connection between my system and left/right brain theory. But my system doesn't try to account for why people do as they do by looking at brain activity. Moreover, my system allows for a lot more individuality than simply labeling people as "left-brained" or "right-brained." That's too simplistic.

So, referring again to the 3-Minute Survey, which side of the divide is your first letter on—the "head" side or the "heart" side? Make note of that. Then look at the second letter of your pattern. It also heavily affects your approach to life. What's the combination of your first two letters? There are three possibilities:

1   Your pattern is led by two "head" letters: TR or RT.
2   Your pattern is led by two "heart" letters: IM or MI.
3   Your pattern is led by a combination of a "head" letter and a "heart" letter: TI, TM, RI, RM, IT, IR, MT, or MR.

What do these combinations mean? In order to keep things simple, let me explain by using the metaphor of boats. There's no particular reason why I chose boats. It's just the sort of thing that I, whose pattern leads with an I, would do. I needed a simple metaphor. I was probably fishing or something at the time I was thinking about this problem. I saw a boat and started thinking about boats. I made an instant commitment. I now use three kinds of boats to describe the three possibilities for combinations of letters in the scoring patterns:

1   *Barges.* If your first two letters are both "head" letters, TR or RT, I call you a Barge. You tend to pursue a focused agenda or plan, not particularly interested in how others are impacted by your actions or decisions, nor particularly concerned with how they "feel" about them. In that sense you're kind of like a barge: you push your way through life and expect others to accommodate themselves to what matters to you.

        "You make it sound like I don't care about people." If you're a Barge and that's what you're thinking at this point, then you're right: I *am* saying that your *first* concern is not people. I'm not necessarily saying that you have no concern for people (some Barges don't). But your *primary* concern as a Barge is with the task, the issue, the plan, the idea, the goal, or whatever. For you (as a Barge) people are a *means* to that end—even if people may benefit by that end.

The amazing thing about Barges is how utterly clueless some of them can be about people. I've met Barges who think of themselves as the kindest, most considerate individuals in the world. Then I meet their spouse, or kids, or co-workers, and boy, do they have a different opinion! The man who regards himself as Father of the Year has no idea that his wife and kids privately think of him as Jerk of the Century (or worse). You think I'm kidding? You think I'm being harsh? I'm not. I'm just shooting straight. Because if Barges want anything, they like for people to shoot straight.

Okay, here it is: if you're a Barge, the 3-Minute Survey ought to be a wake-up call for how you deal with relationships. Food and money probably aren't as much trouble for you, because the structure and control that go with being a Barge make it easier for you to stay within the limits of a diet or budget. But watch out when it comes to people! As a Barge, you need to come to terms with the fact that you are not *naturally* wired to focus on people, which means that it is quite easy for you to ignore or overlook the needs and concerns of people, and *not even realize it*. We'll talk more about that as we go through the book.

2   *Tugboats.* If your first two letters are both "heart" letters, IM or MI, I describe you as a Tugboat. You tend to focus on people through some form of personal

dynamic, such as influence or impact, or perhaps an appeal for compassion. I call you a Tugboat because you tend to come alongside others and either nudge them along or pull them along. Basically, you tug at other people's hearts.

That sounds rather winsome, doesn't it? But therein lies the danger for Tugboats. If you're a Tugboat, you can be so focused on the "soft stuff"—what you or others are experiencing, what you or others are feeling, what people's problems and concerns are, what people need to hear, how to influence them, how to involve them, how to hold their attention—that you ignore the practical realities of life. Things like schedules, deadlines, budgets, logistics, reports, numbers, quotas, supplies, finances, data, profit, costs, calories, interest rates, etc. "Oh, that's for the bean counters to worry about," may be your attitude.

Well, in fact, the "bean counters" (yes, those TR and RT "bean counters," the people who love facts) *will* pay attention to that stuff—and frequently take advantage of you when they do. You see, the problem for you as a Tugboat is that you are not *naturally* wired to "think things through." You think that practical realities don't matter. Well, it's true that they don't matter to you, but that doesn't mean they don't matter. They matter a *lot*. If you don't pay attention to them—and it's not in your nature to do that—they'll come back to bite you every time. In a moment, I'll show you what that means for your lifestyle.

3   *Sailboats.* If your first two letters are a combination "head" letter and "heart letter," TI, TM, RI, RM, IT, IR, MT, or MR, I describe you as a Sailboat. You tend to maneuver back and forth between leading with your

head or your heart, depending on the situation. In that way you are like a sailboat, quite adaptable according to the "winds" that you pick up from a given moment.

So are Sailboats free from trouble? By no means. Look back at your 3-Minute Survey. What were your composite scores for your "head" letters (TR) and "heart" letters" (IM)? If those scores differ by 7 or less, then you have a pretty good balance between them, meaning that both your "head" and your "heart" will affect your behavior about evenly. Sometimes, when it's appropriate, you'll use reason and logic more than feelings and impulse. At other times, when it's appropriate, you'll be more playful and easygoing, rather than strict or analytical. But in the main, you're pretty even-keeled.

What if the composite scores differ by 8 or more? In that case, you'll tend to favor the side with the higher score—which means your behavior will not be nearly as balanced. If your "head" score is higher, you'll quickly go with the plan, the facts, the deadline, or the logic, and only after those have been satisfied will you start considering the human elements of a situation. Conversely, if your "heart" score is higher, you'll be much more inclined to make human experience (whether your own or others') your first priority. Later on you'll start thinking about those "practical realities" that affect the situation.

Each of the patterns—Barges, Tugboats, and Sailboats—is incredibly valuable and tremendously useful in the world. They determine so much about how we live, how we make decisions, how we deal with stress, and how we react to the world around us on a daily basis. For that reason, I like to say, *Know what floats your boat!*

Having said that, I also need to point out that every pattern has a potential "dark side" to it, and that "dark side" can dramatically affect a person's lifestyle, as follows:

- *Barges* tend to be at lower risk for weight and money problems, but at higher risk for relational problems. Can you see why? Barges are great with information and details. They like stability and discipline. Many R's (though by no means all) are particularly strong when it comes to dealing with money. All of that enables Barges to watch what they eat and what they spend. If Barges need to lose a few pounds, it's no big deal to stay on a diet for a while until they reach their goal. Likewise, if they need to pay down a purchase, they find it easy to create a spending plan (a budget), and then work that plan until they've paid off what they owe.

    Where Barges tend to struggle is in their relationships, because relationships are not fundamentally about facts, logic, plans, performances, numbers, and so forth. Sure, those things enter into relationships and affect them. But relationships occur between human beings. Relationships are about connections, feelings, perceptions, time together, shared experiences, stories, trust, understanding, memories, and communication.

    By nature, Barges are not well equipped to function in those areas. They are not always open to new ideas, let alone open to feelings. Indeed, at times they can come across as overbearing, because they assume that everything is about being "right"—and of course they also assume they are "right." Consequently, they don't always listen very well. All of which means they struggle when it comes to people.

    Only they don't struggle, that's the problem. As I alluded earlier, Barges may have a five-alarm fire burning in their relationships at home, yet be utterly calm and collected—utterly clueless—believing that everything is okay. That's why Barges can be so shocked sometimes when one day their spouse suddenly announces, "I've had it! I'm filing for divorce." Barges can totally miss the signals that things are not working in their relationships.

• *Tugboats,* here is where it's your turn to receive a wake-up call: you need to know that *Tugboats are at higher risk than either Barges or Sailboats in almost all areas of lifestyle management.* Tugboats struggle more than anyone else with obesity, debt, and relational troubles. I have ten years of data from using the 3-Minute Survey to support that.

Think about the nature of Tugboats. They are playful and easygoing. They tend to be friendly and outgoing. They'd much rather have fun than stick to a boring old plan. They'd much rather live in the moment than worry about the future. And they approach the world through experience more than reason. Indeed, some Tugboats don't want to think at all: "Just let me live my life. Don't bother me with the facts."

That attitude is perilous for living in this society, because we live in a quick-fix, instant gratification society. Tugboats are easy targets for quick fixes. Are you hungry? Here's a fast-food meal. Here's an all-you-can-eat buffet. Here's a vending machine right within reach. Do you need some cash? Here's an "introductory low-interest" credit card. Here's a convenient ATM machine or debit card. Here's a "special" home equity loan. Are you having troubles with your mate? Here's a perfume that will fix that. Here's a little technique that is guaranteed to remedy that. Here's a TV show that will solve that problem in less than half an hour.

And not only do quick fixes get Tugboats into trouble,

they *keep* them in trouble with empty promises of a quick fix to their troubles. Have you had too much of that fast food, so that you're now grossly overweight? Here's a diet formula that will trim you right down in thirty days. Here's a surgery that will tie off your stomach to keep you from eating so much. Better yet, here's a surgery that will suck that fat right out of you. Are you in over your head financially? Here's yet another credit card, this one advertising "no transfer fees." Here's a debt consolidation plan to lower (and lengthen) your monthly payments. Here's a bankruptcy that will get you back on your feet (and ruin your credit) right away. Are you depressed about all this? Here's a big gulp of calories to drown it all. Here's a cruise to escape from it all. Here's a pill to feel better about it all. And if all that is not enough, you can always overcommit and lose your focus.

Can you see how our society "rewards" Tugboats for not being able to say no? It rewards them with instant gratification. Meanwhile, as we'll see, there's a lot of money to be made in getting Tugboats to eat too much, spend too much, and not set good boundaries in their relationships.

- *Sailboats* tend to make more balanced lifestyle decisions than either Barges or Tugboats. But as I pointed out earlier, a lot depends on your composite scores and the difference between the two. If your "head" score is 8 points or greater than your "heart" score, you can sometimes act more like a Barge than a Sailboat, especially if you're angry or anxious. If your "heart" score is 8 points or greater than your "head" score, you can sometimes act more like a Tugboat than a Sailboat, especially if you're feeling depressed or guilty.

Whether you're a Barge, a Tugboat, or a Sailboat, you have the potential to get into trouble with your lifestyle. But just because you *can* get into trouble doesn't mean you *have* to get into trouble. You can take steps to counter your *natural* tendencies with intentional actions that serve your best interests. You've already started to do that by becoming aware of your attitude and what your natural tendencies are. You've done that by taking the 3-Minute Survey and evaluating your results. That's the first step in the ALTER model:

> **A = Awareness.** Become aware of your attitude, the natural, inborn hardwiring that drives your behavior.
>
> **L = Learn.** Learn as much as you can about your inborn attitude (as revealed by your scoring pattern), and learn as much as possible about the issue you want to work on.
>
> **T = Tactical plan.** Create a realistic and personally meaningful plan for getting the results you want.
>
> **E = Execute the plan.** Translate your good intentions into actual action by working your personalized plan.
>
> **R = Re-evaluate.** Periodically evaluate your progress and use what you learn to develop your next plan of action.

So now that you've completed the first step, Awareness, let's move on to the second step, Learn. In the next two chapters I'll help you figure out what you need to learn and how to learn it in order to permanently ALTER your lifestyle.

CHAPTER 4 You Don't Know What You Don't Know

I need to begin this section by pointing out that "learn" is a negative word for some people. It's kind of like the word "change," which I talked about earlier. "Change" is a negative word for some people because it suggests a complete, 180-degree turnaround. It's too radical. It requires too much.

"Learn" is another word that causes some people trouble, because they've had negative experiences with learning, especially in schools. For them, school was hard, boring, or irrelevant. As a result, they now regard any sort of "learning" as hard, boring, or irrelevant.

On the other hand, some people love the word "learn" because for them school was a very positive experience. They were excellent students and they loved the process. Some of them are even teachers today because they enjoyed "learning" so much in school.

What makes the difference between these two groups? As we've discussed in earlier chapters, it all depends on their wiring. The first group, which sees "learning" as a negative, tends to be Tugboats and playful Sailboats. The latter group, which sees "learning" as a positive, tends to be Barges and serious-minded Sailboats.

But now here's some good news, whether you think you like to learn or not: everyone learns. It doesn't matter how intelligent you are, how quick you are, or how much formal education you have. Everyone learns.

The catch is that *everyone learns differently*. Some people learn by reading, listening, and memorizing. Some people learn by participating in an activity. Some people learn best by personal instruction from a tutor or mentor, someone they can observe and ask lots of questions. Some people only learn if they are part of a team, and the team is learning together. Some people learn by trying things for themselves; they don't need a teacher, they don't want a teacher. There are all kinds of ways that people learn— actually, as many ways as there are people, because every individual learns a bit differently.

How *you* learn depends on your attitude, your "wiring" that we've been looking at in the previous chapters:

- *Barges* like facts and logic. So books that present lots of factual information and give a well-reasoned argument will tend to have appeal to Barges, to the extent that a Barge likes to read. The same might be true for structured, well-researched lectures, to the extent that a Barge likes to listen. Barges also often enjoy learning from spreadsheets, research projects, maps, databases, schematic drawings, and other forms that present data that they can process mentally.

- *Tugboats* like fun and people. So the things they read (if they care to read at all) tend to be books, magazines, and other materials that are entertaining, easy to get through, illustrated by pictures and photographs, full of stories and anecdotes, perhaps emotionally moving, and concerned with human experience. Likewise, Tugboats would rather watch a video than listen to a lecture, unless the speaker is highly captivating through his or her personal dynamic. Tugboats often learn best as part of a team, or when they get personally involved in an activity with others, or when they can get their hands on the activity.

- *Sailboats* can go either way—learning through their head or their heart—depending (as always) on the balance between their "head" and "heart" composite scores. Those that lean toward the "head" will tend to prefer "head styles" of learning: logical, sequential, factually based. Those who lead toward the "heart" will tend to prefer a "heart style": emotionally engaging, experiential, presenting human interest. Sailboats often make the best learners because they can adapt more easily to the demands of various learning situations—everything from the Internet to books, articles, television, radio, seminars, lectures, and so on.

Now I stress this point about different learning styles because I want you to know that when the ALTER model says you need to *Learn* some things, it's using the word "learn" in a very broad sense. I want you to learn what you need to learn, but I want you to learn it in the ways that make the most sense for you, given your hardwiring. That's why the first thing you need to learn about is your scoring pattern. It tells you a lot about *how* you learn in the first place. Knowing how you learn will help you customize the ALTER model to you. And even if some of the learning has to come through ways that don't fit you, at least you can know that and not shy away from those activities just because they feel a little uncomfortable. I'm not asking you to be someone other than who you are.

We humans start learning about lifestyle issues the minute we are born. We start taking in information from an enormous set of sources: our parents and families, our school teachers, our teenage peers, our professors if we go to college, our superiors if we serve in the military, our spouses if we get married, our bosses and coworkers, our adult friends, our spiritual leaders at churches, synagogues, and mosques, entertainers and performers, the media, the government, countless retailers and merchants and their advertising, all of those "quick-fix" organizations we talked about in the last chapter and so on. The point is that we face an unrelenting flood of information coming our way. Information that affects the lifestyle decisions we make.

Some of that information is intended to be helpful. That is, it's intended to guide us toward making positive, healthy lifestyle decisions that will benefit us. On the other hand, some of that information is not at all helpful. In fact, a lot of it is actually intended to cause us to make certain choices that are not in our best interests. It's not that the people giving out that information are out to harm us per se. But the fact is, they have an agenda. They push information that helps accomplish their agenda, and frankly they don't care what happens to those of us who are influenced by their information. If we benefit, fine, but if we get harmed, so what? All they really care about is their agenda (which is usually about making money).

In this chapter, I want to talk about how you can get positive, useful information that will help you ALTER your lifestyle. In the next chapter, I'll talk about guarding against the negative influences of harmful, agenda-driven information.

If you want to ALTER some area of your lifestyle, you've got to *Learn* as much as you can about that area. The fact that things aren't working for you in that area tells you that there are probably some things you don't know about that area, and some things you're not paying attention to.

For example, say your area of concern is weight control. If you want to ALTER your weight, you're going to have to learn some things about nutrition, exercise, food labels, fat content, metabolism, stretching, blood pressure, cholesterol, and other topics pertaining to weight.

Tugboats tend to struggle the most in learning about those things because it takes time, it requires a bit of research, it may mean memorizing some information, and it will certainly take some effort. Most important, it means that they'll have to set some boundaries and make them stick. Tugboats aren't naturally wired to do any of those things, so of course they are the most at-risk for obesity.

Most of the Tugboats I've interviewed who have weight problems don't know the basics about food and nutrition, like how many calories are in a fat-gram, or how many calories are in a carbohydrate. They don't know how to read a food label properly, which means they fall prey to false, misleading, or inaccurate labels—like the ones that advertise "no cholesterol" or "sugar free," yet are full of fat-producing substances. They don't understand that food labels like those are basically hype that tells *what isn't in a product, but doesn't tell what is in the product.* Tugboats are at risk because they tend to trust someone else for the information they learn.

Barges do just the opposite, especially if they lead with a TR pattern. Many Barges will actually study food labels because they've done a bit of research about things like carbs and fats and cholesterol and food additives. They know all about the thirty to forty minutes, three days a week, of cardiovascular activity that are required to set one's metabolism, reduce bad cholesterol, and assist in weight loss and controlling blood pressure. Barges are less at risk for weight problems because they tend to pay attention to information about food and nutrition and use that information to make wise choices.

Sailboats are another matter. Sailboats tend to have the learning style of Tugboats, but the knowledge of Barges. In other words, Sailboats will learn the basics of metabolism, they'll learn how to read food labels, they'll see the value in stretching and exercise and may even do it once in a while because it is fun, but they tend to be easily distracted and won't make a discipline of eating properly, exercising, monitoring their blood pressure, and following the other habits of a healthy lifestyle. They *learn* the information, but lack the *focus* that they need.

Learning about a lifestyle area like nutrition is not a matter of whether or not someone can learn. Everyone learns. It's how one learns that makes the difference. Someone who tells me they "can't" learn something about a lifestyle area is usually saying they "won't" learn about it. It's not their *ability* to learn that's holding them up, it's their *willingness* to learn. If they don't want to learn, I can't help them (remember Ginny in Chapter 1). But if they're willing to learn what they need to learn, I can show them how to do that.

So, for instance, say you're a Tugboat and you learn by participating in an activity. In that case, ask a friend who knows a thing or two about healthy cooking to come over to your house and show you how to prepare some nutritional meals that will help you start eating properly. Or maybe you learn by watching. In that case, check out a video or a TV program on PBS or the Food Network that explains in a very entertaining, engaging way how your body processes food, and the kind of food it most needs. Or maybe you learn as part of a team. In that case, find friends who want to learn about nutrition and team up with them for a month of learning about nutrition. Compare notes, share recipes, trade tips, and work together to take in the information you need.

Do you see my point? If you want to lose weight, you've got to know something about the food you're putting into your body. Some foods are better for your body than others. Some foods are guaranteed to make you gain weight, and some foods will help you lose weight. *Nutrition* is all about food and its effect on your body. There are probably a thousand ways to learn about nutrition. Find ways that fit how *you* learn and get the information you need about nutrition.

I could say the same thing about all the other issues of losing weight. And also for money: issues like budgeting, savings, retirement, investments, insurance, credit cards, and so forth. Here again, *Tugboats* (IM, MI) tend to struggle for the same reasons they struggle with nutrition. They find financial information to be overwhelming—too detailed and structured. Their eyes glaze over if you start talking about credit card interest rates, insurance coverage, the many kinds of investments that are available and how they work, mortgages, car financing, and the like. Tugboats learn with their heart rather than their head, and so anything having to do with finances seems boring and irrelevant. Their focus is on people, not money.

Barges, on the other hand, tend to thrive on doing financial research. Barges learn with their head, and so they'll go on the Internet and research financial topics, they'll subscribe to financial publications, they'll attend financial seminars, they'll review financial reports. Barges often see financial success as a measure of their identity. To them, making money is an irresistible intellectual challenge, a type of sporting event that they must win. Needless to say, Tugboats, along with Sailboats who lead with I or M, are no match for a Barge's financial prowess.

Sailboats tend to do better with money issues than do Tugboats, but again their learning style depends on whether they lead with a head letter (T or R) or a heart letter (I or M). Sailboats who lead with I or M tend to be smart about money in practical ways, but typically they don't take time to research the details of financial products. They learn through trial and error and life experience, as well as from trusted friends. Quite often they overuse credit cards. Sailboats who lead with T or R tend to do more research, and create a more structured approach to their finances. As a result they typically have more in-depth knowledge about things like investments, mortgages, retirement planning, and savings.

What about relationships? Do the three boats handle issues like communication, trust, time management, stress, setting boundaries, and recreation, differently? You bet!

Tugboats have learned over their lifetime to be great communicators. They trust others and like to have fun, and they tend to be active in civic organizations and churches or synagogues. If anything, Tugboats get stressed because they overcommit to others. They constantly struggle with time management. Perhaps the most important thing Tugboats can learn from this book will be to set better boundaries in their relationships and say "no" more often.

Barges have just the opposite problem. They set too many boundaries when it comes to people and say "no" too quickly and too often. As a result, their relationships suffer because no one can get close to them. Barges tend to be the workaholics who neglect time with family and friends because they value success at work more than relationships. The challenge for a Barge is to learn how to play, as well as how to get along with others.

Sailboats, as you might guess, fall in between Tugboats and Barges in the way they handle relationships. That might sound like a good thing, but in a way Sailboats may feel the most stress of all because they are constantly in tension between their head and their heart. They want to have great relationships with everyone—family, friends, community—but also want to be on top professionally and financially. Somewhat like Tugboats, Sailboats can have difficulty in relationships because they have trouble setting boundaries.

For a list of RLM-recommended books and other sources of information for each of the three lifestyle areas—food, money, and relationships—visit www.RealLifeManagement.com/resources.php.

Okay, so let's say that you do as I've suggested, and you start learning about a given lifestyle area. You use your learning style to actively seek out sources of good information, and you have every intention of using that information to make healthy lifestyle decisions. Let me warn you about what's going to happen: unless you pay attention, *you're liable to let your attitude get in the way of your learning.* Isn't that interesting? The flip side of cooperating with your attitude in order to learn in the way *you* best learn is to allow your attitude to keep you from learning. I see that happen all the time. Let me give you an example.

Tom and Sarah are a pretty typical married couple: they are

complete opposites. That's why they fell in love and got married. Because opposites do attract. Eventually, however, opposites repel. And that's also why Tom and Sarah are a pretty typical married couple: they find reasons to quarrel about almost everything.

Tom is a Barge. Sarah is a Tugboat. That's a marriage made in heaven (even if sometimes it feels like . . . well, you get the point). Tom and Sarah need a new car. That's a lifestyle decision. So how will they approach that decision? Let's imagine that they've been reading this book, and they realize that they need to *learn* some things about cars before they go shopping. So that's what they do.

As a Barge (Tom's first two letters are TR), Tom goes right to the Internet and looks at several sites offering consumer guidance for purchasing cars. He gets information on pricing, fuel efficiency, warranties, customer satisfaction surveys, repair costs, dealer locations, histories of manufacturers' recalls, safety records, government studies of crashworthiness, industry ratings of quality, and so on. He then begins to compare specific makes and models. He evaluates different features. He itemizes optional packages. He calculates prices with and without various add-ons. He also looks up financing options. He studies interest rates. He figures approximate trade-in values. He estimates payments. In short, Tom is learning the way a barge would learn: he goes right for the facts.

Meanwhile, Sarah, who is a Tugboat (he first two letters are MI), learns about cars the way a Tugboat learns: She talks to people. She asks her friends what they'd recommend. She looks at what they drive. She notices whether they are smiling or not as they get in and out of their cars. She also notices ads for cars on TV and in magazines. She looks at the people in the ads and imagines herself and her family in the ads. Would that car fit them? Can she see herself driving it? Does she like the color? Does it seem too big for her to drive? Or is it too small, not enough car to protect her? How fast will it go? Will her kids enjoy riding in it? Will it be easy for her to fill up the gas tank? Does it have a DVD player?

As Sarah begins to narrow her selections, she notices that one local dealer is offering four tickets to a football game with any purchase of a new vehicle. She figures that should appeal to Tom. Another dealer is promising a month's worth of free gas to buyers of a particular model. That seems like a bargain. And then there's the dealer who is throwing a big party at his dealership to unload what he says are overstocked vehicles. "Everything's gotta go!" he screams on the TV commercial. He's promising free barbecue, soft drinks, and kiddie rides. Maybe that's where the family should start looking for a new car.

Now notice that Tom and Sarah are doing exactly what I've recommended they do. They are using their learning styles to go out and learn about cars. That's great! The problem comes when they need to learn something important that *doesn't* correspond to their scoring patterns.

In a situation like Tom and Sarah's, where one is a Barge and the other is a Tugboat, it's the Tugboat who usually gets in trouble first. So here comes Sarah, armed with a suggestion for where she and Tom should go shopping for a car. She makes that suggestion to Tom, and that's when it all starts falling apart.

"Why would we want to go there?" Tom asks matter-of-factly. Never mind the fact that it's his wife who is making the suggestion. That alone ought to cause Tom to pay attention. But no. He's already got the make, the model, the dealer, and the deal all figured out in his mind. The facts are the facts. He assumes Sarah will see it the way he sees it, plain as day.

Well, guess what? Sarah doesn't see it that way! She's got a picture in her mind of the "perfect" car. And she'll know it when she sees it. But the only way she'll see it is if she and Tom go drive it. So she's gung ho to hit the dealerships and see what they've got and take some cars out for a test drive.

"That's a waste of time!" Tom says, certain that he's saving the family from an afternoon of futility.

"What do you mean, a waste of time?" Sarah shoots back. "I thought we'd agreed that we need to buy a new car."

"Well, yeah," Tom says. "We need a new car. But not the one you're suggesting."

"What's wrong with my suggestion? You haven't even looked at it. How would you know whether it's the car we want?"

"I don't need to look at it," Tom goes on. "I've already researched all this, and that car didn't even make the first cut. It uses too much gas. It has a lousy repair record. It's overpriced relative to its competitors. The only thing it's got going for it is consumer appeal."

"Well, what's wrong with that?" Sarah says, starting to feel hurt. "*I'm* a consumer!"

"Honey, you just don't understand," Tom replies with what Sarah regards as a terribly patronizing tone. "A car like that isn't worth considering. It may look nice, but it's a piece of junk." He pauses a moment, and then barges on. "Now let me tell you what we really need." He then names a particular make and model, which happens to be a hybrid. He describes the engine, the transmission, the wheelbase, the aerodynamics of the body. He talks about cornering and stopping. He goes into crash tests. He explains the hybrid's exceptional fuel efficiency. He delves into prices. He finally wraps up by talking about an unusually sweet deal on one of the cars that he's found at an out-of-the-way dealership. "So as you can see, that's the car for us, all things considered." He pauses for a second. Sarah isn't even looking at him anymore. So finally he asks, "What do you think?"

Sarah doesn't let Tom know what she really thinks. The truth is, she tuned him out about the time he dismissed her with all that stuff about "consumer appeal." And that's where Sarah made a mistake. (That's also where Tom made a mistake. I'll come back to that in a minute.) Sarah made the mistake of letting her attitude get in the way of learning something important.

You see, Sarah did what a lot of Tugboats do. She got information about cars from her friends and advertisements and other
sources she could *experience*. To her, buying a car is an emotional
decision. But that's what got her in trouble. Because the truth is,
there are lots of *facts* about cars that Sarah needs to take into account. Otherwise, she's liable to make a poor decision that will end
up causing trouble later on. But Sarah closed her mind when Tom
began to share some of those facts with her. That's easy for a Tugboat to do. In fact, it's almost instinctive, because Tugboats don't
learn with their heads as much as with their hearts. In that way
their *attitude* gets in the way of their learning.

Sarah stopped listening, and so she stopped learning. Would
you like to know what she was really thinking as Tom prattled on
and on? "I am married to *the* most rude, insensitive, stubborn,
opinionated, bossy, inflexible, condescending, arrogant bore in the
world! It's leftovers for dinner for him this evening, *and* he can do
the dishes!"

Needless to say, it's going to be a long, tension-filled night at
Tom and Sarah's house! Where did Tom go wrong? Well, he made
a couple of boneheaded mistakes. One is an obvious communication blunder. Tom did what most of us do: he started dispensing
information in the way that made the most sense to him, given his
attitude, but completely overlooked the attitude of the person with
whom he was trying to communicate. In short, he treated Sarah as
if she were a Barge like him, throwing out fact after fact, as if that
would make sense to her. Of course it did not, because Sarah is a
Tugboat. Things might have gone a lot differently if Tom had taken
Sarah's attitude into account, and adjusted his explanation of cars
somewhat to match Sarah's scoring pattern.

But this story about Tom and Sarah is not just about buying a
car. It's a lifestyle story. It's got money issues and relationship issues all tied together. And the stress that comes with the way this

couple is processing the issues creates a potential health issue, as well. See how money, relationships, and health are all interrelated?

Sarah needed to be to be a little more logical in selecting a car. The truth is, if she were going to buy a car by herself, she would want to have some basic questions written down to ask the dealer. Questions such as: What's the markup over the sticker price? (Car dealers typically ask for between 10 and 18 percent over the sticker price.) What's the interest rate for the financing? (Assuming the car will be financed; interest for a car loan is often calculated at the prime rate plus 1 percent.) How does the dealer's lease payment differ from a regular car payment? (It's always smaller, but how does it actually compare in value.) What is the gas mileage for the vehicle? (Nowadays anything less than 20 miles per gallon in the city is unacceptable for most buyers.)

Sarah didn't think about all that information because she knew Tom would. And therein lies the problem. When Tom wanted to buy based on practical information, Sarah became uncomfortable because she truly didn't like his approach to *her*. For her, the issue moved from finances to relationships. Isn't that ironic? Sarah married Tom because she admired his intelligence and the way he made life choices. But now she is unhappy with him for using those very skills to buy a car.

On the other hand, Tom married Sarah because she was fun. Even though she makes quick decisions without a lot of research, she brings excitement to his life. But now he doesn't trust her judgment, even though she's trying to select a car that will bring pleasure to their lives.

How Tom and Sarah process such an issue is not a matter of who is right and who is wrong. It's a matter of their attitudes getting in the way of their communication, and therefore having a negative impact on their relationship. They both need to stop and remember that they are a team. They need to regard each other's opinion as important, and not let their instinctive attitudes dismiss what the other has to say. Both have important points to offer. And before things get out of hand, they need to remember that it is, after all, just a car. Tom could stand a little kinder approach to Sarah, and Sarah could benefit from doing a little more financial research to accommodate Tom.

Well, now that we see how Tom's and Sarah's attitudes affect the way they approach the purchase of a car, let's look at how these two approach another issue, this one involving their parenting. Just to set the scene, Tom has a pretty typical build for a Barge: he's tall, thin, and well groomed. Sarah is very attractive, but she's shorter and about twenty pounds overweight for her frame—not unusual for a Tugboat. Tom likes to exercise, and he maintains a very healthy diet. No sweets for him, except on the weekends. Sarah, on the other hand, does not enjoy exercise, so she doesn't work out. "That's Tom's thing," she says. She has a habit of eating at fast-food restaurants, and she frequently indulges a craving for chocolate.

Now meet Tom and Sarah's oldest daughter, Candace. Candace is a hard-charging, intelligent, competitive child who is about thirty pounds overweight for her frame. She loves her parents and she works hard to make them proud of her. For Dad, she makes good grades. For Mom, she competed and won the role of head cheerleader at her high school, and Sarah couldn't be happier.

You might have guessed that Candace is a combination of her parents. She's a Sailboat whose first two letters are I and R. That makes her fun, involved, and smart and also very active. As a senior in high school, she's constantly on the go, which means she, too, eats a lot of fast food. She charges it on the credit card that she talked her parents into giving her during her junior year.

There's potential trouble brewing for Candace. You see, she's *learning* from her parents as she's growing up. And if she—and they—are not careful, Candace could end up with some real problems. On the positive side, Candace's competitive nature and analytical ability have enabled her to end up in the top 10 percent of her class. And, like her mother, she is loads of fun to be with and she pays attention to the feedback she gets from friends and peers.

But even though Candace admires her father, and he praises her for her good work in school, they struggle in their relationship because he is always talking about her weight. "You need more self-discipline," he tells her. "You need to get on an exercise program, like I do. And stop eating that junk food!" Tom means well, but all his daughter hears is shame. So she turns to her mother for comfort, and guess how Sarah handles her daughter's hurt? Why, she fixes her the most wonderful chocolate desserts! And on the weekends they go shopping. After all, isn't that how a mother shows her love?

There are several lessons to be learned from this family story. The first is that everyone in the family has their own unique attitude. That's actually good news. It means that each of them has a special contribution to make. On the other hand, it means that each of them can inflict harm on the others if their attitude is used as a weapon, instead of their working together and combining their strengths as a team.

We can also see from this family how financial issues, health issues, and relational issues are all tied together. Each issue impacts and is impacted by the other issues. The common thread among them is the core attitudes and beliefs of each family member. Those attitudes and beliefs dramatically affect how each one learns from the others.

Perhaps the most important observation to make is that Candace is learning some negative habits without even realizing it. She doesn't know that her weight is merely a symptom of underlying attitudes of which she is unaware. She doesn't know what she doesn't know.

And that's true for most people. They don't know what they don't know. The most important thing they don't know is their attitude. They just live however they live, unaware that the weight they're carrying, or the debt they're carrying, or the broken relationship they're enduring is not by chance. Those kinds of lifestyle challenges are produced by choices that people make based on inborn attitudes of which they're completely unaware.

By now, though, you are no longer one of those people. You've identified your attitude and started to see how it affects your outlook. You've started to *learn* about who you are, which is the first step in the ALTER process. But now let me help you learn about some people who can get you in trouble as you try to work that process. Some of those people try to look like your best friend, but in reality they have an agenda for you to follow. In the next chapter, I'll tell you who some of those "hidden agenda drivers" (HADs) are. I'll show you who is at risk for their masterful appeals. And I'll suggest some strategies for steering clear of their misinformation so that you can stay in control of your lifestyle.

CHAPTER 5   **Don't Be Had by the HADs**

Does it strike you as curious that when it comes to learning about the three biggest lifestyle problems facing Americans today—obesity, debt, and broken relationships—the one institution of society that is supposed to help people learn is basically missing in action? *Where are the schools?* Why aren't schools teaching our young people about these issues? Why aren't schools preparing kids to take care of their bodies by managing their weight, to take care of their finances and stay out of debt, to take care of their relationships and build healthy families?

As I said in the last chapter, many people look back on their formal schooling as a waste of time. That's because schools teach in ways that don't fit with how a lot of people learn. That's bad enough. But here I'm saying that when it comes to three of the most relevant issues Americans deal with, American schools by and large don't even bring up these issues in the curriculum.

That failure is costing young people big time! For example, did you know that one in six young people between 6 to 19 is now overweight or obese? That's more than 9 million children—about four times the number forty years ago.

It's interesting that if you go back forty years, you'll recall that we were finding out that tobacco companies were targeting young people, trying to get them started on smoking cigarettes. There is evidence that they even colluded with candy makers to sell candy cigarettes to kids to get them pretending that they were smoking. The hope was that later on those kids would try the real thing.[1] The tobacco companies knew that if they could get a kid hooked on tobacco at an early age, they would have a customer for life (or a "customer for death," as it often turns out).

Well, today, forty years later, it's not the tobacco companies that are the biggest danger to our kids, but the snack and soft drink companies along with the fast-food chains and the candy makers that are aggressively pushing food into America's children. I believe the government should put some safeguards in place here, just as it has with tobacco products, because food has become one of the two top drugs in America today (the other drug is money, more specifically credit). Food and money have become "drugs" in the sense that they are sold and used in ways that promote addiction.

For example, 9 million kids are already showing the adverse affects of eating too much. They might as well be smoking, because the excessive weight they are carrying is as deadly as nicotine. Obesity is directly linked to heart disease, strokes, diabetes, various cancers, arthritis, infertility, gallstones, asthma, snoring, and countless other health-related problems later in life. "Weight sits like a spider at the center of an intricate, tangled web of health and disease," says Dr. Walter Willett of the Harvard School of Public Health.[2]

And decades before that weight finally kills the body, it begins killing the soul of the person. I know, because remember, I grew up as "the fat kid." The kid people laughed at, sometimes behind my back, sometimes to my face. It's hard to believe in yourself if people are laughing at you. If people are laughing at you, you eventually start thinking of yourself as a joke.

Not long ago the *Dallas Morning News* printed a feature story about Jim and Jo Ann Tupper of Frisco, Texas, a couple who had lost 300 pounds between the two of them. "People would often ask Ms. Tupper, 32, how she got to be so big," the article said, and then went on to explain, "She suffered no dark childhood traumas, beyond being cruelly teased for her weight."[3]

Excuse me?! How is being cruelly teased *not* a childhood trauma? I understand what the writer intended to say. She meant that this woman's habit of overeating as a child was not a response to physical or sexual abuse. For many, obesity is a self-destructive response to incidents that have destroyed their self-esteem. For others, obesity actually becomes a protective mechanism: by staying fat, they remain unattractive to their abuser, which is exactly what they need to do to survive.[4]

Fortunately, Jo Ann Tupper went through none of that. Her weight, she believes, came from a very simple activity: "Open mouth, insert food. Chew, swallow, repeat."[5] (Can you guess what Jo Ann's scoring pattern might be?) My point is that when an overweight child is called names by other children, or is made fun of, or has jokes pulled on her, or is left out of certain activities, or is unable to belong to a group, or has to sit on the sidelines and watch other kids play or perform, or is otherwise treated cruelly by her peers, the effects of those slights can destroy her sense of worth. And those feelings of worthlessness can last a lifetime and lead to lots of other troubles: abusive relationships, self-destructive habits and addictions, poor decisions, squandered opportunities, even suicide.

"If childhood obesity continues to increase, it . . . could result in our current generation of children becoming the first in American history to live shorter lives than their parents," writes former President Bill Clinton in a *Parade* magazine cover story. Imagine that: the life expectancy of Americans *decreasing*.

"Why is this happening?" the former president asks. "Because children are eating more unhealthy foods and exercising less. Who's responsible? We all are. Too many parents don't have time to prepare—or believe they can't afford—healthier foods. Too many schools have stopped physical education programs, rely on vending machines with sugary treats to raise much-needed cash and don't serve healthy meals in the cafeteria. And too few restaurants and fast-food outlets offer low-fat, low-salt and low-calorie meals."[6]

President Clinton has joined with the American Heart Association and Arkansas Governor Mike Huckabee to support school-based efforts to educate children about healthy eating, increase physical education, improve the quality of cafeteria food, and either eliminate vending machines or fill them with healthier snacks. I applaud those efforts. I also believe that the American Heart Association and policymakers have their work cut out for them.

I say that because schools are starting to become active participants in creating lifestyle problems. For years, the food served at educational institutions was laughed at for its poor quality and bland taste. In fact, the term "institutional food" became synonymous with inferior food service.

No wonder, then, that as the fast-food industry sprouted up in the second half of the 20th century and spread across the land, the franchisers noticed that stores near colleges and universities did a great business with students, professors, and other members of the academic communities. Many students actually preferred to eat off-campus at fast-food joints than to use the on-campus meal plans they had paid for.

Then came the great university marketing blitz of the 1990s. With baby boomers graduated and baby busters coming of age, schools realized they had to become much more competitive. One major area marked for improvement: food service. But how could a university compete with a McDonald's, Wendy's, or Taco Bell? It was only a matter of time before the solution became obvious: allow the fast-food vendors on-campus. In fact, house them right inside university dining halls.

As a result, today's schools don't have cafeterias; they have food courts, just like any mall. Students can order anything they want—pizza, cheeseburgers, French fries, burritos, nachos with cheese. No salaried nutritionists dreaming up meal plans for today's busy scholars! (By the way, this idea of "food courts" featuring fast food sold by brand-name vendors is starting to trickle down to high schools and even middle schools.)

Switch issues with me to the problem of credit card debt. When freshmen show up to register at major universities in this country, one of the first things they often encounter, perhaps online or in the student center or right outside the bookstore, is an opportunity to sign up for a credit card. Usually a "free" credit card. That's what they're told anyway. "Free instant credit." That sort of aggressive marketing makes it extremely easy for students to obtain a credit card.

But what most people don't think about is that in some cases the university is receiving a piece of the action. For every dollar the student charges, the school earns a small "donation" from the credit card company. The more students that sign up, and the more students charge, the more revenue comes to the school. There's no risk on the part of the school. All it has to do is give the credit card company free access to its students. In fact, many of these cards are so-called "affiliation" cards that "co-brand" the school's name and insignia along with the credit card brand. That way the credit card company can appeal to feelings of loyalty that students and alumni have to their school. It all gets marketed as a benign, painless way to support your school financially. All you have to do is charge it!

So what's wrong with this picture? Well, you tell me. In this three-way transaction you've got a multibillion-dollar credit card company, a well-endowed school that's got a billion-dollar annual budget, and an eighteen-year-old kid with maybe $500 in his new checking account. A kid, by the way, who has never had a credit card in his life. Of those three parties, who is most likely to get into trouble? Who is the least responsible? Who has the least maturity? We know that there are entire law firms looking out for the credit card company's interests. Likewise, the university has plenty of legal counsel. But who is looking out for the student's best interests?

In 2000, Nellie Mae, a prominent lender of educational loans, reported that 78 percent of the undergraduate students applying to Nellie Mae for a loan had at least one credit card, and those students were carrying an average of $2,748 on that one card. Ninety-five percent of the graduate student applicants had at least one card, with an average balance of $4,776. On one card! And if that's not enough, 32 percent of the undergraduates had four or more cards.[7] Now why does a college student need four or more credit cards?

The point is that a college student innocently charging a slice of pizza at age twenty-one may still be paying off that pizza at age thirty. "Students figure, 'I'll live like I want to now and then when I get a job it will be easy to pay it back,'" says Gerri Detweiler, an advisor for Debt Counselors of America.[8] But then they don't get the job they expected. Or they don't get paid the salary they'd bargained on. And they discover it costs a lot more to live in this society than they ever imagined. And worst of all, many have student loans to repay—about $20,000 on average, according to the Government Accountability Office (GAO).[9]

Facts like these simply don't support the claim that today's college students are being taught "financial responsibility" by being handed a credit card so easily. Yet the GAO finds that most college administrators view credit card usage by students as something *positive*.[10]

It all sounds well and good to say that when kids graduate from high school they need to "grow up and learn responsibility." Believe me, I'm all for learning responsibility. But I know too much about people. It's not just a matter of maturity, but of *attitude*.

You see, I've been working with the 3-Minute Survey now for about fifteen years. During that time, about 50,000 people have taken the survey. I wouldn't represent that group as a scientific sampling of the population.[11] But given the large number of people who have taken the survey, I feel confident in estimating that about 40 percent of Americans are Tugboats in terms of their scoring patterns (that is, the first two letters of their pattern are the two heart letters, IM or MI).

The fact is, Tugboats struggle with what we call "responsibility." Can you see why? Tugboats have a hard time setting boundaries. They tend to be impulsive, easily enticed by emotional appeals, not particularly punctual, not especially interested in saving money or making profits, more interested in the experience of the moment than in long-term gains, and definitely more interested in excitement and fun than in discipline and routine. I'm not criticizing Tugboats, just making a dispassionate statement of how they tend to approach life.

This means that 40 percent of the population is not predisposed to what we call "responsibility." Please understand, I am *not* saying that if you are a Tugboat you are therefore irresponsible. I am saying that if you are a Tugboat, your inborn wiring predisposes you to struggle when it comes to things that we typically associate with "being responsible." Practically speaking, your wiring puts you at risk for lifestyle problems like obesity and debt. For that reason, we as a society ought to be more careful about pushing fast food and credit cards on young adults who by their very wiring are liable to get into trouble unless significant safeguards are put in place to help them act responsibly.

Instead of helping the vulnerable, we've got whole sectors of our society taking advantage of them. We've got well-funded entities actively pushing information designed to steer as many people as possible into their agendas. There's nothing wrong with having an agenda. I have an agenda in this book. But I've tried to be upfront about my agenda, so that readers can decide whether or not they want to follow it. The parties I'm talking about in this chapter are not always so transparent. For that reason, I call these information pushers the Hidden Agenda Drivers. The HADs, for short.

HADs is just a polite acronym, because in my opinion a lot of these folks are nothing but "drug dealers." I know that may sound like a strong and overly dramatic indictment, but hear me out. I said a moment ago that food and money have become the top drugs in America today. I mean that sincerely. Food and money have become *drugs*, potent means of escaping reality, and just as addictive as cocaine, tobacco, alcohol, or the other things we usually think of as drugs. And just as deadly. Fat kills. Debt kills (debt creates enormous stress, and that stress kills). But whereas we pass laws against crack and heroin, and we force makers of cigarettes, beer, and distilled spirits to put warning labels on their products, food and credit cards remain perfectly legal.

And perfectly moral, even though they could be viewed as the nation's top killers. Food and money are the "acceptable addictions." I mean, when's the last time you went to church or synagogue and heard the minister or rabbi say, "It's a sin to overeat," or "It's a sin to be over your head in debt"? If anything, you've got some churches that I daresay would have a hard time getting people in the door if it weren't for Krispy Kreme! And many a church's building wouldn't exist if the congregation hadn't gone deep in debt to build it.

I don't know why it is that food gets a free pass morally, since the Bible clearly condemns gluttony. "He who is a companion of gluttons humiliates his father," says Proverbs 28:7.

Or go to the New Testament, which tells Christians to "glorify God in your body."[12] There are many ways to glorify God with your body, but loading it up with an extra sixty pounds of flab is not one of them. Excess weight *destroys* the body. And so when I hear someone with an obvious weight problem pray, "Lord, keep me healthy," I can't help but wonder if God isn't sitting in heaven saying, "I'll do my best, but you know what would really help is if you'd drop fifty or sixty pounds."

Do you think God cares if your debt is so big that after you've paid your bills and the monthly minimums on your credit cards, you have nothing left over? Lots of church folk think preachers preach too much about money, but if I were a preacher I'd preach about it almost every Sunday. Because I already know that nine out of ten people listening to my sermon are technically broke. Money is *always* on their mind, so why would I *not* talk about money? Instead, preachers talk about tithing. I think everyone should tithe, but it's hard to tithe when all your money is going to pay interest. (By the way, lots of Christians balk at tithing, but don't you think God is pretty lenient to be asking only 10 percent when some credit card companies have you paying upwards of 30 percent interest?) If churches could eliminate credit card debt, they'd free up so much money for tithing that they wouldn't know how to spend it.

Food and money are the top drugs in America today, and they are perfectly legal. In fact, the folks who sell them to us are lauded as heroes of the American way of life. A great deal of the economy depends on these companies' success. Operating completely within the law, they've devised tremendously powerful strategies for hooking people on food and money.

"But what about individual responsibility?" I hear someone asking. I'm glad you asked, because that's what this book is all about. You can't change the fact that billions of dollars are spent each year to entice you to eat more and charge more. But you *can* develop your own personal strategy to take control of your life and do what's best for you.

However, to develop that strategy, you're going to have to become a lot savvier at filtering the information you get from the HADs. I'm not saying the HADs are evil per se, or that they are intentionally out to ruin your life. But their main concern is *their* interests, not yours. They certainly don't have *your* best interests at heart.

I take pains to point that out especially for the Tugboats, as well as the Sailboats who lead with a heart letter (I or M). If you have one of those patterns, you tend to be a basically trusting person. That's because you see yourself as a basically trustworthy person, and it is inconceivable to you that anyone else would not be trustworthy and would not pay attention to other people's needs and concerns. But that instinctively trusting nature puts you at greater risk for succumbing to the strategies of the HADs. So let me talk about some of the HADs, and as you learn and take in information from them, be advised about what drives their interests.

Food HADS

Fast-food vendors. "Fast food" is a catchall phrase encompassing everything from drive-through restaurants to snack foods and sodas sold in vending machines to popcorn at the theater to novelty treats sold at convenience stores. Indeed, that's the main thing fast-food vendors are selling—convenience. Pay attention to that if you lead with a heart letter! Because your wiring predisposes you to respond to convenience. By nature, you tend to be impulsive, to go for the quick, easy solution. So if you're hungry, what do you do? You grab the quickest, easiest thing that tastes the best and makes you feel good. In other words, you grab fast-food.

The fast-food vendors know that, and their aim—their agenda, if you will—is to get you to buy as much fast food as they can. That's why they've put a fast-food restaurant on just about every street corner in the country. It's why there are vending machines even in supermarkets, of all places. It's why gas stations got rid of attendants at the pumps and instead put in stores carrying sodas, fruit punches, beef jerky, burritos, Big Gulps, Corn Nuts, Weiner Snacks, and Twinkies.

Unfortunately, these fast, "convenient" foods tend not to be very healthy for you, especially in the quantities in which most of them are sold. They are high in fats, starches, sugars, salt, and caffeine. They are high in calories, so it takes more energy to burn them off. They are almost all highly "processed," meaning that their nutritional value has been vastly diminished by what it takes to manufacture them and prepare them to sit on the shelf for months or even years.

Perhaps the worst thing about fast food is that it tastes so darn good. Once you eat it, you instinctively want more. There are powerful physiological and emotional reasons for that, and the fast-food vendors know all about those reasons. That's why they've come up with "super-size" portions (which seem to grow larger in proportion to the obesity of the population). They've also packaged their products quite cleverly. Next time you buy a snack at a convenience store, check out the serving size indicated on the food label. Notice how many servings come in a package. There are almost always multiple servings, but who limits oneself to just part of a package? No, you eat the whole thing, meaning you eat two or three or four or even eight times what a "normal" (i.e., reasonably healthy) serving would be.

The fast-food vendors never point out any of this to their customers. Nothing compels them to do so. Nor is it in their best interests to do so. Instead, they come up with brilliant marketing strategies using clowns and cows and clever slogans and contests and action figures from movies and discount specials and on and on to get people into their stores, buying food. What happens to the person buying the food—well, that's the person's responsibility.

I'm fine about that, but in turn I ask the fast-food industry to be fine about the fact that I am calling them drug pushers, because fast food is one of the top drugs being sold in America today. No one would argue if I told a heroin addict that *he* is responsible for getting off heroin, but that doesn't change the fact that the person selling him heroin is a drug dealer. For millions of Americans, fast food is as much an addiction as heroin, because it is not consumed for nutrition but for escape. It's a legal addiction, but let's call it what it is. All I'm doing is accounting for who is at risk for that addiction, and showing how the fast-food vendors push food to the addicts. There's no argument about who is responsible.

· · ·

The Food and Drug Administration (FDA). I'm picking on the FDA, but I could list any number of government agencies among the HADs. The FDA is the arm of the federal government charged with overseeing the food and pharmaceuticals industries. Can you see the irony in that? The same watchdog that approves the foods we consume also approves the drugs we take to get well from the "approved" foods we consume. Isn't that a conflict of interest?

Another problem with the FDA is a perception issue. Many Americans believe that the FDA exists to protect them when it comes to the things that they put in their bodies, namely food and pharmaceuticals. That sounds about right. Except that "protection" means something different to different people, depending on (you guessed it) their scoring patterns.

To someone whose lead letter is a T or an R, the FDA exists to monitor the safety of food and drugs. That means running studies, checking research, documenting the claims of the food manufacturers and pharmaceutical companies, and otherwise ensuring that what we put in our bodies will do what the makers of it say it will do, and nothing else. To a T or an R, the FDA is a fact-checking enterprise.

But to someone whose lead letter is an I or an M, especially a Tugboat I or M, the FDA is more like a parent who gives permission. The problem is, permission is not the same as approval. A kid who lives in the country may ask his momma whether he can go swimming in the creek near their house. Momma knows that water moccasins have been known to inhabit that creek, so she's not all that keen on letting him swim there. But after he begs and begs, she finally says it's okay. So the boy goes and finds his little brother and says, "Let's go swimming in the creek. Momma says it's okay." In that way, little brother believes that Momma has given her approval. But if asked, Momma would say all she gave was permission.

The FDA does a similar thing as Momma when it allows food

and drug vendors to market a product as "FDA-approved." A Barge understands that to mean that the FDA has checked out the product and found its claims to be accurately represented. The product may or may not be "good" for a person. That doesn't matter. It has been manufactured and sold within the confines of the law. But a Tugboat reads "FDA-approved" as a virtual stamp of endorsement from the government. Because Tugboats believe that the government is their friend and is looking out for their best interests. Of course, that is not the role of the FDA. The FDA only ensures that food and drug makers are not allowed to make products that are inherently dangerous in their manufacture or use. There's a vast difference between permission and approval.

The FDA could help prevent this misunderstanding by having vendors use a less ambiguous term than "FDA-approved." Perhaps "FDA-regulated," or "FDA-passed," or "FDA-inspected." Additionally, perhaps the FDA could do a better job of clarifying its role in the food and drug industries.

Food manufacturers. The FDA requires food manufacturers to place a food label on their products showing "nutrition facts" about the ingredients, calories, nutrients, serving size, and other information about the product. This seems like a straightforward way to enable consumers to know what they are buying. And on one level it is. If you know how to read a food label, you can make healthier decisions about the foods you buy.[13]

But the system doesn't work if food manufacturers play games with the information they put on the package. For example, suppose you are considering a cereal product that contains almonds. The box carries a banner that reads, "Reduces the risk of heart disease!" Sounds good. In fact, the food manufacturer will tell you that its claim is "FDA-approved" (here we go again).

To back up that claim, the manufacturer is required to place the following notice somewhere on the package: "Scientific evidence suggests but does not prove that eating 1.5 ounces per day of most nuts . . . as part of a diet low in saturated fat and cholesterol may reduce the risk of heart disease." So there. The manufacturer has got scientific evidence that their product reduces heart disease. Right?

Not exactly. Notice that what evidence exists "suggests but does not prove" that nuts help to lower the risk of heart disease. Nowhere is the manufacturer required to say how much evidence exists, or what it is, or how much science supports it. Furthermore, notice that the claim of lowered heart risk involves a particular amount of nuts each day, and that other factors have to be involved, as well, particularly "a diet low in saturated fat and cholesterol." Given all these qualifiers, how strong is the claim that the cereal "reduces the risk of heart disease"?

We live in an instant society, and people want their information in quick, easy-to-read snippets. "Just cut to the chase. Give me the bottom line. Give me the *USA Today* version of what you've got to say." Okay, but that's how you end up with "reduces the risk of heart disease" on a cereal box. It's not exactly an outright lie. But it's not the whole truth, either. I could say it's misleading, but the cereal manufacturer would cry that I am impugning their intent. Well, you tell me: what *is* the cereal manufacturer's intent? To sell more cereal, of course. Do they think putting a label on the box that promises lowered risk of heart disease will help? Obviously they do. Do they want to confuse anyone with a highly accurate statement of all the conditions that qualify that claim? Obviously not. So even if the manufacturer's intent is not to mislead, the consumer at least has to be aware that the intent is to sell, and that the consumer's interests only appear to be the manufacturer's first concern.

Buyer beware!

. . .

Surgeons and clinics devoted to weight loss. Have you ever noticed how weight loss gimmicks run in cycles? A few years ago, the drug fen-phen was all the rage until it came out that fen-phen might kill you. Then came liposuction. In one quick procedure, a plastic surgeon could suck out all that nasty fat in your belly and take you from a size 14 dress to a size 4 (or so a lot of people thought). More recently the fad has been bariatric surgery, or "stomach stapling," by which a person's stomach is surgically sewn smaller so that the person eats less. A less radical approach is the lap band, a ring around the top of the stomach that constricts the flow of food.

As long as there are obese people in the world, there will be surgeries for losing weight. And you might think that I would be in favor of those procedures. But I'm not. It's not that I'm opposed to people losing weight, obviously. But I'm highly opposed to any procedure that does nothing to establish lifelong habits of healthy nutrition. How does a quick-fix surgery do that?

I've already pointed out that Tugboats and Sailboats who lead with heart letters (I and M) are the most susceptible to quick, easy solutions to their problems. That's why they gain weight in the first place: because when they feel sad or hurt or upset or some other negative feeling (and they feel negative feelings a *lot*), they turn to the quick fix of fast food. So who do you suppose signs up for a surgery that offers a quick, easy way to lose one hundred pounds? You guessed it—Tugboats and Sailboats who lead with heart letters.

"But Wayne, my doctor told me I *needed* this surgery," someone will say. To which I reply, that may be, but just because they are doctors doesn't mean you should automatically do whatever they say. Especially when they stand to make a lot of money if you agree to the procedure.

"But my health insurance is paying for it." That's even worse! It means that you have even less leverage with your doctor. You're not really his/her customer, you're an insurance claim. Your trusting nature wants to believe that your doctor only has your best interests at heart when he or she tells you you "need" the procedure. Well, I suppose your doctor does care about you, but don't be naive about why doctors are practicing medicine. It's not a charity. There's a mortgage and car payments and private school tuition to pay.

Look, I know I may sound like I really don't trust the medical community. Well, the truth is I don't. Not totally. Just partially. And I think I have a right to be at least a wee bit skeptical when there is significant money involved. It's like the credit card company–university student triangle I mentioned earlier. Only in this case we have a surgeon and the related health personnel and resources, an insurance company, and an obese individual. Whose interests are most likely to be protected in that deal?

Let me say it again: people who lead with heart letters, especially M, tend to be overly trusting, and so they take their doctor's word every time. All I'm telling them is, do your homework. Get a second opinion. Find out your alternatives. Surgery may be indicated for some people. But whether or not it's for you, by all means ask yourself whether the approach to losing weight that your doctor is recommending is a program you can do for a lifetime. If not, walk away from it. It will only bring you trouble.

Diet plans. With all of our obsession with weight, you would think that by now we Americans would have figured out *the* ideal diet plan. Instead, we've got *hundreds* of diets to pick from. It seems like every month brings along a new one. A diet for every waistline. And for every pocketbook.

A study at Tufts–New England Medical Center in Boston, led by Dr. Michael Dansinger, compared four popular diets: the Atkins low-carb, the Ornish low-fat, the Zone, and Weight Watchers. The conclusion? There was no significant difference in the plans' weight-loss potential. "All end up reducing calories," he said. The only thing that matters, regardless of which diet people pick, is whether they actually stay on it.

Easier said than done. Of 160 volunteers in the study, a third dropped out of the Zone and Weight Watchers groups before the yearlong study was completed. Half dropped out of the Atkins and Ornish diets.[14] You know, I've got a pretty good idea of the scoring patterns of those who dropped out and of those who stayed in.

The point is that diets don't work. Eating right and exercising works (as long you're eating and exercising in ways that can last for the rest of your life). Diets don't work because they try to modify behavior without taking into account the underlying attitudes that drive a person's behavior.

But Americans want quick fixes. And so it doesn't matter if they've spent fifteen years bulking up to 250 pounds when they ought to weigh 185. They want to lose the weight in six weeks. So they buy into the extravagant claims of the diet plans.

Makers of diet pills. A moment ago I mentioned fen-phen. In the 1990s, fen-phen was supposed to be the miracle drug that would cause fat to melt away. Millions of people bought it. Then researchers began to discover that people taking fen-phen were susceptible to above-average rates of heart disease and hypertension. In 1997, the government stepped in and asked American Home Products, fen-phen's maker, to take it off the market. Today some fifty thousand product liability lawsuits have been filed in association with fen-phen, and the liability is estimated to reach as high as $14 billion.[15]

I mention fen-phen because it's a classic case of people desperate to believe that there is some magic substance that they can swallow to melt away their weight with no effort on their part. Again, the quick, easy solution. And again, we know who is vulnerable to that pitch.

We all want to believe that there's a pill somewhere that will fix our health problems. Well, I have good news for you. That prescription really does exist, to a point. It's called *exercise*. "We've spent years studying numerous nutritional and lifestyle factors," says Frank Hu, associate professor of nutrition and epidemiology at the Harvard School of Public Health. "Good nutrition is essential for health . . . [but] the single thing that comes close to a magic bullet, in terms of its strong and universal benefits, is exercise."[16] There you have it. That's pretty straightforward information from someone who ought to know.

Health clubs. The point just made about exercise is a good place to talk about health clubs. I'm often asked, "Wayne, are you in favor of health clubs?" My answer is, I'm in favor of exercise. If joining a health club helps you exercise on a regular basis, then that's a good purchase for you. But the membership is not what improves your health, the exercise is.

Most years, the number one New Year's resolution in America is to lose weight. That's why January is the most crowded month for health clubs and fitness centers. They sell tons of new memberships. But guess what? By February, about half the newbies have bailed out, and by March attendance is pretty much back to normal. That's not a bad business model: sell a whole lot of people with good intentions something that most of them won't end up using.

I'm not saying that the health clubs are doing anything wrong. In fact, I'm not talking to the health clubs here. I'm talking to you, the reader. Be careful before you just sign up for that expensive membership. It's great if you have a goal to lose weight. I applaud that. But what's your *plan*? I'm going to say more about a plan in the next section. But don't make the mistake of thinking that purchasing a health club membership is the same as achieving your goal. The *exercise,* coupled with eating right, will achieve your goal.

Remember that the health clubs want your dollars, so they make commercials and advertisements that show pretty girls with great figures and handsome, buff guys exercising and smiling. That's a great picture. It's very compelling. In effect, the commercials are asking, "Wouldn't you like to look like that?" But that's the wrong question. What you should be asking is, "How can I look the best for *me*, for the body *I* was given and the person *I* was meant to be?" There are very few people in this world that were given the genetics to have killer bodies. But *anyone* can be fit and healthy. If joining a club helps you do that, then go for it.

The media. I mentioned commercials and advertisements. That brings me to the role of the media in dispensing information about food and health. Where do I begin? The HADs included in what we call "the media" are so many and so varied that I don't have room in this book to mention them all, let alone talk about their agendas. Suffice it to say that you are literally bombarded every day with thousands of messages attempting to sway your decisions, and most people are unaware of those influences most of the time. But they are powerful influences, noticed or not. And the more aware of them you become, the more cynical you are liable to get, because it seems as if *everything* you are being told through the media has been filtered through lots and lots of agendas.

For instance, have you ever read a newspaper article reporting on some study related to health issues? Most readers don't realize that that article began as a press release from a public relations firm hired by whoever wanted to publicize the findings of the report. Who paid that PR firm? Who paid for the study? What interests of theirs were served by conducting that study? How do they stand to benefit by the publication of the study? Who else stands to benefit? What is the relationship of those parties to the party that paid for the study? Who is quoted in the article, giving their opinions about the study? What are those persons' interests?

Notice that I haven't even talked about the study itself, or the information it offers. I'm just considering the agendas of the people behind the study.

Or take movies. Product placement has become a huge factor in the movie industry in recent years. Product placement means that an advertiser works with the filmmakers to place its product somewhere in the movie in a way that viewers can't help but notice it. And so one of the main characters will open a particular brand of laptop computer or a particular soft drink will be seen on a kitchen counter. The star will wear a certain brand of shoe, or be seen shopping at a certain store.

In the movie *The Firm,* Tom Cruise goes to the Cayman Islands to visit Gene Hackman. Hackman offers Cruise a beer. The beer in question is Red Stripe. When *The Firm* was made, Red Stripe was a little-known Jamaican beer. But within a month of *The Firm*'s release, Red Stripe sales more than doubled in the United States. Not long after, Guinness Brewing bought a majority of the Red Stripe brewery for $62 million. No wonder advertisers want to get their products into movies!

Product placement is an extremely powerful form of advertising precisely because it doesn't *seem* like advertising. It seems like reality, like something we would see everyday. Which is exactly what the advertiser wants: make the product look like it belongs. Advertisers know that people are fully aware that commercials are trying to sell them something. But what if you can catch people off guard and sell them something without looking like you're trying to sell them something? That's the genius of product placement.

And it works, It must work, because advertisers now clamor to get their products into movies. Consider just one film, *The 40-Year-Old Virgin,* released in August 2005. The following brands and products appeared in that film: Apple, Bentley, Budweiser, Carhartt, Chrysler PT Cruiser, Coca-Cola, Dummies, eBay, Excedrin PM, Fanta, Fruit$_2$O, GI Joe, Guinness, Halo, JVC, Kodak,

Lacoste, Magnum, Mentos, Midnight Club, Minute Maid, Monster Cable, Oreo, Orville Redenbacher, Panasonic, Polo Ralph Lauren, Puma, Rolls Royce, Schwinn, Shell, Sony, Testors, TREK, Trojan, Vaseline, Volvo, and Western Bagel.[17]

Did you have any idea that Minute Maid was messing with your mind while you sat in the theater watching *The 40-Year-Old Virgin*?

"Gee, Wayne, you *are* cynical! It seems like you're telling me that I can't believe *anything* I see or hear." That's right. At least, it's almost right. I'm saying don't *automatically* believe everything you see and hear. Test it first. Listen. Pay attention. Make sure you heard right. And then ask: "Is that really true? Is it only partly true? How can I find out what the real truth is? What other sources of information do I need to check out? Whom do I know who could help me evaluate what I'm hearing?"

I'm especially saying that if you're a Tugboat or a Sailboat who leads with one of the heart letters, you could stand to be a little more "cynical." It could save your life!

Money HADs

Credit card companies. If I had to crown one group of HADs as the Evil Empire of hidden agendas, it would have to be the credit card companies. No one is more skilled at seducing people into their clutches. Without a doubt, they are the true masters of the art.

The people who run and work for these companies are for the most part fine, upstanding citizens. So I'm not attacking them personally. But the fact is that credit card companies use many of the same tactics that pimps, drug dealers, and the mafia use to get a firm hold on the unsuspecting and keep them there. The basic strategy is this: Find someone vulnerable who is in need. Make them believe you are their friend. Show them how you can help them with their need. Make it easy for them to get started. Increase their dependence. Increase your demands. Get them in over their heads. Make it impossible for them to ever get free. Threaten them with unthinkable consequences if they try to shortchange you. Control them through fear.

I'm speaking from personal experience. When I was in my late twenties I had so much credit card debt that I was practically on a first-name basis with the people at MasterCard. For a while, I thought they loved me. I mean, credit card solicitors would send me letters that began, "Congratulations, Mr. Nance. Due to your demonstrated financial responsibility. . . ." Man, oh man, did that feel good, that somebody thought I was "financially responsible."

You see, I was a good boy who paid my monthly minimums (monthly minimums are kind of like "protection" money; they never pay off what you owe, they just keep you from getting whacked). I kept paying those minimums, so the credit card companies kept *increasing* my credit limit. Imagine that! With all the debt I had, they wanted me to go *more* into debt. Their strategy was to tell me that I didn't even have to make any payments on the new amounts for six months. I thought, "Wow, they really love me!" But eventually they came calling for their money. And that's when I discovered the truth that if someone's not your momma, they don't love you.

The credit card companies are definitely not your momma. Not when they charge you north of 30 percent interest. So who do you think gets in trouble with credit cards? That's right, the Tugboats and the Sailboats who lead with heart letters (I and M). Those are the folks who are the most impulsive. When they see something they want to buy, they buy it. A credit card makes that incredibly easy. Probably too easy. Tugboats and I or M Sailboats are also the folks who don't keep a budget, so they don't always have enough money at the end of the month to pay off their credit card purchases. And since they also don't read the fine print, they overlook the consequences of minimum payments, late payments, and missed payments. Pretty soon, they're looking at serious debt.

"That's not our problem," the credit card companies will say. "We spell everything out in writing. We can't be held responsible for people's excesses." No, but then how is it that the more credit card debt one has, the more offers one gets in the mail for additional credit cards? If a bar serves an obviously drunk patron more liquor, and the drunk kills someone driving home, the bar is liable to get sued. It's an irresponsible thing to do. But when a credit card company signs up a debtor for even more debt, it's the credit card company that is allowed to sue the debtor if the debtor runs into trouble.

In the end, it's irrelevant to debate the credit card companies' responsibility for people's credit problems. The fact is that the companies are in business to make as much money as they can. That's what I want to call the reader's attention to: *the credit card company wants to make money off of you.* Period! They are not your momma. They are not your friend. They don't love you. They do not exist to help you. They will not and cannot provide a way out of your financial troubles. Use a credit card if you must for convenience and to avoid carrying cash. But don't get sucked in by their come-ons.

Period!

Consumer credit counseling agencies. "Surely you must approve of consumer credit counseling, Wayne." Well, guess what? I don't. Not the way most are currently set up.

Let's start with the fact—largely overlooked—that consumer credit counseling organizations were created by the credit card companies in the first place. Did you know that? No altruistic third party ever looked at people struggling with credit card debt and said, "We should help those people. We should set up an agency that steps in and tells the credit card companies to ease up while we help these folks get control of their finances and start making regular payments that they can manage." It didn't happen that way.

No, if you go back to the mid-1900s, you'll find that credit cards originally were something only rich people could have. Rich folks were the only people lenders would extend credit to. But with the growth of the middle class and the growing wealth of the middle class in the 1960s and 1970s, more and more people qualified for credit cards. Merchants figured that out and began accepting the cards. Before long the words "charge it" had become a standard part of the American vocabulary.

Then came a few blips in the economy, and a lot of folks began defaulting on their credit card payments. A whole collections industry sprouted up as a result (because remember, the credit card companies want their money). Eventually the excesses of that industry caused the government to step in. It was in that climate that the consumer credit counseling agencies were born.

The credit card companies figured out that sitting down with a creditor and talking things over and working things out is a much better way to get a debt repaid than to hound someone mercilessly until they either pay up, skip town, or blow their brains out. But make no mistake: the objective of the consumer credit counseling agency is not to make the creditor feel better, or to make them a better person, or even to make them a more responsible person. *It's to get the credit card company its money.*

It was a stroke of genius to use the word "counseling" to describe these agencies. "Counseling" is a friendly, soft, warm word. It's a word that has tremendous appeal to the very folks who get into the most trouble with credit cards—the Tugboats and I or M Sailboats. To them, the idea of going to someone for "counseling" connotes understanding, empathy, patience, and respect. And I daresay that a lot of the "counselors" who work for consumer credit counseling agencies probably extend all of that.

But just because the "counselor" is kind and respectful doesn't change the fact that they are there to collect a debt, not to be your friend. Keep in mind, they are ultimately paid by the credit card company.

I'm not saying that any of this is underhanded. It's a lot better than having some guy interrupt your dinner with the family by calling to say, "If you don't pay up we're going to sue you." I just want the reader to be clear on how things are set up if you turn to a credit counselor. That counselor is paid by the credit card people not to "help" you repay your debt but to *ensure* that you repay it. The counselor is not your momma any more than the credit card company is.

There's a second reason why I frown on consumer credit counseling: it's just another quick fix that fails to address the underlying issues that have gotten someone in trouble in the first place. If Bubba and Bertha have maxed out five credit cards because their hardwiring predisposes them to be impulsive and irresponsible with money, how does consumer credit counseling help them become disciplined and responsible?

The counselor is going to work with them to create a monthly payment that the counselor believes they can afford. Let's say for the sake of argument that they manage to make that payment over all of the months that it takes to pay off the debt. If you're a T or an R, you'll look at that and say, "See, paying off that debt taught them to be responsible." But in fact it did not. As soon as that debt is gone, guess what Bubba and Bertha will do? Get another credit card. Start working on a new debt. I see it happen over and over. Because unless someone intentionally follows a plan to ALTER their behavior, they'll never change.

Consumer credit counseling is a quick fix. It's no different from dieting. You can go on a money diet for sixty months or whatever, but just as most dieters gain back the weight they lost plus 10 percent, so most debtors will go back into debt, oftentimes worse than before. Consumer credit counseling is a quick fix, and quick fixes don't work. The only plan for managing your money that "works" is a plan you can follow for a lifetime. And you can't do that unless you take into account your inborn *attitude*.

Bankruptcy lawyers. Did you know that in America you get multiple times to file personal bankruptcy? That's great, because it means you get to practice a few times until you finally get it right.

Bankruptcy has come a long way, for sure. There used to be a terrible social stigma attached to filing for bankruptcy. But now it's almost commonplace. Kind of like credit card debt, isn't it? Or obesity?

The thing you have to remember about a bankruptcy lawyer is that they are not your friend. They are your advocate in a legal proceeding, and they get paid a fee for representing you.

I's and M's are particularly susceptible to thinking that the bankruptcy lawyer is their friend. After all, he's in their corner, fighting on their behalf. And so their trusting nature leads them to view their attorney as their buddy—not unlike the way they tend to view a credit "counselor" as their buddy. That's flawed thinking.

A bankruptcy attorney gets paid if you file for bankruptcy. That in itself creates a potential problem. Have you ever seen newspaper ads or TV commercials for a bankruptcy lawyer? They almost always say, "Free consultation!" That makes you think, "Gee, it won't cost me anything to just check out my options." But what do you expect the person at the law office is going to tell you when you go in for that consultation? Are they going to say, "Mr. Nance, we really would advise you *not* to file for bankruptcy"? No way! Just like a plumber gets paid to roto-root and a surgeon gets paid to cut, so a bankruptcy lawyer gets paid to file for bankruptcy.

So don't go to a bankruptcy lawyer to "check out your options." Talk to an accountant or read a book or consult some other neutral source to decide if bankruptcy is your best alternative.

And remember one other thing: bankruptcy is another quick fix. It may be the worst quick fix of all, because even though it gets your creditors off your back, it saddles you with a poor record for a long, long time. And it does nothing to put you on a plan that you can follow for a lifetime.

Retailers. By now you're probably realizing why my blood starts boiling when people (usually Ts and Rs) shake their heads at folks who are struggling with their weight and/or money and say, "Those people just need to learn some personal responsibility!" I detest the self-righteousness of people who say that. But I have to admit, they are right. The key to getting one's lifestyle under control is to start taking personal responsibility for one's lifestyle. That's what this book is dedicated to helping readers do.

But here's the real point of this chapter, and it's very fitting to emphasize this point as we come to retailers. The point is that each of us needs to exercise individual responsibility because we live in a society that has created a vast network of interlocking systems that are quite powerful and effective at exploiting our weaknesses. Put simply, America has so many fat, broke, and divorced people because our economy is set up to produce them.

Look, I'm as proud to be an American as anyone, and I support our way of life. But a fact is a fact, and the fact is that there's only one person who is (or ought to be) looking out for your personal interests, and that's you. *You* have to take responsibility for you, because no one else will. No one else does. That's what this chapter is saying. All of the entities I've mentioned have their own agendas. That doesn't make them evil. It makes them interested in their own benefit *first.* If your interests happen to coincide with theirs, fine. But their primary concern is their agenda. They deal with you to the extent that you benefit them.

But know this: if you aim to take control of your lifestyle, realize that you are up against a whole system that, to put it bluntly, wants control of your lifestyle. And the face of that system that smiles at you first and foremost is the retailer. Beware of that smile!

Be especially aware if you live in Collin County, Texas. Or Fairfax County, Virginia. Or Santa Clara County, California. Or McHenry County, Illinois. Or any of the other counties that have the highest incomes in the United States. There is no product or service known to humankind that has not been placed within easy reach of such affluent communities. This makes them breeding grounds for the must-have lifestyle.

That lifestyle is rooted in the subtle but extreme power of peer pressure. You know how that works. The lady in the cubicle next to yours comes to work wearing a new belt, or carrying a new purse, or talking about the expensive camp where she and her husband are sending their kid next summer. And you think, "Wow, that's really nice." And then, "I'd like to have/do that, too." And then, "I deserve that." And finally, "I've got to have that."

Or say your fourteen-year-old son comes home and says, "Guess what, Dad? The Joneses got a new TV. Forty-two-inch plasma screen on their wall. It's awesome! Can we get one?" The must-have mind-set doesn't think about saying no. It thinks, "Hmmm, those things are pretty pricey." Then it thinks, "I make more than Larry Jones. How is it he can afford a high-definition TV with a plasma screen?" And finally, "I don't want my family to feel like we're falling behind. I better get over to Best Buy and check these things out."

Parents of teens worry about peer pressure in schools, but they ought to be more concerned about the pressure at their own peer level, especially in affluent communities. Adult peer pressure is far more powerful. I know, because I've lived there. In fact, it's their parents' envy of other parents that teaches kids to think they are better than their peers if they have better stuff than their peers.

As you might guess, Tugboats and Sailboats who lead with heart letters (I and M) are the most susceptible to peer pressure, and therefore to the retailers and their advertising, as well. Tugboats and I and M Sailboats love to please, so it's quite easy for them to overindulge their kids with Christmas and birthday presents. They love to meet the needs of others, which means they'll buy things they think their spouse "needs," whether or not those things are actually needed. And they tend to be impulsive, which means that sending them to a mall with a credit card is like turning a child loose at a candy store with the instructions, "Enjoy yourself, but don't spoil your dinner."

But now if you're a Barge, don't think for one minute that you are immune from peer pressure. If anything, you may be gripped by a far more serious kind of peer pressure, which is the desire to make others envy you. You see, Barges have a way of assuming they are better than everyone else; buying expensive things becomes a way to prove that. Barges also tend to be great with money, so they often use money to keep score. Buying their wife that expensive jewelry, taking the visiting executive to the top restaurant in town, flying first class, and similar luxuries become ways of saying to everyone else, "I make a lot of money. Let me show you how much."

It's a power game, a one-upmanship that can extend to prom dresses, plastic surgery, second homes, private schools, weddings, funerals, even charitable giving. And by the way, the credit card companies understand that game. Whom do you think they invented the "platinum" card for—the impulsive Tugboats who get in over their head, or the sophisticated Barge who buys for status?

The must-have lifestyle thrives among two-income families with younger children and teens. The kids are key, because then every purchase becomes emotional. The purchases made out of guilt. The ones made for security and safety. The ones made to please. The ones made to get your kid off your back. And especially the ones made to prove to your peers that you are a loving parent who really is devoted to your child.

Retailers love two-income families not because those families can afford to buy, but because they view everything they buy as stuff they *need*. It's the must-have lifestyle. It's the two-income lifestyle. And a lot of it—in some places most of it—is built on credit card debt.

One way you discover that is by watching what happens when the economy takes a downturn and one of those two incomes goes away. You would think that the loss of a job would result in downscaling the family's lifestyle. But all the evidence shows that many families try to *maintain* their lifestyles when someone loses a job, basically to keep up appearances. Usually that means living on credit cards and racking up debt. And for families that have already racked up debt, it means significant credit problems, and eventually disaster.

When you look at the situation that way, you realize that when a retailer picks out a nice, affluent community in which to plant a store, it's the equivalent of finding out where the highest number of alcoholics are living and then opening a bar there and going out of your way to invite them in.

I'm completely serious. Money has become one of the two biggest drugs in America today. And if the credit card companies are the drug dealers, then the retailers are basically their collection agencies. The retailers make it irresistible to spend money—money that in many cases doesn't exist yet, because it hasn't even been earned. "But you can charge it!"

Relationship HADs

Talk Show Hosts. I wish I had 3-Minute scoring patterns on a cross-section of viewers who watch Oprah, or Dr. Phil, or Regis and Kelly, or the other television talk shows. I'm willing to bet that a disproportionate number would having scoring patterns that lead with I's and M's.

I believe that, because television talk shows are designed perfectly for I's and M's. They are hosted by extremely engaging personalities who are fun to watch and listen to. They feature guest celebrities, brilliant experts, emotionally gripping stories, dramatic turnarounds, controversial topics, and books that make a powerful impact. Being television, they tend to be visually interesting to watch. And above all, they are great entertainment. I's and M's love entertainment.

I have nothing against entertainment. But I think you can see that if someone is going to address relationship issues (or any other lifestyle issue) on a talk show, that issue has got to be turned into entertainment. And that's the hidden agenda behind the talk show: first and foremost, it is entertainment. It is designed to capture and hold attention. Which means it has to make its topics visual, dramatic, and fun. There's nothing wrong with that. Except, what about the parts of a lifestyle issue that are not visual, dramatic, and fun? Somehow those parts tend to get edited out.

It's a situation ripe for the quick fix. I mean, what could be more compelling than to bring out a couple whose marriage was saved after the wife agreed to shed two hundred pounds through bariatric surgery—complete with before-and-after photos? Or maybe have a program on out-of-control high school kids whose parents have let them rack up thousands of dollars in credit card debt. Or let the couple who can't stop fighting meet on-air with the amazing communication expert who pinpoints their problem *and* its solution all in less than forty-three minutes of airtime.

"Wow!" viewers will say. "If only I could have that expert talk to me and my husband." "Maybe I can get my kid to start being more responsible the way that author suggested." "I'll bet if I had that surgery, my spouse would start loving me again."

If only life were that simple. The talk shows imply that it is. By now, I hope you can see that life isn't that simple, and why quick fixes don't work.

I'm not suggesting that you stop watching talk shows. I'm just saying that the next time one of them presents someone who has experienced a dramatic turnaround with his health, finances, or one of their relationships, don't just accept the story at face value. Look a little deeper. What might be the person's scoring pattern? What did it actually take for him to turn things around? How long did it take? How long will it last? Is this person actually living differently, or is he just experiencing the momentary effects of a quick fix? What would it take for you to ALTER your lifestyle in that way?

Authors and seminar presenters. When we get to the folks who write books and lead seminars on relationships, I can speak from firsthand experience, because I am one.

The first thing you need to be aware of is that a majority of the most effective seminar speakers have an I as the first or second letter in their scoring pattern. Can you see why? I's tend to be lots of fun, very engaging, quick on their feet, and highly expressive. They love to get a reaction. They also love to make an impact. If they have any verbal ability (and a lot of I's do), they do well in front of a crowd. And if they gain some expertise on a topic (a lot of seminar speakers also have an R as one of their first two letters) and work it up into a compelling talk, they've got a bright future as a popular speaker.

Now there's nothing wrong with being engaging. I think most of us would rather listen to someone fun and interesting talk about a lifestyle issue than someone who sounds as if he's reading out of the phone book. But watch out for that energetic I. Just because he's entertaining doesn't mean he's right. And remember what I just said about entertaining talk shows. They are designed to hold your attention. So it is with the entertaining I. He's a master at holding your attention. He's also a master at painting a compelling picture of what life could look like if you follow his advice. That can be very motivating. But don't mistake that momentary, positive response for real change. That response may turn out to be a first step toward change, but a lasting ALTERation of your lifestyle will take a process, over time.

The other thing to remember with seminar presenters and authors is that they make money by selling books. Now I'm all for selling books, obviously! Books are wonderful tools—as long as they actually have something to say, and as long as they actually get read and acted on. I do believe books can change lives. Indeed, I want this book to ALTER your life.

But let's be honest. When you attend that seminar or workshop with the rah-rah speaker, the presentation is designed, among other things, to get you to go to the resource table, where you'll find all of the presenter's books and audiocassette series and DVDs and so on. By all means, buy those resources if you believe they will help you. But don't just whip out your credit card and make an impulse purchase. Buying the book will not change your relationships, any more than buying a health club membership will cause you to lose weight. *Exercise* causes you to lose weight. By the same token, practicing the things taught in the book will begin to improve your relationships.

Divorce lawyers. Anyone contemplating divorce should be required to watch *The War of the Roses*, a cautionary tale about a couple who literally end up dueling to the death as they fight their way through a divorce. Danny DeVito, who plays a lawyer representing the husband, gives a rather stark summation of things by saying, "A civilized divorce is a contradiction in terms."[18] Whether you're a Barge, a Tugboat, or a Sailboat, you are well-advised to heed that warning when you consult an attorney about a divorce: there is no such thing as a civilized divorce.

So Tugboats, listen up! A lot of what I said earlier about bankruptcy lawyers applies to divorce lawyers, as well. Divorce lawyers earn a living by filing your divorce or representing you if you get sued for divorce. In other words, they are your advocate in a legal proceeding. They are not necessarily your friend. They are a hired gun.

That's why they say there are no winners in a divorce except the lawyers. Cynical, yes, but largely true. Just ask anyone who has ever gotten divorced. No matter how the divorce was settled, no matter how either party felt about the settlement, the lawyers got paid.

When a business files for bankruptcy, its lawyers get paid first because the court considers them part of the reorganization expenses. Needless to say, there's a significant incentive for bankruptcy lawyers to string out a reorganization for as long as possible. In a similar way, there's an incentive for divorce lawyers to string out divorce proceedings for as long as possible, especially where a couple has significant assets to work with.

Barges tend to play right into this trap. Barges typically get tough in a divorce proceeding. Indeed, they are often the party that files. So they instruct their lawyers to "go after the money," and they play hardball. And sure enough, unless the Tugboat in the marriage hires a mean, tough Barge to represent them, that Tugboat is liable to get mauled by the settlement.

But as I say, it's really only the lawyers who win. Imagine a Barge who is bound and determined to keep as much of the assets as possible away from his Tugboat wife. His attorneys keep filing motions and doing discovery and subpoenaing records and statements. And let's say that by the time all the dust settles, that Barge has succeeded in protecting assets from his wife. But not from the lawyers. Legal fees will have significantly whittled down the assets from what they would have been. So the Barge doesn't really win.

There's another great line in *The War of the Roses*. After DeVito's character goes out of his way to scare one of his clients by telling him the sad story of the Roses, he proposes an alternative to divorce: "You can get up and go home and try to find some shred of what you once loved about the sweetheart of your youth."[19]

That's good advice, especially if you are a Barge who wants to quickly get out of your marriage. Why don't you slow down and try working on the relationship before you just throw it away? You see, the problem for a Barge is that the divorce system works *too* well for you. It takes advantage of your dispassionate way of looking at things. For example, your lawyer knows full well that you don't regard him as a friend, but rather as a tool you're using to do an unpleasant job. He has a vested interest in carrying out that job, so he certainly is unlikely to counsel you to hang in there with your spouse. Indeed, the odds are that he is a Barge himself. If so, he is supremely equipped to go get the settlement you want. In that way, the system feeds on the worst side of your makeup.

Do you realize that? Barges have a much higher risk for divorce than Tugboats or Sailboats because marriage is a relationship, and relationships are not a Barge's long suit. A Barge's long suit includes things like money, decision-making, getting facts right, and analyzing legal matters. Which means, to put it bluntly, that if you're a Barge you'll do better at breaking up your marriage than you've done at building it. How about that!

I know I'm coming down on Barges here, but for good reason. Throughout this chapter I've been telling Tugboats to become more responsible. Well, now I appeal to the Barges: why don't you become more relational? You have no problem telling Tugboats to start using their head. Well, why don't you start using your heart? Why don't you start paying attention to the things that will build your marriage, like trust, commitment, communication, emotional honesty, patience, affection, laughter, and respect? Become a human, for crying out loud!

I'm fully aware that it goes against a Barge's nature to attend to those kinds of things. But how is that any different from Tugboats going against their nature to attend to things like budgets and deadlines and chores and boundaries? It's no different. It's the Barge's version of "taking responsibility." So if you need to consult a professional, such as a marriage counselor or a therapist, to help you work on these things, do it. Take responsibility for how you do relationships!

Churches. What I'm about to say is specifically directed to churches, which I and my co-authors know something about, but not to synagogues, mosques, and religious communities of other traditions that we know little about. Some of what I say may apply to those other institutions. I simply don't know.

But I do know something about churches. The first thing to say is that there are all kinds of churches, so it's tough to make universal statements about them. What is true of one church may not be true of another. So all I can say is that *some* churches are HADs in that they have a bias when it comes to relationship issues.

Let me illustrate. Daniel and Sherry are a middle-aged couple with a troubled marriage. One day Sherry hears a talk show guest implore listeners that if they are experiencing a particular problem in their marriage, they should seek out a counselor. Since that very problem exists in Sherry's marriage, she pays attention, and that night she asks Daniel if he will go with her to talk with someone about their problem. Reluctantly, he agrees.

So Sherry makes an appointment with one of the ministers at their church. That's fairly common, by the way. Clergy are among the first professionals that people turn to for marital help.

Now let's say that when Daniel and Sherry meet with the minister, the first thing he does is have them fill out the 3-Minute Survey. Daniel's pattern is RTIM. That's a Barge. So it's no surprise that Daniel is smart, savvy, and driven. He's a no-nonsense guy. He owns a business and he's making a lot of money from it. That's because he spends almost all his time on the business.

And that's Sherry's first complaint. She feels neglected. She feels like her children are getting neglected, too. Sherry's scoring pattern is MTIR. That's a Sailboat who leads with a heart letter. In Sherry's case, the M means that her first concern is other people. The T after that means she wants structure and order. That combination actually makes her rather accepting of the fact that Daniel needs to devote so much time and energy to the business. She can appreciate that.

But she and her kids have needs, too, and one of their most important needs is for a husband and a father. Unfortunately, when the family gets Daniel, they seem to get the worst of him. He comes home surly, critical, mean-spirited, and self-absorbed. In fact, Daniel treats his family a lot like I was treating my family a few years ago, as I've described in an earlier chapter. Daniel has a different scoring pattern than I do, but he is basically being a jerk, like I was.

And that's essentially what Sherry is hoping the minister will tell Daniel, just like Shannon told me: "You're acting like a jerk." Maybe the minister will say it using church language that's a bit more finessed, but the message needs to be clear: "Daniel, you're acting like a jerk." Because, in fact, that's how he's acting.

So is that what the minister tells him? Well, maybe if Daniel and Sherry were newcomers to the church and the minister had never met them before, he might be so bold as to suggest that Daniel pay attention to how he's doing his family relationships. But that's not the case here.

In this illustration, Daniel and Sherry are longtime members of the church. And Daniel is a major financial contributor to the church. That puts the minister in a very difficult spot. He certainly doesn't want to offend a key donor. Churches, after all, are non-profit organizations that depend on donated funds to operate.

So what is that minister going to say? Well, a lot depends on his scoring pattern. If he leads with an I followed by an R, he might be impulsive enough to shoot straight and let the chips fall where they may. On the other hand, if that second letter is an M, he'll shy away from any potential conflict. Other patterns would produce other possibilities.

But quite apart from the minister's scoring pattern, can you see how the situation tempts the minister to be a bit biased? Church attendance and membership are voluntary, not compulsory. Church-goers vote with their feet. So no church leader wants to give someone an excuse to leave.

That's why I count churches among the HADs in that they have a vested interest in not making people uncomfortable. Certainly not at a personal level. It's okay to preach about love in the home. Just don't take Daniel aside and personally confront him by saying, "Daniel, it's great that you provide so well for your family. That's a form of loving them. But in the process you're neglecting them, and that's not very loving. What can we do about that?" In many a church, it's just safer to let Daniel remain a jerk.

This raises an interesting question for any reader who is part of church: what lifestyle area would you have to seriously start paying attention to if the leaders at your church were willing to tell you the truth? Suppose they told you you were overweight. Suppose they looked at your checking account and your credit card statements and told you that your finances are a wreck. Suppose they informed you that no one in the church wants to be on any committees with you because you're too hard to get along with. Would you be open to that kind of straightforward honesty?

"Well, Wayne that would be meddling. It's none of their business how I live my lifestyle." I disagree, of course. Church has a *lot* to say about how we live our lifestyles. Why do you think the Old Testament includes the book of Proverbs, which is all about every-day issues like contracts and debt and marriage and discipline and wine and integrity? Why do you think there are all those teachings in the New Testament about relationships and how we treat one another?

Jesus said the greatest commandment is love. If the issue of relationships isn't about love, I don't know what is. For that reason, churches ought to be the institution that takes the *lead* in helping people with every kind of scoring pattern address their relationships. But doing so takes courage, because it means telling the truth. Churches, of course, are supposed to be about truth, as well as love. But if a church compromises honesty out of fear of making people uncomfortable, then it's nothing but a HAD. It's telling people what they want to hear instead of what they need to hear. When that happens, the church is no longer effective. It may be entertaining, but when it comes to real life, it's irrelevant.

Relationship HADs in the workplace. Up until now I've mostly talked about relationships in families, and to a degree relationships in general. But now let me focus specifically on relationships in the workplace. Many of us spend the bulk of our day at work, and most of the people we interact with are at work. If we examine those interactions, we discover people in the workplace who have agendas for us, too, just like all the other HADs. Remember that a HAD is a party with a vested interest behind the information or advice they give us.

So who might be some of those workplace HADs? Well, in a sense, everyone at work is a HAD in that everyone has an agenda. Everyone has a job to do, and they need you to cooperate with them in order to get that job done. So in that sense there's a vested interest behind everything people in the workplace do. But I don't want you to get suspicious of everyone's intentions. After all, most people are not exactly hiding their agenda, which is what real HADs do.

The HADs you really have to watch out for are the ones with *malicious* intent—the backstabbers, the ruthless, the devious, the liars, the swindlers, the manipulators, the predators, the betrayers. Folks like these often have charm and wit and remarkable people skills. But it's all a ruse. They mask their true colors in order to prey on the unsuspecting. When the time is right, they make their move. They are out for themselves, and they leave behind a trail of disappointment, anger, lawsuits, broken relationships, and sometimes failed companies.

Sometimes the law catches up with those folks and they end up doing time. But many never get "caught" because they aren't exactly doing anything illegal. They're just selfish troublemakers. For instance, people who make careers out of filing false sexual harassment claims or worker's comp claims.

But it's not just individuals who are HADs in the workplace. Employers sometimes operate with hidden agendas, as well. My co-author Bill once had a senior executive at a major real estate firm explain his company's strategy for holding on to the best and brightest young talent: "We like to get a kid who's about twenty-eight years old and has had some experience. We set him up with a really nice draw on commission, and encourage him to buy a house with a big mortgage in a really nice neighborhood. We expect him to lease a high-class car. And we kind of make it a part of the corporate culture for everyone to put their kids in private schools. By the time it's all said and done, the guy ends up at thirty-five with so much overhead to cover that he literally can't afford to leave us, and he's too scared not to perform." Talk about a hidden agenda!

As in all relationships, relationships in the workplace have to be based on trust. The problem is, workplace HADs bank on the fact that others will trust them. That's what makes them so dangerous.

The only real protection against those HADs, aside from legal safeguards and careful background checks, is discernment. And here is where Barges and Sailboats who lead with a head letter have a decided advantage over Tugboats and Sailboats who lead with a heart letter. The latter tend to be overly trusting and not very discerning. They want to believe that everyone is their friend, and they want to accommodate everyone's needs. That leaves them open to manipulation and abuse.

Is there anything you can do if you are a Tugboat or a Sailboat like that? Yes, you can ask the people who care about you, especially any Sailboats who lead with a head letter, to help you evaluate the motives of other people. Again, the point is not to be suspicious, but self-protective. A lot of the relationship problems that you have may be largely of your own making, because you don't set good boundaries. You think that a boundary is a sign that you don't trust others. But it isn't. A boundary is an invitation for others to demonstrate that they are worthy of your trust. Let them show you that first. Then you can see about satisfying their agenda.

Conclusion

There are other HADs I could mention for each lifestyle area. By now, I hope you take the point. Each of us must take personal responsibility for our lifestyle decisions, not just because no one else will, but because if we don't the HADs will take control.

This brings me to a final observation before we leave this topic of *learning* in the ALTER model. I've been showing how vulnerable Tugboats and I and M Sailboats are to the hidden agendas of the HADs. So who runs the HADs? Who is in charge at the fast-food vendors and the food manufacturers and the credit card companies and the retailers and the law offices and the media and all the rest? The answer is that T's and R's run the HADs. T's and R's run the American economy. The majority of people who sit in executive offices and boardrooms and decide the policies and strategies for marketing to the general public are smart, objective, stick-to-the-facts, results-oriented, bottom-line-driven T's and R's. A lot of Barges and a lot of Sailboats who lead with head letters (T and R).

I think that's interesting. In simple terms, it means that the T's and the R's have created a system that takes advantage of the I's and the M's. Call that an oversimplification if you want. But I believe a careful analysis will show that on a broad scale that's exactly what has happened. And it accounts for why our society has gotten so affluent while at the same time producing so many fat, broke, divorced people.

The T's and the R's control the I's and the M's. So who's responsible? We *all* are. Every one of us is responsible—and in two ways. First, each one of us needs to take personal responsibility for the lifestyle decisions we make. We can't blame anyone else if we're overweight, or deep in debt, or failing in our relationships. Yes, there are certainly the influences of the HADs working against us. But in the end, each one of us makes our own, individual lifestyle decisions. So let's own that responsibility and start living responsibly—that is, living like we matter, like our lives count.

But each of us also has a responsibility to the people affected by how we live. And here I would throw down a challenge to the T's and R's associated with any of the HADs like the ones mentioned in this chapter. I've urged my readers to become more discerning consumers. Now I challenge you to become more conscientious producers. Own your responsibility for how your product or service affects real people.

CHAPTER 6 **A Plan for Health and Fitness**

There's an old saying: "Most of us don't plan to fail, we fail to plan." That sounds good, doesn't it? Unfortunately, it's not exactly true. For one thing, it's not true that *most* people fail to plan. A lot of people actually love to plan—notably Barges, as well as Sailboats who lead with a T. If you're one of those, life just doesn't seem right unless you've got a good, solid plan to follow. So it's not true that most people fail to plan.

But it's also not true that just because you have a plan, you won't fail. Even those quintessential planners—the Barges and Sailboats who lead with a T—don't always achieve their carefully crafted schemes for improving their lifestyles. It's not for lack of a plan. Yet ironically they often end up as frustrated as everyone else in achieving their goals. So where's the problem?

Well, here's the real truth: most of us don't fail to plan, but *we fail in the way we plan.* In other words, we may come up with a plan, but you won't get the desired result if it's the wrong plan. This is particularly true for lifestyle issues.

For example, say you've decided that you need to lose some weight. You're a hundred pounds overweight, and this is the year in which you've decided to get that weight off once and for all. So here you are. At this step, it's finally time to come up with a *Tactical plan.* What's your first thought about what that plan will entail?

"I need to start on a diet."

Is that what jumped into your mind? If so, then you may be surprised to hear me say, "No, that's the wrong plan."

Or take the area of finances. Let's say you've decided that this is the year you're finally going to get your spending under control. To that end you've picked up my book, and now you're at the *Tactics* step, where it's finally time to come up with a plan. What's your first thought about what that plan will entail?

"I need to go on a budget."

Is that what jumped into your mind? If so, then you may be surprised to hear me say, "No, that's the wrong plan."

Or again, say your area of concern has to do with your marriage. You and your spouse have been struggling for years, and this is the year you've decided to really work on how you communicate. On the recommendation of a friend you've picked up this book, and you've read all the way to this point, the *Tactics* step, and now it's finally time to come up with a plan for improving your marriage. What's your first thought about what that plan will entail?

"He's going to tell me that I need to spend more time with my spouse."

Did something like that jump into your mind? If so, then you may be surprised to hear me say, "No, that's the wrong plan."

You heard me right. A diet is not the right plan for losing weight. A budget is not the right plan for getting your spending under control. More time with your spouse is not the right plan for divorce-proofing your marriage.

I know, I know. What I'm saying goes against every lifestyle guru you've ever come across. But that's my story, and I'm sticking to it. And for good reason: If dieting is the right plan for losing weight, then why are two-thirds of Americans overweight? If a budget is the way to cut spending, then why are so many people drowning in credit card debt? If time alone with one's spouse is the key to building a marriage, then why is the divorce rate just as high among actuaries as it is among traveling salesmen?

Remember, most of us don't fail to plan, we fail in the way we plan. Our plan doesn't work because *it's the wrong plan.* It's the wrong plan for at least three reasons.

First, it's wrong if it doesn't take into account that everyone is different. Everyone does life a bit differently. So one-size-fits-all plans don't work and won't work. People need a plan that is customized to their particular wiring.

Second, it's wrong if it's not a plan you can follow for the rest of your life. Quick fixes don't work. They only provide temporary solutions for what turn out to be permanent, lifelong issues.

That brings us to a third reason why most of us fail in the way we devise lifestyle-altering plans: we follow the parts of a plan that fit our particular scoring pattern, but ignore the parts that don't fit our pattern. For example, when it comes to health and fitness, Tugboats don't mind getting exercise through activities that are fun and/or group-oriented. But the part of the plan that calls for watching what they eat is a lot harder for them to do, so they'll skip that part. Another example is the Barge who is meticulous about scheduling her annual physical, but ignores the part of the plan that calls for stress management, because she's got so much to accomplish.

In this and the next two chapters, I'm going to lay out an overall plan for each of the three lifestyle areas we've been discussing: health and fitness, money and finances, and marriage and relationships. For each area I'll explain what motivates the three different boats to start paying attention to that area. Then I'll give a checklist of ten steps that *together* comprise a comprehensive plan for dealing with that area.

Now let me forewarn you about the steps: *if you want to ALTER your lifestyle in a given area, you've got to work all ten steps in the plan for that area, and you've got to work those steps in their given sequence. You can't skip steps.*

I stress that because some of the steps you will like, but some you will immediately dislike. Only you probably won't come right out and say that you dislike them. You're more likely to dismiss them by saying, "Oh, I don't need to do this one," or "That one doesn't really apply to me." But you can't skip the steps you don't like. Nobody likes all of the steps. But that's okay. Life doesn't cater to our every whim. Not everything has to be easy. The good news is, I can help you work the steps that you don't instinctively enjoy, so that you realize the real benefits that you're seeking.

A Plan for Health and Fitness

What Motivates Someone to Take Action?

1 A life-changing event, such as a graduation, getting married, giving birth to a child, getting divorced, taking a new job, and such.

2 A fad diet or workout program that has captured your interest.

3 A diagnosis from your doctor that you have a serious illness or condition, or advice that you are at risk for such an illness or condition and you should take action.

4 A personal decision to obtain counsel about your health, physical fitness, and/or nutrition.

Each boat will tend to respond to these motivators differently, as follows:

Barges like order and control, so they try to regain control of their health and physical welfare quickly after a life-changing event, or upon experiencing a traumatic health event or receiving a life-threatening diagnosis. Many Barges tend not to seek health counseling on a regular basis because they are busy overachievers who won't hear of sitting around a doctor's office waiting for a checkup.

Tugboats are not particularly interested in health and fitness to begin with, but they can be drawn into taking action by the lure of a fad diet or the clever appeal of a health club or any gimmick that offers a quick fix. Life changes involving rejection, such as losing a job or a relationship, will trigger initial sadness and depression, but many times that will be followed by a burst of energy for a new exercise program or diet—which usually goes away once the newness wears off. As a rule, Tugboats will not take responsibility for getting regular health counseling, and they are not likely to follow the instructions of their doctor or health professional.

Sailboats take action according to the lead letter in their scoring pattern. If their pattern is led by a head letter (T or R), they are more likely to start paying attention to their health and fitness if they experience a major life-changing event, or a significant disease or illness. If their pattern is led by a heart letter (I or M), they will talk about losing weight, but their strategy will be to get on a fad diet even as they continue their habit of eating fast food. They don't like structure, so the advice they receive from doctors and other health care professionals may be followed, but not very consistently.

A 10-Point Plan for Health and Fitness

1   Annual checkup
2   Reality check
3   Stress management
4   Nutrition
5   Water intake
6   Stretching
7   Strength training
8   Exercise and activity
9   Relaxation
10   Health assessment

Remember, the sequence of the steps is crucial, and *all* the steps must be followed, not just the ones that appeal to you. So let's get started.

1. *Annual checkup*. Suppose I called a travel agent and said, "I want to fly to New York." What's the first question the travel agent would ask me? "Where are you traveling *from*?" It makes no sense to plan a trip unless you know what your starting point is.

Yet that's exactly what many people do when they decide to get serious about their health or fitness. They just start in. They wake up one morning and say, "Man, I need to get in shape. I think I'll go jog a mile." Never mind that they are fifty-two years old and haven't run since they were seven.

"Well, Wayne, I don't need a doctor to tell me that I'm one hundred pounds overweight. All I have to do is step on the scales to see that."

Great, so you can see you've got a weight problem (although, if you're a hundred pounds overweight, you don't need a scale to see that). So does that qualify you as a doctor? What exactly is the right amount of weight for someone of your height and build? What about your blood pressure? What's going on with your blood chemistry? What are your cholesterol levels? Do you have any indications of diabetes? Do you have any history in your family of heart problems? Are there any issues that might suggest what kinds of exercise would be best for you, or, conversely, exercise that you should *not* engage in? Are there "X-factors" related to your lifestyle that might be affecting your health, such as smoking or excessive drinking? If you're a woman, are you pregnant? Are you trying to get pregnant? Are you in menopause? If you're a male, what's going on with your prostate?

These and scores of other questions need to be considered if you want to gain control of your health. So the first step in your plan for pursuing fitness should be a comprehensive checkup by a qualified professional. All the other steps will depend on the information you gain from that audit of your physical body.

"But Wayne, I saw my doctor last winter when I had the flu. He weighed me and told me to lose a few pounds, and then he gave me some meds. Doesn't that count?"

No. Going in to see your doctor about a single issue like the flu is not what we have in mind here. You need as much of a comprehensive physical exam as you can afford. A truly complete physical involves a thorough examination of your body by a trained professional, who uses his or her expertise in conjunction with laboratory tests to evaluate all of your body's systems—the major organs in your abdomen, your pulmonary and vascular systems, your muscles and skeleton, your vital signs, your neck and thyroid, your eyes, ears, and throat, and your blood chemistry.

Do you want to get control of your health? Then put down this book and phone up your doctor and schedule a physical. That way, you'll be ready to work the next step.

How do the three boats tend to work this step?

- Barges tend to get an annual physical when it is necessary for work, or if they are ill. They also are more likely to make it a routine habit than other patterns.
- Tugboats tend to be overcommitted, so scheduling a physical gets put off. However, at the slightest sign of sickness the physical moves up on their priority list.
- Sailboats tend to put off getting a physical unless they lead with a head letter (T or R). For sailboats that lead with a heart letter (I or M) it's just not a priority.

2. *Reality check.* A physical is going to generate lots and lots of data about you. A lot of it you probably won't understand. That's why it's important that once all of the information is gained from the examination, your doctor sits down with you and explains in

plain English the highlights of what he or she has found, as well as recommendations for what you need to do and/or be aware of when it comes to your health. (Many doctors used to furnish that in a written report in addition to a verbal summary, but that doesn't always happen nowadays with the time-is-money pressures facing doctors.)

Once you've had that conversation with your doctor, you're ready for a *reality check,* a brutally honest, realistic appraisal of where you stand physically—the good, the bad, and the ugly. As the term implies, a reality check means you face facts. Do you weigh thirty pounds more than is indicated for someone of your age, height, and build? If so, the reality check says, "Okay, I'm thirty pounds overweight." Are you low on iron? If so, the reality check says, "Okay, I need more iron." By the same token, is your "bad" cholesterol lower than it was the last time it was checked? If so, the reality check says, "Okay, I'm doing better with my cholesterol than I was the last time." A reality check takes an honest look at your body and says, "It is what it is."

The reality check is a critically important step because people who gain control of their health live in reality. Remember what I said above? If I want to travel to New York, the first thing I have to know is where I'm starting from. That gives me some idea of what sort of journey I've got to prepare for. You see, there's a big difference between starting out to New York from Hackensack, New Jersey, than from San Diego, California. Those are two different trips, requiring different plans.

In a similar way, there's a big difference between starting out one's "fitness journey" from a position of fundamentally good health as opposed to one of serious health concerns. You can end up in good health—or at least better health—from either starting point. But those are very different "trips," requiring very different plans.

A reality check is the place to start thinking realistically about what you want to accomplish in terms of your health and fitness. And you can make that objective anything you want it to be. There is no one "right" or "best" outcome.

For instance, say you learned from your physical that you are, in fact, thirty pounds overweight. You also learned some other facts about your physical condition. And after adding up all those facts and hearing your doctor's advice and taking a long, hard look at what matters to you, maybe you decide that you're going to be satisfied if you drop twenty pounds. That's it. That's your target weight. That's what seems realistic to you, and that's what you're comfortable setting as a key fitness objective. That's great! No one says you have to lose thirty pounds. For that matter, you may decide that, for now, you'll be happy if you only shed five pounds. The point is, *you* get to determine what to do about the realities you are dealing with.

For that matter, nothing says that your objective even has to be about your weight. You may decide on other goals in light of your particular situation. For example, to reduce stress. To eat a healthier, more balanced diet. To get more physical activity. To get more sleep and better sleep. To drink more water and fewer soft drinks. To lower your "bad" cholesterol. To take up swimming or biking. To run a marathon. To take a walk every day. To practice relaxation exercises for fifteen minutes a day. In fact, maybe your objective is just to feel better about yourself. The possibilities are endless.

Whatever objective you choose, based on your reality check, *write it down*. Write down what is important to you, and why it's important, so that you have something to go back to and remind yourself when the going gets rough and you feel like quitting. The reality check says, "Here's who I am, here's where I'm at, here's where I want to go, and here's why." There's a lot of power in making that declaration, because it means basing your life and your decisions on reality, not fantasy.

In this connection, let me mention one other reality to consider. Recognize that there is a cost associated with good health. Not just a personal cost, in terms of resolve and commitment, but a financial cost as well. For example, you can get junk food at a relatively cheap price, but you may pay a little extra for something nutritious. However, that small difference in cost is well worth the money. Anytime you pay more to pursue a healthy lifestyle, you are investing in your long-term future. You'll never be disappointed.

How do the three boats tend to work this step?

- Barges tend to be so busy working that they don't think about the reality of their health goals.
- Tugboats tend not to be goal-oriented, so they rarely formulate goals. Instead, they focus on the negative: "I'm too fat."
- Sailboats tend to do the best with setting health and fitness goals. They know they want to lose weight, eat better, and exercise more.

3. *Stress management.* If you stop and think about it, safety and stress go hand in hand, don't they? Have you ever been in a hurry and driven recklessly through traffic? If so, you probably noticed that doing so causes your heart to race and your blood to pump like crazy, and if you're late for something really important, like a job interview or a critical business meeting or your wedding, what do you feel? Anxiety, of course. In short, behaving in an unsafe manner puts a lot of stress on your system.

But then, let's turn that around and point out that stress itself can be dangerous for your health. Not all stress. There is actually a good kind of stress that propels people to do their best stuff. For instance, a lot of NFL quarterbacks love—or at least revel in—the stress of being behind by ten points with 1:45 left on the clock. They don't like being behind, but they enjoy being on the field and thereby having control over the outcome of the game. They love to rise to the moment.

Some people reading this book can relate to that, especially at work. That's where they feel in control, doing their thing and doing it well. There may be lots of stress and tension in the job—deadlines, demands, political pressures, crises, or whatever. But if they love their work, do it well, and feel that it matters, then even though they feel stressed, it's a creative kind of stress that motivates them to do their best.

But then they come home, and what happens? Maybe they face stress there, too, only it's not creative stress, it's stressful stress. It's the stress of a bad marriage, or a teenager that they are worried about, or financial debt, or a neighborhood with high crime. It's the kind of stress that brings them down. If they're a Barge or a Sailboat who leads with a head letter (T or R), it's stress that causes them to feel angry, and they tighten up and seize control and become demanding. If they're a Tugboat or a Sailboat who leads with a heart letter (I or M), it's stress that causes them to feel guilty or depressed, and they look for escapes, and they compromise, and they open themselves up for manipulation.

Negative stress becomes distress, and it is literally a killer. Regardless of its source—and there are countless sources—that kind of stress contributes either directly or indirectly to every one of the six leading causes of death in the United States: heart disease, cancer, respiratory disorders, accidental injuries, cirrhosis of the liver, and suicide.

What stresses you in a negative way? If you're a Barge or a Sailboat who leads with a head letter (T or R), your biggest stressor is probably people, especially people who lead with the heart letters, I and M. People stress you because it's hard to control people.

People have an odd way of being, well, human. Which means less than perfect, irrational, emotional, and needy. People make demands. People interrupt. People get in trouble. People cause trouble. People get on your nerves.

If you're a Tugboat or a Sailboat who leads with a heart letter (I or M), your biggest stressor is probably people, too, only in a different way. For you, negative stress comes from feeling that you can never please the important people in your life—your spouse, your kids, your boss, your pastor or rabbi, your therapist, your parents. You feel that you care so much and you try so hard. But it's never quite enough.

"Wayne, my biggest stress comes from not having enough time," someone will say. "I've got too much to do and not enough time to do it in." I can empathize with that. But time is actually not the core issue. Time is the one resource we are all given exactly the same amount of. How we use our time makes all the difference.

So what determines how we use our time? You guessed it—our underlying attitude. Both Barges and Tugboats tend to be overcommitted, and therefore frequently stressed out. But they are overcommitted for very different reasons. Barges like to be in control, so they try to control all of their work and end up working too much. Tugboats tend to let other people control their time, so they end up running around satisfying other people's agendas. Sailboats have a bit more balance, but can go either way depending on their lead letter.

It's crucial that we figure out which negative stressor we are most prone to because the number one reason people don't eat well is that they feel stressed. By knowing your primary stressor, you can take heed when that stressor shows up and you start feeling the negative feelings associated with it. Then, when your body tells you to make a poor food choice in order to comfort yourself, we can recognize that impulse for what it is, and choose something that is healthier. You don't have to be at the mercy of our stress.

How do the three boats tend to work this step?

- Barges find stress management to be a tough assignment. They feel as if they have so much to do and accomplish, so many people to straighten out, so many money issues to keep track of. All of it causes them stress.
- Tugboats can't seem to make everyone happy, so they feel significant stress and don't pay enough attention to themselves to manage that stress.
- Sailboats tend to have the most balance when it comes to stress management. But their many activities with their work, family, and community, and their inclination to run all of them, pulls them off that balance—as always, in ways that depend on their lead letter.

4. *Nutrition.* Whenever I talk about food, you'll notice that I almost always talk in terms of "nutrition," never in terms of "diets." That's because I hate diets! Diets are quick fixes. Diets mean deprivation. Diets mean being the odd duck at the table. There's your family or your friends or co-workers sitting there, enjoying themselves over a meal. But for you it's, "No, I can't have any of this," and, "No thanks, I'd love some, but I'm on a diet, you know." Pretty soon, nobody wants to ask you whether you want anything. You're the odd duck of the party. Unless, of course, you cheat. Then you feel guilty. And what do you feel like doing when you feel guilty? Why, eat, of course. (Or spend money. Or yell at your spouse. Remember, health, money, and relationships are all interrelated.)

I hate diets. But I love food. Because I love nutrition. And that's really what nutrition is all about: eating *and enjoying* foods of all kinds in ways that nourish your body. Notice I said *nourish* your body. *Nourish* means to feed your body, to supply it with the nutrients it needs for growth and health.

"Well, that's not why I eat," someone is saying. I know. Sadly, you don't eat to nourish your body. In fact, the reason you eat has nothing to do with your body. It has everything to do with your emotions. You feel bad, so you eat badly. In fact, you don't really eat, you just consume. You ingest food because it makes you feel better—for a while. But the food does your body more harm than good (because your body doesn't need more food), and it doesn't come close to meeting the emotional needs you have, either. For you, food is nothing short of an addiction.

If you want to regain control of your lifestyle, you have to pay attention to your nutrition. And here's a concept to grasp: there are only two kinds of nutrition—good nutrition and bad nutrition. Good nutrition means eating in a way that builds up your body and makes it healthy. Bad nutrition means eating in a way that tears down your body and makes it unhealthy. It's that simple.

"But Wayne, what about carbohydrates and proteins? What about cholesterol and fiber and folic acid and vitamin B_{12} and anti-oxidants and all that?"

What about it? If you want to get technical and study up on all that stuff and really get into the science of it, go to it. I did, for a number of years when I was learning about my body and its need for food. It was fascinating. For instance, I didn't know that if I eat too many carbohydrates (like rice, pasta, or potatoes), it turns to sugar. That was news to me, and it helped me understand why I would enter a marathon and run like a rabbit for the first five miles, but then at about mile six or seven they'd practically have to carry me back on a stretcher. I'd eaten too many carbohydrates and not enough proteins.

My in-depth study of nutrition was invaluable and continues to help me to this day. But that's not what enabled me to lose one hundred pounds and keep it off. In fact, I know people who weigh one hundred pounds more than I did when I was one hundred

at was bad. I didn't know anything about nutrition back then,
t I didn't have to. All I had to do was look in the mirror and I
uld see that I wasn't eating right. I was taking in bad nutrition.

If you're eating fast food every day for lunch, do you think
at's good nutrition or bad nutrition? If you're eating a couple of
nuts and coffee every morning for breakfast, do you think that's
od nutrition or bad nutrition? If your dinners consist mostly of
ings like pizza, hamburgers, Mexican food, and Chinese takeout,
ashed down by beer, do you think that's good nutrition or bad
trition? You don't have to be a nutritionist to answer those ques-
ns. All you have to do is look in the mirror. All you have to do
think about how you feel physically most of the time.

God made potatoes, but humans made french fries. God made
erries, but humans made pies. God made beef, but humans made
uble-patty cheeseburgers. God made pigs, but humans made pork
ds. God made water, but humans made Big Gulps. God made
gar, but humans made Twinkies. In fact, now humans are mak-
g fried Twinkies. Fried Twinkies! Can you imagine that? Do you
ink that's good nutrition or bad nutrition?

If we humans would stick closer to what I call God's Diet
an, the better our nutrition would be and the healthier we'd all be.
d's Diet Plan means staying as close to natural foods—properly
oked—as possible, and making those foods the bulk of our diet.
n not saying to swear off Mexican food. That's fine on a Satur-
y night. The question is, what are you eating on Friday night?
d every other night? What are you eating for lunch every day?
hat about that bag of M&M's in your bottom desk drawer?

Obviously, you can eat any way you want. It's your choice.
st remember that there are two kinds of nutrition—good nutri-
n and bad nutrition. If you're going to stay on this health and
ness travel plan we're building, you're going to have to turn more
your bad nutrition choices into good nutrition choices.

But whatever you do, stay off diets!

pounds overweight who know vastly more about nut
ever hope to know. Yet that knowledge hasn't do
ounce of good. Because obesity isn't about knowledg
attitude—one's wiring and emotional beliefs.

That's actually good news, by the way. It mean
have to become a nutritionist to practice good nutriti
need to know is that there are only two kinds of nutri
nutrition and bad nutrition.

I have to look at it that way because I'm an I, and
keep things simple. You see, I can go to a supermarket
the incredible foods that God made: eggs, potatoes, beef,
grains, juices, oranges, even brussels sprouts (why God m
sel sprouts is beyond me; maybe they were intended as a
to see if we'd really eat them). Lots and lots of tasty, hea
foods. If I eat a variety of all those foods in their natural st
get most of the nutrients my body needs.

But that's not what most people do, is it? That's certa
what my momma did. When I was growing up, Momma ha
of chicken-frying nearly every dish she put on the table. N
chicken. We had plenty of fried chicken. But every other
meat, too. One time she brought home filet mignon, and I
her beating it with a mallet, then dipping it in milk and e
flour before dropping it into a skillet of frying oil.

That's not healthy. Fried food tastes great, which of cou
why she cooked it that way. But the frying loaded us up wit
Nothing wrong with fat—until you get too much of it. And u
tunately, it doesn't take much fat to get too much of it. So if
had fried chicken one night a week, that would have been fin
on another night we'd had fried Tater Tots, that wouldn't h
been so bad. If on yet another night we'd had fried okra, t
wouldn't have been good, but it still wouldn't have been bad. I
the truth is we were having fried something *every night of the wee*

How do the three boats tend to work this step?

- Barges can struggle with their nutrition if they keep irregular hours. They tend to eat in the context of workplace settings, which means longer lunches, drinks after work, and late-night snacks at the office.
- Tugboats tend to be impulse eaters, which means fast food and snack foods.
- Sailboats tend to have good intentions to eat in healthy ways, but if they have a busy schedule they just keep grabbing those cheeseburgers and pizzas.

5. *Water intake.* The body of an adult male is made up of about 60 percent water, on average. An adult female is made up of about 55 percent water, on average. In light of that, water intake becomes a main issue for developing a personal plan for health and fitness.

And here's another factoid: fat tissue does not hold as much water as lean tissue, which means that fat people are made up of less water (as a percentage) than skinny people. So if you're overweight, you need to pay extra attention to water. You're probably not getting enough.

Water irrigates the body. Every system you have relies on it. In fact, if you get dehydrated and lose even 1 or 2 percent of your normal water level, you will feel tired. Water flushes out the toxins and other nasties in your system and holds down infections. And if you're trying to lose weight, drinking lots of water is one of the most important things you can do.

Now when I say drink water, I mean *water*, not coffee, not soft drinks, and certainly not alcohol. Plain old water, nothing added. It doesn't have to be bottled water that has a fancy name. It just has to be pure water. How much? That varies from person to person, but a good rule of thumb is the "8 by 8" approach: eight 8-ounce glasses of water every day (taken throughout the day, not all at once). Another way to think about it is to drink a glass of water when you wake up, another at breakfast, one at midmorning, one at lunch, one in the afternoon, one when you get home from work, one with dinner, and one at bedtime.

An interesting sidelight to this issue of water is that when people go on a diet, the first thing they start to lose is water. At first they may appear to be losing pounds quickly, but mostly they are just losing water. That's not healthy. (The second thing to go, by the way, is muscle tissue. Fat is the last thing your body will burn. So if you want to lose fat, don't stop eating. Eat in a way that nourishes the muscle and starves the fat. And keep drinking water!)

How do the three boats tend to work this step?

- Barges fall into two extremes when it comes to drinking water. Some turn their natural discipline and structure into a habit of religiously having a bottle of water at hand throughout the day. Conversely, others are so enmeshed in their work that they don't allow time to drink eight glasses of water a day.
- Tugboats don't mind drinking water. But since there's no "wow" in doing so, they find it easy to skip it unless prompted.
- Sailboats tend to just not think about this step.

6. *Stretching.* An auto mechanic will tell you that the greatest wear and tear to a car's engine occurs at start-up, especially in the morning. The car has been sitting all night, and most of the oil that lubricates the engine has drained to the bottom of the crankcase. That leaves the metal parts of the engine sitting right next to each other with very little lubricant remaining between them. So when the starter kicks in and those parts start rubbing against each other,

they grind away for a moment until the oil pump starts washing oil over the engine to smooth things down. By then, however, the damage is done.

A similar principle applies to your body. When you've been sitting or lying for a while, doing nothing, the muscle groups in your legs, back, and arms relax and less blood flows to them. If you were to suddenly jump up and start running or jumping, you would be asking those muscles to do something for which they are totally unprepared. And as with the parts of an automobile engine, you run the risk of damaging your muscles and their connective tissues by suddenly jerking them into action.

Stretching is a way to prepare your body for action. For that reason, any fitness trainer will tell you that before *any* type of exercise, you need to stretch the major muscle groups of your body. However, stretching should not just be limited to fitness training, but to any physical activity you undertake: taking a walk, climbing stairs or a ladder, doing yard work, throwing the ball with your kids, even getting out of bed in the morning.

Indeed, a regular daily regimen of stretching is a key part of an overall health and fitness plan. Think of stretching as a way of giving your muscles a big breath of fresh air. Actually, that's exactly what you are doing, because stretching improves the circulation of blood to your body, bringing oxygen and other nutrients to the tissues and carrying away the wastes. Stretching keeps your muscles and joints flexible, and can actually increase your range of motion. Your posture will improve, or at least maintain. And the overall increase in circulation and oxygenation of muscle tissue helps to relieve tension and reduce stress.

Experts in physical training and therapy have developed literally hundreds of stretching exercises, so I won't go into detail on ways to stretch here. You can go online and find any number of fine Web sites that show you how to stretch. Many are tailored to specific activities you plan to do, such as running, swimming, walking, or lifting.

A few essentials to keep in mind, however:

- *Warm up before stretching.* Walk around for a few minutes and rotate your arms in order to get your blood circulating. Never start stretching when your body is "cold."
- *Hold a stretch for between 30 and 60 seconds.* Opinions vary on how long you should keep a muscle in flex, but most experts seem to agree on a minimum of 30 seconds and a maximum of 60 seconds. This gives the muscles time to stretch out.
- *Don't bounce.* Keep the stretch even and steady. You can create small tears in your muscles and/or connecting tissues by "bouncing" the stretch.
- *Put a demand on the muscle, but not to the point of pain.* If a stretch is hurting, you are pressing too hard. Let your muscle tell you how far is far enough.
- *Breathe normally while stretching.* Don't hold your breath.
- *Stretch both sides of your body.*
- *Don't forget to stretch after your activity.* Your muscles actually need more stretching after you exercise them than before. Failing to stretch afterward will increase soreness and stiffness.[1]

How do the three boats tend to work this step?

- Barges tend to run a tight schedule, so when they arrive at their health club they are stretched for time (no pun intended), with the result that stretching is not a priority.
- Tugboats can't see any immediate value in stretching. It just seems like an extra step that wastes time. So they tend to skip it.

- Sailboats are more prone to stretch than the other patterns, but a lot depends on their lead letter, as well as their second letter. Sailboats who have a T as one of those first two letters are the most likely to stretch because the T in their pattern tells them that stretching is part of the routine.

7. *Strength training.* I want you to notice that to this point in my health and fitness program I haven't asked you to do anything physically difficult or demanding. But now we come to strength training. And here I need to tell you straight out: you're going to have to make some physical effort on this one, and you may not like it at first until you start to see some gains from the process. Strength training means putting demands on the muscles in your body in ways that build them up and make them stronger.

Our objective is to turn flabby, weak muscles into healthy, vibrant muscles that do what muscles are supposed to do—supply strength.

Let me tell you a story. After I lost a hundred pounds and got my weight down to 215, I decided I wanted to start jogging. So I went to an exercise physiologist with a Ph.D. and told him what I wanted to do. I expected him to immediately fit me with a pair of running shoes, draw out a cross-country course, and send me off. Instead, he just laughed. "When's the last time you went jogging?" he asked me. I told him, twenty years. "That's what I thought," he replied. "I'll tell you what, before you get back to running, why don't you spend about three weeks here in the gym, walking on the treadmill for ten minutes a day."

I felt a bit humiliated, but it was the smartest thing he could have done. You see, I didn't realize that after twenty years of inactivity I didn't have the muscles to run anymore. Through lack of use they had atrophied. If I had jumped right in and hit the pavement, not only would I have tired very quickly—and probably given up on jogging as a result—but I might very well have injured myself. The fact was, I didn't have the *strength* to run. So before I was ready to do real exercise, I needed *strength training*.

Everyone who is in good physical condition will tell you that regular strength training is a key part of their fitness regimen. That's because muscles require regular use in order to stay toned, supple, strong, and useful. A hundred and fifty years ago, few people needed to worry about strength training because most of them worked on farms or in factories, they had no cars, and they had few "labor-saving" devices to do their work for them. In short, their muscles got lots of use.

Today, however, it's become the norm for many people to basically sit all day—in a chair, on a seat in a car, on the recliner at home. They don't use their legs or arms for much of anything. Two things happen as a result. One is that they don't burn off the calories they take in, so they get fat. The other is that their muscles atrophy through lack of use. As a result, they have very little strength.

My point is that strength training is now a requirement of a healthy lifestyle because our way of life in this society makes few demands on us physically. We have to intentionally find ways to exercise our muscles if we want to keep them strong and useful.

Does that mean we have to join a gym? No, although joining a health club that has free weights and what are called "resistance machines" (machines that require one's muscles to push or pull against weights or friction) can make it convenient to do strength training. But you can do strength training at home with some barbells in the garage or even small handheld weights in your bedroom.

The point of strength training is that you make your muscles do repetitive work on a regular basis. That builds them up. As with stretching, there are plenty of books and online resources you can turn to for various workouts, so I won't go into those here. If you join a health club or gym, you will have access to a trainer who can show you some basic exercises that will work for you.

I personally believe that if you've never done strength training before, it's a good idea to enlist someone to help you or do it with you. Not only can he explain what to do, he can encourage you to actually follow through on doing the exercises. You see, this is the part of the plan where you actually make your body strain a little bit. You push your muscles beyond what they are used to. Those muscles have gotten lazy with you sitting on your rear all day, every day. Now all of a sudden you're telling them to push that bar up and lift those weights. And they won't like that. "Hey, what's the deal?" they'll start asking. "What are you doing? Why are you making us do this? This doesn't feel good. This takes effort. Stop pushing us! Let us rest! This is not good! This is too hard!"

It's at that point that many of us—especially Tugboats and Sailboats who lead with a heart letter (I or M)—need another person to hold us accountable and help us "hang in there." Someone who can encourage us by saying, "Keep going! You can do it! Almost there! One more! That's it! Good job!"

As I said earlier, you may not like this part of the plan until you start to see some gains from the process. My challenge is to give it 91 days (I'll explain that magic number in a later chapter).

The first three or four weeks can be hard, no doubt about it. But in truth, they are not that hard. It's just that if a person has been doing nothing physically for twenty years and suddenly starts pumping some iron, it's going to *feel* hard. Your muscles are going to react by feeling sore for a while. You're going to breathe hard. You're going to sweat (sweating is actually a pleasurable thing once you get used to it, but if you're not used to it you can think something must be wrong). It takes three or four weeks to get past that initial shock to the system. So a lot of people get tempted to drop out, with the attitude, "This isn't for me."

But if you would just hang on another couple of weeks—and a trainer can help you do this—you would start to see and feel some noticeable benefits from your efforts. For one thing, the strength training exercises would not feel so difficult. In fact, at some point you will actually desire *more* resistance in the exercise. Your muscles will start to get firm and toned. Your breathing will become easier and stronger. You will start to notice that you don't feel as tired when lifting or reaching. You might feel your pants or skirts fitting a bit looser around the waist. You start to look forward to the mixture of relaxation and energy they feel immediately after working out. You feel less tired in the afternoon. Amazingly, you find yourself actually looking forward to working out, and even missing it if you have to skip a workout. And perhaps most amazing of all, you will find yourself having a greater desire for foods that build up your body and give it strength, and less desire for foods that add nothing but empty calories.

Some of you can't imagine these things happening to you. Sadly, some of you have never in your life experienced any of these things. But you can! I promise you benefits like these are true and absolutely worth the effort. How do I know? Because I, too, have complained and moaned when it comes to strength training. I don't like the process any more than the next person. But I've never, ever regretted doing it because to feel strong, to feel vibrant in my muscles, to feel healthy in my body is infinitely better than anything I ever felt as a fat man. Nothing feels as good as strength and health. Nothing!

How do the three boats tend to work this step?

- Barges will actually enjoy some weight-lifting, because they feel they need to look good.
- Tugboats as a rule don't enjoy lifting weights at all.
- Sailboats find lifting to be fun because it makes them look good and promotes self-esteem.

8. *Exercise and activity.* Exercise doesn't begin with your body, it begins with your mind. Before you *do* anything, I want you to stop

and *think*. I want you to think about the most enjoyable physical activity you've ever done in your life. What would that be? If you have to, go all the way back to your childhood and recall the one physical activity you liked doing more than any other. Maybe it was biking all over town with your friends. Maybe it was playing soccer in elementary school. Maybe it was taking hiking trips with the Scouts. Maybe it was swimming in the creek behind your house. Maybe it was throwing a Frisbee to your dog.

Here's the point: in this part of the plan I'm asking you to engage in some sort of physical activity or exercise on a regular basis, and the only exercise I want you to do is exercise that you enjoy doing. So if you already know of an activity that you find pleasurable, you're ready to get started.

On the other hand, I don't want you to start an exercise activity that you hate. That would be crazy. In fact, it would be punishment. For instance, I'll never tell you to start jogging if you hate jogging. (I might suggest you try jogging if you've never even tried it, but if you've tried it and already know that jogging is not for you, then so be it.) If you can't stand a particular activity, you won't stick with it.

So what kinds of activities am I talking about? Well, there are really only a couple of criteria, aside from liking the activity. The first is that it has to be something that involves your whole body. So playing cards won't do. Watching TV won't do. Driving the kids to and from school won't do. (Some readers are wondering whether napping will do, since it involves the whole body. Nice try!)

Exercise means getting up and doing something. Something that involves your whole body. There are a lot of activities that qualify on that score. We typically think of fitness activities like running, walking, swimming, cycling, working a treadmill, aerobics, or rowing. But there are many other things people can do to exercise their bodies: basketball, soccer, racquetball, water skiing, snow skiing, wind surfing, in-line skating, vacuuming, raking leaves, chopping wood, walking (briskly) through a mall, climbing stairs, building a deck on the back of your house. The idea is to get off your rear and do something active with your body.

What if you are physically challenged, perhaps in a wheelchair or bedridden? In that case, your options are more limited, but that doesn't mean you can't get exercise. You should discuss the possibilities with your physician, but see if there isn't some activity you can do with the parts of your body that *do* function properly.

For instance, a lot of wheelchair-bound folks have learned to play basketball, as well as to do long-distance "running" (or rolling) in their wheelchairs. Likewise, a man who was unable to get out of bed rigged up a bar by which he could lift his upper body and exercise his arms. In my opinion, folks who find ways to exercise despite their physical challenges are not only an inspiration to the rest of us, but also a rebuke to those of us who have everything physically and yet don't even use what we've been given.

The second criterion for an exercise activity is that it gets your heart rate up. That means challenging your heart but not taxing it. The idea is to get your heart working harder than it does when you are just sitting. To do that, you'll need to engage in the activity for at least twenty minutes.

Now I realize that there are a lot of different people reading this book. Some are ready to go out and jog a mile or two right now. Others are a heart attack waiting to happen. That's why the first step in this health plan is to go get a physical. If you did that, you should know the relative strength of your heart. If you didn't, you need to go back and schedule a physical with your doctor before you start exercising.

"Getting your heart rate up" means exercising to a point at which your heart is actively pushing blood through your system. You'll know that is happening when you start breathing more heavily. If you keep up the activity long enough, you will also probably start perspiring. Now if you get to the point where you are breathing *hard,* then slow down or stop. You don't need to kill yourself!

Some readers will be familiar with the term *aerobic.* It was coined by Dr. Kenneth Cooper, founder of the Cooper Aerobics Center and Cooper Clinic in Dallas, Texas. *Aerobic* refers to a zone of heart rate that is ideal for exercising. If you're interested in learning more, consult Dr. Cooper's books or website that explain how to calculate the aerobic zone for you. I'm not going to get into that in this book because it's an advanced concept, and I want to stick with the basics. If you're a woman who is 5' and weighs 285 pounds, or a man who is 5'9" and weighs 315, you don't need to be worrying about your "target" heart rate just yet. You need to start very slowly and just get some physical activity before you embark on an intensive aerobic exercise regimen.

So let's say you are that worst-case scenario—seriously obese and confused as can be. You've read to this point, and the idea of doing *any* physical activity seems overwhelming. Let me suggest a way for you to get started. I want you to set this book aside, get up, and walk to the end of your block and back. (If your street isn't on a block, then I want you to walk whatever distance you can walk in five minutes, then turn around and come back.) That's it. That's your exercise for today.

When you're finished, I want you to write down in a journal that you walked for ten minutes today (I'll say more about keeping a journal in a later chapter). Tomorrow I want you to walk ten minutes again—five minutes out and five minutes back. I want you to do that again the next day, and the next, and to keep doing that for four weeks. By then you will have developed your muscles to the point where you can increase your walk to twenty minutes—ten minutes out and ten minutes back. At that point, you're there! You're exercising twenty minutes a day. Fantastic!

By the way, most experts agree that twenty minutes is about the minimum amount of time required to get the real benefits from any sort of physical activity or exercise (although *any* amount of exercise is preferable to no exercise). If you engage in the activity twenty to thirty minutes a day, three or four days a week, you will reap significant benefits like the ones I mentioned earlier. And if it's an activity you enjoy, it's a no-lose proposition: your body gets fit while you do an activity you like to do. Whoever said "no pain, no gain"? (Probably a Barge!)

One last point about exercise: it's one part of your life over which you have total control. If you were born ugly, that's too bad and you can blame your parents for it. But just because you're ugly doesn't mean you can't be fit. Or maybe you are, in fact, one of those rare individuals who have an underactive thyroid. Great, blame Mom and Dad for that, too. But just because your thyroid is underactive doesn't mean everything else in your body has to be underactive as well. Get up and do something! Nothing is standing in your way to find some activity that you enjoy and is healthy for you. You may have been dealt a bad hand in other parts of your life, but when it comes to exercise, you hold all the aces.

How do the three boats tend to work this step?

- Barges tend to prefer games with rules and competition for exercise, such as golf or tennis. They may work out at a health club, but they tend not to exercise as much as they should because work comes first. Also, they are most likely to have a home gym and will enjoy working out alone.
- Tugboats will engage in exercise as long as they feel it is fun and it's an activity they can do with friends, such as bowling, riding bikes, or playing basketball.
- Sailboats generally prefer sports or activities that involve others as opposed to working out by themselves unless they lead with a head letter (T or R).

9. *Relaxation.* Okay, now we come to the part of the plan that everyone likes. Well, not everyone. Believe it or not, Barges and Sailboats who lead with a T or an R actually have trouble when it comes to relaxation. I guess you could say they have a predisposition to not lightening up.

And that's what relaxation is all about: lightening up. Pulling back. Doing something fun. Obviously that varies from person to person. I myself like to fish. I find it very relaxing. Other people like to play golf, but for me golf is anything but relaxing. Golf stresses me out!

The whole point of relaxation is to do something that de-stresses you. It's really the other part of step 3 above, in which I talked about figuring out what creates negative stress in your life. Relaxation is about figuring out what relieves your stress.

Tugboats and Sailboats who lead with a heart letter (I or M) are naturally inclined to do something stress-free. Oftentimes they find that people are a way to de-stress their life. So, for example, they may throw a party, and for them that's a very relaxing activity. Or they'll go to the lake with friends. Or they'll get out a jigsaw puzzle and put it together with their kids. They find enjoyment in the people and the relationships, and those interactions help them escape from the pressures and tensions of their world.

Barges could probably take a lesson from that. I said earlier that Barges often find people to be their greatest source of negative stress. And yet people can also relieve stress—*if* you don't try to control them. Only people can laugh and tell jokes. Only people can give affirmation and a sense of belonging. Only people can be creative and entertaining. Only people can talk.

How do the three boats tend to work this step?

- Barges believe that relaxation is something you do when your work is completed. But of course their work never seems to be completed. So they rarely relax. They're liable to tell their family, "Just go on to the party without me."

- Tugboats love to relax. Almost any activity will do: watching movies, playing games, visiting friends, going to the lake. Of all the patterns, Tugboats find this step to be the easiest.
- Sailboats can enjoy relaxation, as long as it's with friends. However, sometimes they have a tendency to overcommit, which can hamper their attempts at relaxation.

10. *Health assessment.* This step brings us full circle. We began with a physical, an audit of our body to find out where we were. Then we did a reality check to face facts and set our objectives. In this step, we assess our health and fitness after having worked the plan for a while, to see how far we've come toward accomplishing our objectives.

You'll notice that this step is consistent with the ALTER model. R in the ALTER model stands for *re-evaluate.* I'm a big believer in the idea of evaluating our progress and then using what we learn from that evaluation to improve our efforts. That's how we create a plan we can work for the rest of our life.

Let me suggest that if you get an annual physical, you should plan on doing an annual health assessment, too. Maybe a month ahead of your physical would be a good time to schedule that. The idea is to sit down with the 10-point health and fitness checklist, along with your journal, and look over the previous year. Here are some suggested questions to ask yourself:

- What were the objectives I set out to accomplish as a result of my reality check?
- Which objectives did I actually accomplish? What did I actually do to accomplish them?

- Were there any objectives that I accomplished beyond what I expected? What accounts for that?
- Which objectives did I not accomplish, or not as well as I would have wanted to? What accounts for that?
- As I think through each of the other nine areas in the health and fitness plan, which steps in the plan did I do the best? Which ones need more attention?
- What are some benefits that I can point to as a result of following this plan? How do I feel about those gains?
- What were my dominant emotions as I worked this plan? (I'll say more about tracking your emotions in the section on journaling.) What do I think is the source of those feelings? How are those feelings affecting my behavior?
- What questions should I prepare to ask my doctor as I go in for my next physical?
- What new goals and objectives would I like to start thinking about as I cycle through this plan again?

By the way, you may find it helpful to go through your health assessment with someone else, especially someone who has a different scoring pattern than you. You're liable to overlook some things. And it's just human nature to be harder or easier on yourself than is warranted. Someone else who knows you well and has your interests at heart can help you keep a realistic appraisal of things.

How do the three boats tend to work this step?

- *Barges* tend to view this step as a huge imposition on their time. "I got a checkup before," they'll say (if they got a check-up in step 1). "Why do I need a health assessment. It's a waste of time."
- Tugboats tend to skip this step because it gets them into too much technical information.

- Sailboats may seek out an annual health assessment if their lead letter is T or R, but probably not if it's an I or M.

Before I end this section on the health and fitness plan, I want to congratulate you on working this plan. If you've made an honest effort and done at least something in all ten steps of the plan, then guess what: you're ahead of 98 percent of everyone else in the country toward health and fitness. That's a fact! I'm not saying you're there yet. But you're on the way, and that's what really matters. You're gaining control over your life. That's what you ultimately wanted, isn't it—to develop positive behaviors that you can follow for the rest of your life? If you keep following them, it will be a healthy life. And nothing feels as good as health. Nothing!

CHAPTER 7 **A Plan for Financial Fitness**

What Motivates Someone to Take Action?

1 A significant financial setback in one's life, such as a business partner filing for bankruptcy or the loss of a career.

2 A major life event, such as getting married, getting divorced, having a child, the death of a loved one, and the like.

3 Receipt of a large sum of money such as an inheritance, the rollover of a retirement plan, a large settlement from a lawsuit, or a substantial cash prize.

4 A personal decision to obtain counsel about your personal finances.

Each boat will tend to respond to these motivators differently, as follows:

Barges are not keen on calling a financial consultant because they tend not to trust salespeople, and they tend to do their research on their own—by reading books or journals, or browsing the Internet. Ironically, even though Barges are methodical and risk-averse, they tend to procrastinate on financial decisions because they fear failure. When they do seek out financial professionals, they usually are seeking affirmation of their decision, not information. For these reasons it often requires a disaster or life-changing event to motivate a Barge to take action in this area. Also, this pattern is most likely to have their financial house in order.

Tugboats struggle the most when it comes to money and financial matters. They are motivated by people, not by finances. It usually takes a crisis—loss of a loved one, being turned down for a mortgage because of bad credit, impending bankruptcy—to get them to pay any attention to their financial condition. Tugboats typically do not seek out financial counseling because they don't know where to start, whom to talk to, or what questions to ask. They feel inadequate and totally overwhelmed when it comes to money issues. They also fear that a financial advisor will put them on a budget, which means they'll have to make decisions about how much money to spend—or not spend—and that will feel like deprivation.

Sailboats are an interesting lot on the subject of financial fitness. Their motivators tend to shift as they go through the steps of financial fitness. If they have an M in the first or second position of their scoring pattern, they'll tend to procrastinate on financial matters because they don't want to be wrong. They fear failure, and they don't want to make any decisions that might hurt a loved one. If they have an I in the first or second position of their scoring pattern, they'll tend to take action more quickly on financial issues but will be more susceptible to get-rich-quick schemes. They'll also struggle with follow-through when it comes to working the steps of a financial plan. These kinds of Sailboats tend to be afraid of not winning, and so they will take unwarranted risks and may fail to stay focused. Sailboats that lead with a head letter (T or R) tend to be more balanced in this area.

A 10-Point Plan for Financial Fitness

1   Cash flow analysis/One line budget
2   Reality check

3   Legal advice: wills and trusts
4   Life insurance
5   Medical, disability, long-term care, and casualty
6   Freedom funds
7   Short-term investments
8   Long-term investments
9   Retirement planning
10   Financial statement

Just as the 10 steps for health and fitness need to be followed in their given order, so the order of the 10 steps for financial fitness is crucial. Likewise, *all* the steps must be followed, not just the ones that appeal to you.

I stress that because the Hidden Agenda Drivers (the HADs we talked about in Chapter 5) of the financial services industry don't really want you to know about these steps—especially the HADs who have something to sell, like the life insurance companies, the stock brokerages, the investment companies, and the banks. They'd rather convince you that the most important financial move you can make is to buy their product. And they can be very persuasive in doing that. Their advertisements are everywhere—in magazines and newspapers, on TV, online, on banners and kiosks at airports. They promise security, wealth, extra spending money, financial independence. The key is to buy their stuff. Needless to say, they'll never tell you about all 10 of the steps above. As a result, many people don't even know about some of these steps, with the result that their financial house is in peril.

So let's take each of these steps in turn:

1. *Cash flow analysis/One line budget.* I spent the first twenty-five years of my career in the financial planning business, and the one thing both my clients and I could always agree on was cash flow: yep, their cash was flowing right out the door!

Seriously, though, it's always true that "cash is a-flowin'." By "cash a-flowin," I'm talking about a very simple concept. First figure out the amount of cash you have coming *in* every month. Then figure out the amount of cash you are paying *out* every month. Then subtract cash out from cash in. That figure is your "cash flow" and is what you have available to fund your Financial Fitness plan. We'll be using that figure throughout this section, so it's crucial that you know what it is.

The One Line Budget is this total amount of money you have to do Steps 3 through 10 in the plan. Remember, the plan is going to help you figure out your financial needs for the rest of your life. So once you figure out what those needs are, the One Line Budget will be the money you can use to fund your plan. You may not be able to fund all of the steps at once, so retain a competent financial advisor, who can help you develop a customized and workable strategy to begin funding all of these important steps. This is all a part of the Reality Check that we will cover in the next step.

How do the three boats tend to work this step?

- Barges tend to know their cash in and cash out on an annual basis. However, Barges that lead with the RT pattern don't care for the details of keeping track of money in and out, and so they either won't do it or they'll hire or marry someone with a T as their lead letter to handle those details.
- Tugboats tend to be unaware of their actual income or outflow. They usually only think about their net income on a weekly or monthly basis, and don't pay attention to their gross income. Nor do they factor in other sources of income besides their paycheck, such as interest and dividend income. As for cash out, they have little desire to know exactly where their money is going.
- Sailboats whose lead letter is T or R tend to be more like Barges and have a handle both on the money coming in and

the money going out. However, Sailboats whose lead letter is I or M will tend to be more like Tugboats and be unaware of both actual total income and total outflow.

2. *Reality check*. If you've looked at the 10-Point Plan for Health and Fitness (chapter 6), you'll notice that the second step in that plan is a reality check. The same need for a reality check applies here (and with the relationships checklist in chapter 8).

A *financial reality check* means an honest, realistic appraisal of where you stand financially, especially in light of your cash flow. It starts with a simple premise: if you've got more cash flowing in than flowing out, that's good; if there's more cash flowing out than flowing in, that's not good.

So what is that cash flow figure (cash in minus cash out)? You could have $15,000 a month flowing in, which is a very nice income ($180,000 a year). But if you've got $14,750 flowing out, that's only a net positive cash flow of $250 a month, which is not a lot of cash relative to what you're making. One serious financial demand, like your kid needing braces or your teenager totaling the family car, and your cash flow will be headed the other way. (By the way, just *assume* you will have serious financial demands sometime in your life.)

Obviously things are much worse if you've got $15,000 a month flowing in and $15,750 flowing out. In that case you're paying $750 a month that you don't have. The question is, do you realize that?

Some readers will assume I am being silly by asking such a question. But I'm totally serious. You see, there are lots of people making $15,000 a month and more who have a negative cash flow, not of $750 a month, but of $2,500 a month, or $5,000 a month, or even $15,000 a month. I'm not kidding! You know what they are living on? Credit, not cash. Credit and hope. Or rather, credit and an assumption. Their assumption is that the future will cooperate with them. Their assumption is that at some point they will get the big bonus, make the big commission, sell the property at a big profit, or hit the big jackpot, and suddenly their cash flow will go positive. They'll pay off their excesses.

If you're living that way, I wish you well, and I hope your assumption pans out. But I'll tell you one thing: if you're living that way, you are *not* in control of your finances. Fate is in control of your finances. The interest rates are in control of your finances. The price of oil is in control of your finances. But you are certainly not in control of your finances.

People with a negative cash flow of $15,000 a month scare me. But the ones who really scare me are the families who are grossing $4,500 or $5,500 a month *between two incomes,* and they've got a negative cash flow of $350 or $400 a month. There are far more people in that boat than in the $15,000 boat. And while $350 or $400 may not seem like much to some people, for a couple grossing $4,500 or $5,500 a month that overage is more than 6 or 7 percent of their income. This means that in a year's time that family will be a full month's income under water. They are headed for disaster.

Now having said that, let me pause right here and say something important: the fact that you have a negative cash flow does not make you a bad person. Do you hear that? It's terribly important that you do. You see, I can almost guess what some readers are thinking, or maybe even saying, at this point. For instance, I can almost hear a couple arguing by the time they finished the preceding example. One of them is a Barge, and she's quoting from the book: "See! Nance is saying what I've been trying to tell you forever. We're going broke! We're spending more money than we're making!" And she's delivering those lines to her spouse in a harsh, accusing tone that's really saying, "*You* are causing us to go broke! *You* are the irresponsible one! We wouldn't be having financial problems if it weren't for *you! You* are at fault!"

In turn, the spouse hearing these words is probably a Tugboat or a Sailboat who leads with a heart letter (I or M), and he's thinking, "Man, oh, man. What a miserable human being I am. She's right. I'm the irresponsible one. I'm lousy with money. I'm going to bankrupt our family. I've gotten us into trouble. There's no way we'll ever get out of it. It's hopeless. And it's all my fault."

If you and/or your spouse are having any sort of thoughts or conversations like that, may I ask you to just stop it, right now? It's not going to do any good. It will only do harm. And that's not what should happen by doing a reality check.

The way to get control of your finances is not through shame, blame, guilt, anger, or any other negative emotion. By the same token, it's not through denial, or by pretending that nothing is wrong, or by fantasizing that luck, a bank error in your favor, your rich uncle, the Powerball numbers, or a miracle by God will magically rescue you. No, gaining control of your finances begins with honesty about your situation. What is the figure for your cash flow? And is it positive or negative? Just as with your physical health, a reality check for your financial health is critically important because you can't set any financial goals or develop an overall game plan without it.

So let's go back to the couple who is grossing $5,500 a month on two incomes, but they've got a negative cash flow of $350 a month. Just by doing their cash flow analysis, they've already identified one obvious objective: they've got to come up with $350 a month, through some combination of reduced expenses and increased income, in order to break even.

A financial reality check is the place to start thinking realistically about what you want to accomplish in terms of your money and finances. And you can make your objectives anything you want them to be: saving for a down payment on a house, beginning a college fund for your child, paying down—and ultimately paying off—your credit card balances, turning a hobby into a money-making business, maybe just breaking even on your cash flow for a change.

The next 8 steps in the plan are designed to help you determine what those financial objectives should be, so that you end up in a position of financial fitness. By working through those steps, you'll be able to come up with what I call your One Line Budget. Imagine that—a budget that has only one line item to it. Pretty good, huh?

The One Line Budget is the total amount of money you'll need to do the following 8 steps of this plan. The plan is going to help you figure out your financial needs for the rest of your life. Once you figure out what those needs are, the One Line Budget will be the money you budget to pay for that plan.

How do the three boats tend to work this step?

- Barges tend to know their financial objectives fairly well, and they can stay very focused on their goals. But unless they have a strong T and a penchant for data, they don't care for keeping budgets and financial spreadsheets.
- Tugboats give very little thought to financial goals, and they certainly don't keep a budget. For that reason, they tend to like the idea of a One Line Budget, because it's simple and they only have to focus on one number a month.
- Sailboats tend to work with goals, and even multiple goals. They also like the idea of a One Line Budget because it simplifies their bookkeeping by combining their savings, insurance, and retirement into one figure.

3. *Legal advice: wills and trusts.* Perhaps the single most common financial mistake that people make today is that they don't have a will. Some estimate that more than half of all Americans die without a will.[1]

Why is that a mistake? Because dying without a will places an unbelievable burden on the survivors, as every little financial decision becomes an order of the court. Do you want someone else deciding how your property and assets get distributed after you die?

Do you want someone else to decide who will take care of your minor children? If not, then it's a mistake not to indicate your desires—your *will*—while you are still alive and of sound mind. Please take care of this step right away.

But there are lots of reasons why people never draw up a will. One of the biggest reasons is their inborn attitude. Barges don't think they're going to die. That may sound silly, but it's true. Somehow they feel that just because they have stayed in control of everything else in their life, they can control whether or not they die. My research indicates that death *always* wins, 100 percent of the time. But who says attitudes are rational—even for Barges?

Meanwhile, Tugboats neglect to create a will because they don't know anything about legal matters, and it all becomes very confusing and intimidating (especially if their lawyer is a Barge). Tugboats also shy away from the discussion about a will because they love their loved ones, and they don't like to talk about anyone dying.

There are other reasons why people don't draw up a will. One of them is that financial planners, insurance brokers, stockbrokers, and other salespeople in the financial services industry don't make a dime of commission off someone drawing up a will. So there is no incentive for them to press it. As a result, they typically just blow right by this step. If a client wants to go get a will drawn up, that's fine with them. But it doesn't affect them one way or the other.

However, a will *does* affect you, the reader. And so as your "virtual financial coach" I'm telling you to get a will if you don't have one. Have it customized to fit your particular situation and your unique needs. And make sure it fits the size of your estate. And if you already have a will, take it out and review it. Consider whether it needs to be updated in light of changes and developments in your situation, especially if the document was drawn up some time ago.

Now let me talk straight here. As a former consultant to the senior management of a life insurance company, I realize that death is not a subject that most people enjoy talking about. But as I say, all the research shows that 100 percent of us are going to die. It's not a question of if, but of when. So if you died tonight, what would happen to your children? What would happen to your pets? Who would make decisions about your money? Who would decide what happens to your house and property, your furniture, your fine china and silver, the ring you got from your Great Grandma Myrtle?

Do questions like these make you feel uneasy? If so, there are two things you can do. One is what most people do: put your head in the sand by putting off any discussion of these matters and live as if you're never going to die. But that's dumb. That's not living in reality. The wiser alternative is to create peace of mind by creating a will. Sit down with a legal pad and make a list of all the things you care about—your family, your possessions, your assets, your pets, your causes. Then answer the question, *What do I want to happen for these concerns after I'm gone?* Doing that will help you gain clarity about what you want in a will. Then find a lawyer who specializes in wills and pay him/her to draw up a will for you.

"Do I really need a lawyer?" the T's and R's will ask. Always looking to save a buck, they figure they can just adapt some generic boilerplate for a will out of a book or off the Internet. But I don't advise that for at least two reasons. First, in light of estate laws at both the state and federal levels, you want to make sure that your will is drawn up correctly so that you maximize deductions and exemptions to pass value to your heirs. Secondly, the judge who is going to look at your will when you die is going to be an attorney. Attorneys don't like it when people try to circumvent their legal system by using something out of a book. It's like doing surgery at home off the Internet. So I don't recommend it. Go ahead and pay an attorney to do the job right, because they went to school to learn to do that. Their fee doesn't involve any hidden agendas (unless you are guided into trusts and shelters which you may not need). Basically, I have no problem with people making money by doing what they are trained to do as long as the service is appropriate for your situation.

How do the three boats tend to work this step?

- Barges whose pattern leads with TR will typically have a will customized for their estate. Barges whose patterns leads with RT will typically avoid wills because they don't like or trust attorneys. Moreover, they act as if they think they are somehow going to have a trailer hitch on their hearse and cart all their money possessions with them to the grave, where no one is going to touch them.

- Tugboats are open to drawing up a will because it affects their loved ones. But getting the job done may be easier said than done because it's a legal matter, and therefore complicated and not much fun.

- Sailboats tend to seek legal advice, and they'll learn about what information they need to furnish for a will, but then they'll get distracted before they're finished.

4. *Life insurance.* What's the most important thing you need to know about life insurance? Probably 99 out of 100 people would say, knowing what kind of life insurance to buy. Not so. The most important thing is to coordinate your life insurance with your will. That's why life insurance is step 4 in my plan, following step 3, getting a will. Oftentimes people buy life insurance and designate the beneficiaries of that insurance. Then later they draw up a will that tells who is supposed to get what after they die. Unfortunately the names of the beneficiaries in their insurance disagree with the names of the beneficiaries in their will, and then they have a problem.

So what kind of life insurance should you buy, once you've drawn up a will? A whole bunch of readers (especially Barges) are immediately thinking "term." Because how many times have you heard that the only kind of insurance to buy is the cheapest? So what's the cheapest kind of insurance? Some companies have made a fortune by convincing everyone that term life insurance is always the cheapest. The premiums are lower than for "whole" or "universal" life, so obviously term is the cheapest, right? "Don't waste your money on cash-value policies," goes the received wisdom. "Buy term and invest the difference. You'll come out way ahead."

A lot of Barges, as well as Sailboats who lead with an R, have bought into that thinking. So they buy term insurance because they want to beat the system. But you know what? Automatically concluding that term is the cheapest, and therefore the best, insurance to buy is a form of a quick fix for which Barges and Sailboats who lead with an R are suckers. Those Barges and Sailboats think they are sticking it to the insurance companies by refusing "more expensive" products in favor of term. But who is really getting taken? During the four years I spent consulting with that insurance company I mentioned a moment ago, the standard joke in the boardroom was: "We love selling term. It's the most profitable product we've got, and everybody thinks they're getting a bargain!"

Term insurance covers a specified period of time. And it's the perfect insurance to buy if you know exactly when you're going to die. Just tell your agent when that's going to be, and he can write a policy for that term period. Then when you die at the appointed time, it all works out perfectly. Right?

Seriously, term insurance has its place. But don't settle for a temporary fix to a permanent problem. If you buy term because it's the cheapest (supposedly), you're liable to quit paying the premiums once they get too high, and then you'll die uninsured. And whatever type of life insurance you buy, you've got to *make sure that it will be in force on the day you die.*

The only way to know what kind of life insurance is best for your situation—and your pocketbook—is to do your cash flow analysis, take a realistic look at what's important to you and what your financial objectives are, and to evaluate what you and your family need to have happen when you die. Armed with that information, you can then approach an insurance agent and *tell him what your needs and desires are,* not the other way around. (Tugboats take note!) If you let an agent tell you what you need before they understand your situation and goals, you're dealing with a HAD. I'm not saying the agent is dishonest, just that he has a vested interest in looking out for his concerns more than yours. What you want is for the agent to customize his products to *your* needs, not the other way around.

How do the three boats tend to work this step?

- Barges are averse to buying life insurance because they tend to think they'll never die. If they do buy it, they almost always buy term because they assume they're saving money.
- Tugboats are open to buying life insurance out of concern for their loved ones, but they rarely know how much they really need, so they're liable to be overinsured or underinsured. Tugboats need to have their premiums payroll-deducted or bank-drafted or else they won't always get paid.
- Sailboats tend to put off buying life insurance because they are waiting for a friend to talk them into it.

5. *Medical, disability, long-term care, and casualty.* Step 4 dealt with the financial protection you need to have in place after you die. This step deals with the protection you need to have in place while you're still alive. Maybe you already have plenty of life insurance, so your heirs will be all set when you pass on in thirty years. But what happens if you get sick or injured in the next thirty years? What happens if your illness or injury keeps you from working? What happens if you get sick after you retire and you need medical care for ten or fifteen years?

A lot of people leave it to their employers to provide those kinds of insurance as part of their benefits package. That's great if your employer does that, but don't let your employer determine what you need. As with life insurance, the place to start with health insurance, disability, and long-term care coverage is to work steps 1–3, so that you have a handle on what your real needs are and what you are trying to accomplish. That information should guide any conversations you have with an insurance agent about medical, disability, or long-term coverage.

Do you really need those kinds of insurance? Well, of course you do. They're protecting *you*! People will insure their possessions for more than those possessions are worth, but they won't put any insurance on themselves, except for if they die. Now how does that make sense?

Notice that to this point in the 10-step plan I haven't said anything yet about investments. That's because before we talk about making money, we need to know where the money we are already making is going, we need to establish some financial goals, we need to have a will, and we need to put in place various kinds of insurance. That's what the first 5 steps of the plan do. They form what I call "estate protection." They create a nice, safe haven for the money you're going to make in steps 6–10.

You see, what if I helped you make a whole lot of money, but you didn't have that protection? A whole lot of trouble and disappointment could result. For example, the government could take a lot of your money for taxes. Your family might not get everything that's coming to them. You could run up significant legal fees. Your assets could be ravaged. The steps of estate protection can help you avoid all of that.

How do the three boats tend to work this step?

- Barges typically have medical and disability coverage through their work, and the premiums are payroll-deducted. But they tend not to buy long-term care insurance because

...onths. So you need a safety net. Your freedom fund allows ...eedom, or latitude, while you get back on your feet.

...o where should you park that freedom fund money so that ...n access it very quickly if you need it? A common answer is ...ficate of deposit (CD). That way the money can earn a little ...st while it sits idle. The problem with that strategy, however, ...t a CD locks up your money for a period of time, even if it's ...six months. In a true emergency you would need the money ...er than that.

Furthermore, short-term CDs today don't pay very much in-...t. As a matter of fact, they haven't paid very much interest for ...past seventy-five years. On average, they've paid 3.5 percent. ...ay of comparison, annuities have averaged 4 percent, and the ...k market has averaged a little over 7 percent. So CDs are not ...great of an investment, whether they are short-term or ...-term.

My suggestion is to put your freedom fund in a money market ...ount where you can get your hands on it quickly when you ...ly need it.

But wherever you park your freedom fund, beware of placing ...vith a financial institution that wants to redirect it to a short-...m or long-term investment or a retirement plan (steps 7–9 be-...v). You'll know that's what they want to do if early in your ...nversation with them they start recommending an investment or ...etirement plan. *Walk away from that conversation!* You're deal-...g with a HAD.

You see, no one makes any commission off of this step 7. ...our freedom fund is just cash that is parked somewhere. So a ...AD will try to get you to commit that cash to something that will ...ay a commission—and also tie up your cash so that it's no longer ...ee. Watch out for that!

How do the three boats tend to work this step?

they believe they'll never have a long-t
condition.

- Tugboats may have medical and disabi
  their employer, with the premiums pay
  not through their employer, they alm
  their own. Nor do they purchase long-
  They don't understand it, and they don
  for it.
- Sailboats may have medical and disability
  their employer, with the premiums payr
  they probably don't have long-term care
  they are not clear on what it is.

6. *Freedom funds*. A freedom fund is a stash of
"liquid," meaning you can put your hands on it
cause it's not tied up in an investment. Traditiona
ners call this an "emergency fund." But you know m
about freedom more than emergencies. "Emergency
sis. And in fact that's what these funds are for. But i
to keep my freedom. So I call this money a freedom

The rule of thumb for calculating how much mo
in your freedom fund is: three times the second num
up with in step 1, the amount of cash flowing out. In
if you've got $2,000 a month going out, you need to
in your freedom fund. Or, if you're like that family that I
going out each month, you'd need $44,250 in your fre

Where does that calculation of "three times cash
from? Well, if you lose your job, you need a cushion.
"money for a rainy day," as it's sometimes called. You
fund provides backup to see you through the storm unt
another job. The same thing applies if you are disabled.
ability policies don't kick in for three months or six month

- Barges tend to keep cash available in some sort of freedom fund that they have easy access to.
- Tugboats almost never have enough savings because their freedom fund tends to become their "fun fund." They live with the attitude, "If I have the money in the bank, why can't I spend it?" They are especially tempted to spend that money on others. Tugboats tend to use their credit cards as their "freedom funds."
- Sailboats tend not to have enough savings on hand, either because they spend it on shopping or they give it away.

7. *Short-term investments.* A short-term investment means an investment with a five-year objective in view. For example, a high-growth stock might be a short-term investment for people who are seeking fairly hefty returns in the near term. They don't expect the stock to grow dramatically forever, but they'll give it five years to play itself out. Another example of a short-term investment that involves considerably less risk would be a sixty-month CD.

The reason you want to have at least some short-term investments is that you don't want to tie up all your assets in long-term investments. You and your family have needs on the horizon for which you want to set money aside in a way that you can get to that money when the time arrives—for example, the down payment on a house, saving for a car, college tuition, or a twenty-fifth anniversary vacation.

By the way, just to clarify terms for some readers, an "investment" means a transaction set up to earn you money, not spend it. That doesn't mean an investment will always make money for you; sometimes you lose money, as with a stock that tanks. But at least the purpose of investing in a stock is to make money. By contrast, a car is not an investment. Yes, you "invest" (i.e., spend) money to buy a car, but a car is not intended to make you money, it's a means of transportation. And it's a "depreciating asset," meaning it loses value every day you own it. So don't confuse the meaning of the term "investment" to mean anything you want to put money into.

How do the three boats tend to work this step?

- Barges tend to be visionaries who see the big picture and plan for the long term. So they don't bother much with short-term investments. They prefer long-term planning.
- Tugboats have probably never even thought about what a short-term investment is.
- Sailboats rarely take the time to worry about short-term investments because they are too busy and to them short-term investing is not a priority.

8. *Long-term investments.* This is where you want to sock away your assets and accumulate wealth. These are the investments you have no intention of liquidating anytime soon—certainly not within five years. For most Americans, their home is their primary long-term investment. Some people buy mutual funds or stocks on a long-term basis, with a "buy and hold" philosophy, especially "blue-chip" companies that have a long track record of positive performance. Other examples of long-term investments might be an addition to an existing home, second homes, rare coins or other collectibles, Treasury notes, oil-and-gas partnerships, and works of art.

The challenge with long-term investments is finding a balance between security and value. You certainly want your investments to be safe and sound. On the other hand, if you were to just put all of your wealth into a savings account at a bank, the interest would be so low that you would actually lose money over the long haul. That balance between security and value differs from family to family, and also varies throughout the various stages of life.

Perhaps the primary strategy for achieving that balance is to diversify your investments as best you can. In other words, spread your risk among several investments, and don't put all your eggs in one basket. Your entire assets as a whole are called your "portfolio." You want to divide up your portfolio into different investments, so that your investments as a whole achieve a balance between security and adding value.

For some families that will mean that 90 percent of their long-term investments are tied up in their house. Is that wise? Well, given that housing values have basically kept going up over the past century, that's probably prudent. A local or regional housing market will experience a downturn occasionally. But home ownership has so many advantages that for most people it's a good long-term investment (as long as they are wise about buying the house and its mortgage to begin with).

What about the other 10 percent of their long-term investments? Well, here they have to evaluate their tolerance for risk, as well as prudence about a given investment. But again, the key is to diversify. Some assets might go into ultra-safe investments like T-notes or municipal bonds. Others might go into more aggressive mutual funds or stocks. And a little bit may go into deals that have significant upside potential, even though that means higher risk.

How do the three boats tend to work this step?

- Barges tend to have balanced long-term portfolios with diversified holdings.
- Tugboats do not put a lot of time or thinking into any kind of investment strategy. Long-term planning is not something they like to do, so planning a long-term investment has no appeal. Besides, why would anyone want to tie up their money for ten or twenty years? What's the point of that? Especially when there are so many things you could do with that money now! If a Tugboat does have a mutual fund or a house or some other long-term investment, it's probably because a friend or loved one talked him into it.

- Sailboats tend to have long-term investments that are tangible, like a home, land, or a business.

9. *Retirement planning.* One of my main motivations for writing this book is that 85 percent of Americans will retire broke. I think that's a crime. And it's downright scary to ponder. Especially as we see the world changing into a much more precarious and expensive place to live. I'm afraid that many folks who have been living it up—largely on credit—are in for a rude awakening when they get into their sunset years.

But that doesn't have to happen for you. Your retirement planning will fall into place if you do steps 1–8 above properly and *then* add to it a qualified retirement plan that is tax-deferred—a 401(k), a SEP, an IRA. If you've got those, you've got a retirement plan and you'll be ready when retirement comes around.

How do the three boats tend to work this step?

- Barges may have multiple retirement plans—perhaps a 401(k) or 403(b) at work, but often supplemented by additional retirement plans, like IRAs.
- Tugboats will have a retirement plan if it's provided by their employer and is payroll-deducted. They'll understand very little about that plan and will remain unaware of the various choices they have within that plan. Tugboats will usually trust someone else to invest their retirement savings.
- Sailboats are likely to have a 401(k) plan at work, or an IRA, or both. But they are not totally clear about what they are or how they work. They just know that a retirement plan is necessary.

10. *Financial statement.* There's an old joke about businesspeople, that they have three financial statements: one for the government that says they don't have any money, one for the bank that says

they've got a lot of money, and the real one that they don't want anybody to see.

Now that's quite a contrast to the average person on the street who doesn't even have a financial statement. In fact, the only time most people come up with a financial statement is when they want to get a new credit card, or they go to a bank to get a loan or refinance their mortgage.

That's not the reason to have a financial statement. The reason you need a financial statement is that it is just like the health assessment I gave you in step 10 of the health and fitness plan (chapter 6). Just as the health assessment helps you evaluate how well you have been working the steps of the health and fitness plan, a financial statement helps you evaluate how well you have been working the steps of the financial fitness plan.

So what should you include in your financial statement? Here's a list:

- *Gross income.* Consider personal earnings in all forms, such as salary, commissions, rental income, child support and alimony, royalties, etc.
- *Total expenses.* Consider where you spend your money in all areas, such as medical, credit card interest, mortgage or rent, other household, personal, entertainment, vacation, insurance, auto payments or leases, any repair and maintenance. Do not forget the taxes that directly reduce your gross income.
- *Net income or loss.* Subtract your total gross income from your total expenses.
- *Total assets.* Consider personal assets, such as the value of your home and property, investments, possessions that have monetary worth, etc.
- *Total liabilities.* Consider all of your debts, such as your mortgages, car loan, boat loan, credit card debt, etc.

- *Net worth*. Subtract your total *liabilities* (or debt) from your total assets.
- *Debt ratio*. Divide your total liabilities by your total assets. A debt ratio *greater than 1* means that you have more debt than assets. A debt ratio *less than 1* means that you have more assets than debt. Your debt ratio is one indicator of how "strong" or "weak" you are financially.

Your financial statement is really a scorecard of steps 1–9 above. It allows you to go back and evaluate how you've done in each step, and how far you've progressed by working all the steps in sequence. You'll certainly see some room for improvement. But the main thing you'll see is that you've paid attention to all the key areas. In some of them—hopefully in all of them—you'll see that you've made progress.

And that's an incredible feeling, to know that you are making progress with your money and finances. It relieves a *lot* of stress. As I've said repeatedly, the number one cause of stress in America is money. So to get on top of where things stand financially, and to take steps to protect and strengthen your financial position, and to not leave any holes—I mean, that's better than any sleeping pill! You can just go right to sleep at night when you know you've gotten control of your finances.

How do the three boats tend to work this step?

- Barges tend to know exactly where they stand financially. How they represent their financial condition to others depends on what they stand to gain or lose by the disclosure.
- Tugboats almost never have a financial statement. They don't know how to prepare one, nor do they have much interest in learning. They may not even be sure why a financial statement is needed.

- Sailboats whose pattern is led by a T or an R will tend to have a financial statement. But if the lead letter is an I or an M, they probably will not—not unless they needed one to get a loan.

My real objective in offering you this plan for financial fitness is to give you peace of mind and confidence. Confidence is a tremendous hedge against all the HADs out there in the financial services sector who want to earn a commission off of you. I'm not saying everyone in financial services is bad. I'm just saying it's a fact that they all have something to sell. It's a lot easier to sell to someone who has no confidence and is intimidated when it comes to money.

You no longer have to be intimidated. If you've worked all 10 steps of the plan, you're not only miles ahead of most people, but miles ahead of most financial planners. I say that because I personally have been training financial planners in the 10 steps of this plan for years, and I estimate that only 10 percent, maybe 15 percent at most, of the financial planners in America today recognize these steps and teach them to their clients.

So congratulations! You've accomplished something rare. For one thing, you've acquired some knowledge that you never were taught in school (unfortunately). And perhaps more important, you've gained an awareness of how *you* do finances, based on your inborn attitude. That's incredibly valuable! In fact, that's really your greatest financial asset, because every decision you make about money will be affected by that inborn attitude. How's that for something you can take to the bank?

Remember, you have a choice: you can control your finances or your finances will control you.

CHAPTER 8 **A Plan for Relationship Fitness**

What Motivates Someone to Take Action?

1   A major life event, such as getting married, getting divorced, sale of a business, retirement, and the like.
2   A fad self-improvement program has captured your attention.
3   A career or business relationship has created stress and/or financial troubles.
4   A personal decision as a result of being unhappy to obtain counsel about marriage, family, or workplace relationships.

Each boat will tend to respond to these motivators differently, as follows:

Barges instinctively focus on their goals, especially those related to careers and money. Oftentimes it takes a fractured relationship at work, school, or home to get Barges to stop and consider how they are relating to other people. The start of a new romantic relationship, the start of new job, a marriage or the death of a loved one or a valued colleague will focus a Barge on relationships and family issues. Unfortunately, Barges struggle the most when it comes to relationships. Perhaps the one bright light in this regard for some Barges is that as they grow older and work begins to wind down they seek love and often find time for their grandchildren and enjoy doting on them and bragging about their accomplishments.

Tugboats are all about people, so they have a natural advantage motivationally when it comes to relationships. They love almost everyone they know. The Tugboats desire and need relationships more than any other pattern. They tend to welcome life-changing events—even the tough ones, such as divorces, diseases, and deaths—as new opportunities to serve people. Tugboats look forward to sharing accomplishments and life events such as weddings, graduations, and children. They are the most social of the patterns.

Sailboats have a number of innate motivations to work on the relationship steps. For example, they tend to want to make sure their family will be taken care of when they get around to retirement. Sailboats tend to be comfortable living with others as well as living alone. They get excited thinking about the future, and they tend to be extremely proud of their spouses, children, and grandchildren. The Sailboats are the most encouraging of the boats and their "families" can extend to their team, their friends, neighbors, and co-workers. However, if Sailboats lead with a heart letter (I or M), they may struggle to save enough money to provide for all the life events they are looking forward to. If they lead with a head letter (R or T), their struggle may be to avoid overworking and not leaving enough time for the people in their lives. Sailboats tend to be pretty good at relationships in general, but they can send mixed signals to others when they are under stress.

A 10-Point Plan for Relationship Fitness

1   Communication/Reality check
2   Trust
3   Commitment
4   Conflict management

5   Fun and relaxation
6   Career management
7   Finances
8   Extended family
9   Romance and sexuality
10   Spirituality

Remember what I said in the two previous chapters: each of these steps for relational fitness need to be followed in sequence, and *all* the steps must be followed, not just the ones that appeal to you.

Also note that while I'm primarily addressing marriage relationships in this chapter, the principles apply to relationships elsewhere in life—dating, families, parents and children, the workplace, schools, etc.

1. *Communication/Reality check*. Perhaps you've seen the *Far Side* cartoon in which a man is scolding his dog. The first panel is captioned, "What people say." In it the man is shouting, "Bad dog! Bad! Very, very bad! Bad dog!" The second panel is captioned, "What dogs hear." In that panel the man is also shouting, but his words are, "Bark bark! Bark! Bark, bark bark! Bark bark!"

I think that pretty well sums up how communication—or lack thereof—takes place in all too many relationships. For instance, a wife says something to her husband. She is absolutely certain that her words are as clear as day. And she's utterly convinced that what she is saying makes all the sense in the world. But later, her husband confides to a friend, "I don't have a clue what she was talking about."

"Bark bark! Bark! Bark, bark bark! Bark bark!"

I can guarantee that if you're a parent, you are unintelligible to your kids much of the time. "I told you to do your chores! I even left a to-do list on the kitchen counter! Why haven't you done your chores? This happens every time! I'm sick and tired of having to clean up after you. I'm not asking a lot! All I'm asking is . . ."

Meanwhile, your kids look at you with that blank stare. They know you're going on about something, but heck if they know what it is! All they're hearing is the *"Peanuts* voice." You know, from the *Peanuts* cartoons that were produced for television? In *Peanuts,* whenever adults intervene, you see the kids looking up to listen, but all they hear is a bunch of droning notes: "Wah, wah, wah, wah, wah!" It's the *"Peanuts* voice," Charles Schulz's version of, "What parents say, what kids hear."

I suppose every marriage expert in the world has their own take on what accounts for miscommunication, and how to transform it into good communication. Maybe the most prominent is John Gray, who says it's all about male-female differences: men are from Mars, women are from Venus. Men hold on to their feelings and don't talk, while women are highly expressive with their feelings and must talk. I think Gray is clever. But my research suggests that things are a bit more complicated than that. You'll find men who are highly emotive and talkative, and women who are quite reserved and silent.

At Real Life Management, we have a tool for understanding how someone communicates that is far more accurate than simply saying, "You're a man, so this is how you communicate," or "You're a woman, so this is how you communicate." Our tool is the 3-Minute Survey that was discussed in Chapters 2 and 3. It's more accurate because it gets at the core of the person, down to his or her *attitude.* We profoundly believe that attitude drives behavior far more than gender.

So if you want to promote communication, whether at home, at work, in your place of worship, or wherever, start with the 3-Minute Survey. It will be a *reality check* for you as it reveals your attitude and communication style. Have the people you're trying to relate to go through it.[1] It will give you a reality check not only on yourself but on what is really influencing your communication. Once you've determined everyone's scoring pattern, a whole lot of insight and understanding will come to light.

For one thing, you'll quickly see that other people are *not like you*! Can you believe it? For example, your spouse and children are not like you. Right there you've gained an insight into how you and your family communicate—or *mis*-communicate. It explains why sometimes when you talk to your spouse, it's as if your words go right in one ear and out the other: "Bark bark! Bark! Bark, bark bark! Bark bark!" It accounts for why, when you talk with your daughter about being responsible, she just sits there and gives absolutely no response: "Wah, wah, wah, wah, wah!"

Attitude is the major thing that drives behavior, including the behavior of communication—both how one gives it and how one receives it. And by now I think you can predict how the different scoring patterns do communication:

- *Barges* lead with two head letters (TR or RT), so they tend to be factual and logical. If they lead with a T, they pay attention to the accuracy of the facts. They expect you to cut to the chase, get to the point, don't beat around the bush. If they lead with an R, you'd better make sure that what you're saying makes sense, because if you don't they'll tell you all the ways in which you are not making sense.

  Barges often struggle in relationships because they feel more comfortable keeping things at a factual and rational level. But of course relationships are also emotional in nature, and that can be threatening to a Barge. For that reason they'll tend not to talk about their feelings, except in a roundabout way. For example, they may give you an analysis of their feelings (instead of a feeling itself). Or they may express a negative feeling by accusing *you* of doing something wrong. Many will make feeling statements that are passive in nature, as if someone is doing something to them, instead of owning their feelings outright: "I'm being neglected," as opposed to, "I feel all alone."

- *Tugboats* lead with two heart letters, so they tend to be playful and gregarious. If they lead with an I, they are not shy about initiating a conversation, and by the same token there's no guarantee they won't break off a conversation to go talk with someone else. I's also like to keep things light; they may use lots of humor, and they're always looking for a response. If Tugboats lead with an M, they are prone to hold on to a conversation for as long as they can. They want to hear all about the other person's feelings, needs, problems, concerns—all that "soft" stuff, the "touchy-feely" stuff.

  Tugboats are quite endearing, but sometimes they have a hard time getting to the point. Indeed, oftentimes they have no real "point" to make, because for them communication is not about presenting an argument or establishing who is right or wrong, but just the experience of "being" with one another. Indeed, some Tugboats will "tune out" if things get a little too abstract, technical, or "heady." They may stay in the conversation and smile, but inside their head all they are hearing is, "Wah, wah, wah, wah, wah!"

- *Sailboats* tend to do better at all aspects of communication because their combination of head and heart letters as the first two letters in their pattern gives them a balance between the two. It makes them more adaptable. Sailboats who lead with a head letter (T or R) will be like a Barge in that they prefer to deal with facts and reason first. But they can quickly adjust if the person speaking to them leads with a heart letter and is communicating in a heart manner. Likewise, Sailboats who lead with a heart letter (I or M) will be like a Tugboat in that they prefer communication that is relaxed and personal. But they can quickly adjust if the person speaking to them leads with a head letter and presents them with facts and logic to consider.

Now these descriptions have to be qualified just a bit. They are not hard and fast rules, because remember, communication is a two-way street. A lot depends on whom one is dealing with. For example, Lakeisha, who is a Tugboat (IMRT), has no trouble talking about her day—the people she met, the phone calls she got into, the places she went, what her friends told her, on and on. She'll talk your ear off if you let her.

Well, her daughter Deiondre doesn't mind that at all. Deiondre happens to be a Sailboat. Her scoring pattern is MRIT. She and her mom talk on the phone all the time—sometimes several times a day, and for extended periods of time. Deiondre loves hearing from her mother. She feels privileged to have such a great relationship with her mom.

But things are much, much different between Lakeisha and her husband, Michael. Michael is a big old Barge (TRIM). He married Lakeisha because he'd never encountered such a beautiful creature, and it felt great when Lakeisha kept telling him how smart he was. But once they were all settled into their new life together, Michael realized he was living out the blues song that Lowell Fulson and Ferdinand Washington wrote called "Honey Hush."

Over time, Michael has found a hundred ways to "tune out" his wife (I'm not saying that's a good thing to do, I'm just saying that's what he does). And by now, Lakeisha has learned to "hold" her tongue at the supper table, or in the car, or at bedtime. She's still a Tugboat, but she's not talkative—at least when she's around Michael. However, once he goes off to watch TV or retires to his home office to do his budgets and financial matters or whatever, she just phones up her daughter or a friend or a neighbor, and away she goes.

Can you see how attitudes dramatically affect our communication? If we want better relationships, we've got to do a couple of things in this department. The first one I've already alluded to: we've got to respect that those around us don't communicate the same way we do. That means we've got to respect their style for what it is. We may find that style difficult to understand at times, but that doesn't make them a bad person, just a different person. Different from us.

So it's no good to yell (or even think), "What's the matter with you?! Why can't you *communicate*?!" The answer is, they *are* communicating, they're just doing it differently from you. Try a little understanding first before you shame them for being who they are.

The second thing we can do to improve communication is to adjust to the other person's scoring pattern. I teach the 3-Minute Survey to a lot of salespeople, and I always make a big point out of this. Salespeople can double and even triple their sales if they'll start paying attention to people's scoring patterns and tailoring their sales style and strategy to fit the various patterns. Most salespeople sell in only one way—according to whatever their own scoring pattern is. They act as if everyone is like them. For instance, maybe they're an IRMT, and they're just as bold and brassy and boisterous as they can be. Well, guess what? That don't sell to the Barge who doesn't "do" bold and brassy and boisterous.

The same principle holds true in marriages and families. It's all about putting your message in terms that the other person can hear. So back to Lakeisha and her husband Michael. Let's say Lakeisha wants to go to the seashore for their summer vacation. What are the odds that she's going to "sell" Michael on that prospect? You think he's going to get excited about spending a week on the beach with that voice? If Lakeisha talks to him in Tugboat language, the conversation will be over before it starts.

But now suppose Lakeisha does as I've suggested and has Michael take the 3-Minute Survey. And suppose she does the wise thing and actually studies both her pattern and her husband's pattern and ponders their significance for their communication. She comes to realize that a TRIM is going to want to see a solid plan that makes a lot of sense and saves a lot of money. In truth, a TRIM may not care to go on a vacation in the first place, but he just might if it's a good plan and is presented in the right way.

The point is, Lakeisha's got to learn to talk Barge, and specifically TRIM Barge, if she's ever going to get the communication going again with her husband. Yes, we could also say that it would help if Michael learned to interpret Tugboat language, which was my previous point. But I'd say that more of the burden of "translation" is on the person initiating the communication than on the one receiving it. In *Far Side* terms, if humans want to talk to dogs, they've got to learn Dog first before they try to get dogs to speak English or Japanese or French or whatever. Otherwise, it's just "Bark bark! Bark! Bark, bark bark! Bark bark!"

Now I can't talk about this area of communication without letting you know that there's a wild card in the deck that sometimes pops up in a relationship. That wild card is the fact that some people are simply not hardwired to communicate through verbal means. Please understand: everyone communicates, but some people are naturally more inclined to speak nonverbally than verbally. For example, many artistic types are Tugboats who pour their soul into musical compositions or paintings or theatrical performances or whatever. These folks are brilliant and highly expressive in their art, yet they struggle to put into words even the simplest of their own thoughts, feelings, and needs. On the other hand, you'll come across an engineer, accountant, researcher, or other "head" person who is a Barge that is amazing at dealing with extremely technical subjects, but can't articulate his own concerns verbally except in the most rudimentary, clumsy way.

Unfortunately, these "silent types" may not even be aware that they are not being heard, because they don't think in terms of verbal communication. Instead, it's the people around them who are most troubled by the situation. For that reason, if you are married to someone like the ones I'm describing, then I appeal to you to take the initiative. Tell your partner that you are not getting enough communication from him/her. Explain that that doesn't make your partner a bad person. It's just that you need to know more of what's going on in his/her mind and heart.

But don't leave it there. Your spouse may understand what you are saying, but may not have a clue how to give you what you need. Again, that doesn't make your spouse a bad person, just a different person. So help out by coming up with some practical ways for your spouse to give you what you need by way of verbal input.

For instance, one wife made sure that every Saturday morning she had breakfast with her nonexpressive husband. All during the week leading up to the breakfast, she would make a list of the things she needed to hear him talk about. Then, while they ate, she would work her way through her list, prompting him to "download" his thoughts and feelings about various topics. Granted, that's not the ideal way that that wife would have wanted her husband to communicate. She would have preferred to have much more spontaneous conversations. But that weekly breakfast—even if it may sound a bit wooden or contrived—provided a way for her to get what she needed. The key is that the couple did something intentional to make sure their relationship was working. They didn't just give up.

But now let me say a word to the person who is not very verbal or conversational. I've stressed several times that your reserved style does not make you a bad person. However, you need to know that your style is definitely affecting your relationships, especially those who are closest to you. They can't read your mind, and you can't expect them to guess at your feelings. So unless you find ways to let them know what is going on inside you, *they will not know*. Do you want to be misunderstood? If not, you've got to find ways to verbalize what your thoughts and feelings are.

That will probably feel a bit unnatural to you. You may think, "Don't they just know?" The answer is no, they don't. You may also think, "Why should anyone care?" Well, forget why; they *do* care, that's the point. So seek out ways to communicate yourself to them, not because *you* need it, but because *they* need it. If you have to, set as a goal that three times every day you're going to stop and take five minutes to talk to your spouse in person or by phone in order to tell him/her what you are thinking about or what you are feeling. Even if all you can do is just state or announce your thoughts or feelings, great! I guarantee your marriage will become more of a *relationship,* where you and your spouse actually connect, rather than a placid ocean where ships are passing in the night.

How do the three boats tend to work this step?

- Barges tend to like e-mail as opposed to phone calls, and their style is straight to the point. Sometimes they can be insensitive to others, especially Tugboats, whom they tend to dislike.
- Tugboats have a natural bent toward open communication, whether by phone, e-mail, or in person.
- Sailboats tend to be pretty good at communication. If their lead letter is an I or M, they may be challenged when it comes to follow-up and handling details that have come out of the communication.

2. *Trust.* Trust is to a relationship like oxygen is to the body. A relationship simply can't survive without it. That's true in business partnerships and manager-worker relationships. It's especially true in marriage, because a marriage is the joining together of two people in an intimate relationship where each one's vulnerabilities, fears, and truest selves will be revealed. Unless there's trust that one's partner will remain true as these things come to light, intimacy is impossible and the relationship will collapse.

This brings us to the question: can *you* be trusted? Everyone wants the other person to be trustworthy. But trust actually begins with you. Trust is a matter of character. Character is not something you are born with, but something you develop over time. So if you're not an especially trustworthy person, don't just accept that. Own it, but accept responsibility for making trust a key quality for you to develop. It's the only way your marriage and family relationships will prosper.

So how do attitudes factor into this issue of trust? Well, all of the patterns are capable of being trustworthy, but all of them are also tempted to break trust in one way or another:

- T's are the most reliable of all the scoring patterns. They can especially be trusted with facts. If a T tells you there's $1,048.93 in a checking account, you can trust that. It's probably accurate right down to the penny. Where T's are less trustworthy is when they are afraid. They desperately need structure and a plan, so if things are not going according to plan, they start to feel anxious and uneasy. Only they tend not to be honest about those feelings. Instead, they mask them behind anger and a drive to reestablish control. T's don't always realize that their anger causes the people around them to distrust their motives and wonder whether they even care.

- R's can be trusted to think things through. They often end up in leadership in businesses and organizations because people instinctively trust that they know what is going on and will lead with greater wisdom. However, R's sometimes have a way of being sarcastic and condescending, and that behavior undercuts trust in ways that an R can't even imagine. R's also tend to be very analytical and logical, which is tremendously helpful in some situations. But in relationships, that approach to things can erode trust because others can never figure out what the R is *feeling,* and where his heart is.

- I's have an infectious way of getting people to warm up to them quickly, which leads to quick rapport and trust. However, that immediate likability has a definite downside, in that first impressions sometimes disappoint—and that is especially true for an I. I's have a way of creating expectations, but then their spontaneity and impulsiveness sabotage the trust they've generated by drawing them away to other people and pursuits. "I thought he was my friend," someone is liable to say of an I after being disappointed. Ironically, when the I comes back, he can usually reignite the relationship in such a way that all is forgiven. But that means the disappointment will only be greater the next time around. In short order, an I can become perceived as unreliable—perhaps the least to be trusted among all the patterns.
- M's have a long suit for loyalty. That means you can trust the faithfulness of an M forever. They will stick with you through thick and thin, and it's arguable whether a true M would ever file for divorce. Of course, the dark side of an M's ability to please people is a tendency to be dishonest about true feelings and opinions. An M is liable to say that everything is "fine" in her marriage, when in fact the marriage is in serious trouble. M's tend to pay little attention to facts and figures, so M's are not always trustworthy with a checkbook or credit card.

Now my point in describing how these four letters handle the issue of trust is to show tendencies, not hard and fast rules. (And of course a lot depends on the second and third letters in the scoring pattern.) Just because you are prone to operate a certain way doesn't mean you have to do it that way. Indeed, my objective is to help you avoid falling into the traps associated with your pattern.

However, two tendencies are especially worth emphasizing, because they are particularly common, and both create untold problems for many relationships. The first is that Tugboats tend to trust *too* much, and that gets them into a lot of trouble. Tugboats instinctively see the good in people, and they expect the best from people. However, the cold fact of the matter is that not everyone in the world is trustworthy. So Tugboats get taken advantage of time and again. They trust people who should not be trusted, people who are not worthy of their trust. Sometimes they even marry such a person. "Oh, but he'll change," they may say. "I'll change him." It's a noble aspiration, but doomed to failure.

Tugboats' trusting nature causes them not to set good boundaries, as I've mentioned before. So even if they are married to someone who is quite reliable and compassionate, Tugboats can still find their needs being overlooked. It's not that their spouse doesn't care, it's that their spouse can't be expected to know everything that the Tugboat needs.

For example, Tom and Lucinda have three small children. Tom works as a salesman for an auto parts distributor, and he's on the road twenty-one weeks a year. That much travel is tough on family life, but Lucinda is very supportive, and the couple have a great relationship. Tom usually arrives home from his travels on a Friday night. For a long time, he spent Saturday mornings on the golf course with his buddies. It was a great way to unwind from his trips.

But then one Saturday afternoon Tom found Lucinda crying her eyes out. Tom is a Sailboat (ITMR), and he's quite compassionate. So when he saw Lucinda's tears, he immediately dropped everything and took her in his arms. "What's up, honey?" he asked.

Lucinda just cried for a while, comforted that Tom was finally paying attention. Lucinda is a Tugboat (MITR). Finally she began talking, and after a good long while of conversation (it often takes a Tugboat *time* to feel safe and secure enough to risk getting down to the real issue), Tom discovered what she was upset about. "I feel like I never get a break," she said, still sniffling. "When you're away, I've got the kids all week. And then you come home, and I know you're tired and you need to relax. So I don't mind you going out with your friends on Saturday. I really don't. But I just get so tired of being with them! I sometimes think I'm going to scream. It's not like I don't love my kids. Honestly, I do. But I get to the point where I'd give anything to just be by myself for a little bit. Is that a terrible thing?"

Tom had absolutely no idea that his wife was feeling overwhelmed. She had never said a thing about it until that point. Indeed, all he saw when he got home was smiles. You see, Lucinda was not doing a very good job of articulating her needs. She was not asking him to respect any boundaries—namely, a bit of time for herself, to regroup and refresh her energies as a mom. Tom didn't do anything wrong, and yet out of ignorance he was living his life in a way that took advantage of Lucinda. To his credit, once Tom realized what was going on, he helped Lucinda formulate a plan by which she could get some breaks from the children. Their marriage grew stronger as a result, and the whole family benefited by having a happier mother.

At the end of the day, each one of us has to take responsibility to see that our needs are being expressed and met. We can't leave it to someone else to pay attention to all that we need, much as we might like for that to happen. It simply won't happen, and it's irresponsible to live as if it should. If you're a Tugboat, you've got to "go against pattern," as it were, and be a little "selfish" sometimes. Let your needs be known, and establish some boundaries to see that they get met. You're not helping anyone by suffering in silence.

A second tendency that I want to focus on is that some Barges have low self-esteem, and as a result they have an especially hard time trusting anyone at all. You can imagine how that could happen. A little boy who is a Barge (RTIM) grows up in a home where love is inconsistent, affection is lacking, and the father keeps telling the boy how "stupid" he is (even though he's actually quite bright).

The impact of those conditions is that the boy's self-confidence withers. He doesn't believe in himself, and so he doesn't try very hard. As a result, he underperforms; he settles for much, much less than he is actually capable of. He may even end up grossly overweight, which is very uncommon for Barges. But even a Barge can overeat because food is one of the quickest ways to assuage feelings of inferiority.

That Barge's inability to trust is especially troublesome, because it ends up poisoning all his relationships. At a very deep level, the Barge expects everyone to think poorly of him. So he finds ways to come across as incompetent, even though his natural disposition is to be highly competent. He makes sarcastic comments about others, but his most disparaging remarks are reserved for himself. In short, he keeps people at a distance in order to avoid going back to the conditions in which he grew up. But the sad thing is that that's exactly where he ends up, because no one knows him, and he sets thing up such that he can't receive people's love.

If I'm describing you or someone you know, then I implore you to seek out professional help in addressing these issues. You are letting the most valuable things in life pass you by—all because someone planted lies in your mind and heart way back in your childhood. Isn't it time you sought out the truth, and set yourself free?

Trust is one of the primary building blocks for building successful relationships. So what are some ways for developing and maintaining trust? Let me suggest five things you can do:

1   *Honor your word.* It should be obvious that following through on commitments and expectations is the way to convince people that they can trust you. Kids are especially perceptive in this regard. How many times have you told your son or daughter that you would do something with them as soon as you have the time, only to forget about it? I assure you they won't forget

about it. Only they may not ask a second or third time. Rather, they'll gradually come to the conclusion that their parent is not to be trusted, no matter their good intentions.

2   *Live consistently.* Suppose I sent you my address, and then a year later sent you a new address, and then six weeks after that sent you still another new address, and so on. Then imagine I told you I was moving into your neighborhood, where I was planning to "settle." Would you believe me when I said I was planning to stick around? Probably not. More likely you'd be very careful about establishing a relationship with me, because you would assume that I'll be gone in a few months.

Well, that example illustrates how a lot of people cause others not to trust them because their lives are so erratic and inconsistent. Today they've committed to one thing, tomorrow they're on to something else. Today they've got a plan of action, tomorrow they've got a completely different plan. As a result of their unpredictability, no one quite believes them. If you want your family to trust you, you've got to satisfy the expectations that you create.

3   *Say you're sorry.* None of us is perfect. That's okay, because I've discovered that none of us expects anyone else to be perfect. We just assume that people are going to make mistakes, let us down, and sometimes even hurt us. So what do we expect when they do? An apology, of course.

Well, that same expectation applies to us. It's inevitable that we're going to do things that offend others and disappoint them. So when we do, the fastest way to reestablish trust is to come clean about our screw-up and make an honest apology. Let me just say that Barges have the hardest time with this one, because Barges never want to be wrong. But guess what, Mr. or Ms. Barge? The people in your world respect you, not for always being right, but for being honest on those rare occasions when, oops, you're human and you're wrong. Just own it. You'll end up with a lot more trust if you do.

4   *Respect the concerns of others.* If you want to earn people's trust, pay attention to what matters to them. If you don't, they'll conclude that you don't care about them. This is a lot easier to say than do, of course, because our attitude gets in our way. We naturally focus on whatever our pattern predisposes us to focus on. So we can fly right by the interests of others and not even recognize it. Sometimes we do that even when someone tells us in no uncertain terms what matters to them.

For instance, many a T has explained to his I or M wife that it's very important to him to be on time. He has said it in anger, and he has said it in love. He has said it a thousand times. He has explained that being late puts him in a foul mood. He has done everything he knows how to communicate the importance to him of being on time.

So here comes the most important function of the year at his company, and he's all dressed and ready to walk out the door. And what is his wife doing? Why, she's still getting out of the shower and putting on her makeup! She didn't plan her afternoon very well, so she got home late. And even though he tried to tell her that time was running out, she chose to get on the phone with her girlfriend and chat for a while. So now she's . . . *late!* Which means *he* is going to be late.

Now let me ask: what are the odds that that man is going to totally believe his wife later that evening when they get home and she retires for the night with the words, "Good night, sweetheart. I love you"? You have to wonder what she means by "love." Because he is probably thinking, "If you loved me, you'd be on time. If you loved me, you'd pay attention to what matters to me. If you loved me, you wouldn't violate a boundary about punctuality that is very important to me." And he's right. Trust requires that we provide people a basis for believing what we say.

5   *Use touch to communicate trust.* The Barges and the Sailboats who lead with a T or an R will struggle with this one, just a bit. But the truth is that touch has a powerful way of communicating trust. It's part of why people shake hands when they meet: anthropologists suggest that a handshake is reassurance that the parties have come unarmed.

If you never touch the people in your life, you are denying them an important means of trusting you. A hand on the arm or shoulder, a pat on the back, a light jab on the arm, a hug, a kiss. All of these are ways to say, "You can trust me. I'm for you. I'm with you." Obviously you have to determine what sort of physical communication is appropriate to the person, the relationship, and the situation. But use touch to say what words cannot quite convey.

Tugboats come by this more naturally than the other patterns. It's the Barges and the Sailboats who lead with a T or an R who could profit the most by it. So if you're one of those, I would ask: when's the last time you kissed your spouse? When's the last time you hugged your child? When's the last time you gave a firm handshake or a pat on the back to that person who reports to you at the office? If it's been a while since you've come across with behaviors like these, you might be surprised at how much distrust has built up. And if not distrust, at least wondering: "Does s/he really care about me?"

By the way, if you're the father of an adolescent daughter, you should especially pay attention to this point. Adolescent girls need more physical affection from their fathers than at any time previously in their life—in a healthy and appropriate way, obviously. But as their bodies change and they grow into mature women, the physical touch of their father is extremely important in reassuring them of many vital things: security, protection, acceptance, attractiveness, and confidence, to name just a few.

I know many a father who is all worried about how boys treat his daughter. Talk about a trust issue! But one of the best ways for that father to head off trouble is to hug his daughter at least once a day, and to reassure her of his love. Believe it or not, of all the men in the world, *he's* the one whose love she most wants to have at that point in her life. Trust me!

How do the three boats tend to work this step?

- Barges frequently struggle with trusting others, and they often are mistrusted by others because they appear to be concerned with rules, details, and money more than people.
- Tugboats are instinctively trusting—in fact, too trusting at times. They assume the best in people and oftentimes that gets them in big trouble.

- Sailboats who lead with a T or an M tend to trust others more quickly than other Sailboats. Sailboats who lead with an I or an R can come on a bit strong early in a relationship, and that can generate some mistrust in others.

3. *Commitment.* Commitment goes hand in hand with trust. When it comes to marriage (as well as all other relationships), commitment is the glue that holds the marriage together, especially during hard times.

Let's make sure we're clear on what we mean by commitment. You see, with the breakdown in the institution of marriage nowadays, there's a lot of confusion on this point. It's now become common for people to talk about being in a "committed relationship," which means they are not married, but they are somehow "committed." My question is, committed to *what*?

People today make "contingency commitments": they're committed until something better comes along. But that's not commitment, that's just attachment. Commitment means you're in to stay. You've made up your mind. You're not going anywhere. You're determined to make it work.

There's an old story that clarifies what "commitment" is really about. A chicken and a pig were talking. The chicken was just so proud of herself for contributing her eggs to the family breakfast table. She allowed as she was thereby "committed" to the welfare of the family. But the pig would have none of it. "Chicken," he said, "for you, breakfast is just something you're involved in. But for me it's a commitment."

Are you just involved in your marriage, or committed to it? As an I, I have to tell you that I's really struggle with this one. That's because I's are easily distracted. I'm not saying that I's are unfaithful to their partners, any more than the other patterns. But commitment in marriage is about more than just sexual fidelity. It involves that.

But it involves more than just avoiding certain behaviors that erode trust. It means actively pursuing behaviors that build trust. And that's where I's really struggle, because they have a short attention span and like to be in control.

Commitment means that you're able to go the distance. It means you can be relied on to hang in there when the going gets tough. Because it's a foregone conclusion that in a marriage, things are going to get tough. A young couple stands at the altar exchanging vows, and it's so sweet. They're pledging to be there for each other, "for better or worse, for richer or for poorer, in sickness and in health, 'til death do us part." What a powerful set of commitments!

But when you're twenty-two or twenty-four or whatever, you don't know what you don't know. You don't know about layoffs or downturns in the economy. You don't know about breast cancer or adult onset of diabetes. You don't know about two o'clock feedings or diapers. You don't know about menopause or trophy wives. You don't know about impotence or low sperm counts. You don't know what you don't know, and you certainly don't know what the future holds. As a result, the biggest thing you don't know is what commitment means. Commitment doesn't mean making a promise, it means *keeping* a promise. Most of the time, keeping a promise is hard—especially when you have other options.

So you have to decide somewhere in your heart that you are going to make your relationship work. You effectively cut off any other option, because otherwise it's too tempting to bail if you don't like the way things are going. I know that sounds a bit old-fashioned, but that's the way I see it. I don't think Shannon and I would still be married if we had left ourselves open to splitting up. We just decided that we had to figure out how to make our marriage work, and I'm glad we did, because the best stuff in marriage lies on the other side of "working things out." If you quit too soon, you miss that.

sn't matter what the topic is, it's the attention and time that
ter. That activity reassures her that her husband cares, and that
is secure in the relationship.

Conversely, it's very difficult to feel that someone is commit-
to you when that person never spends time with you, and acts
f he/she'd rather be with others than with you.

Pursue common interests. Someone has well said that the great-
enemy of marriage is "creeping separateness." Most marriages
deteriorate don't do so because of sudden crises or out-of-the-
affairs. Rather, they die through a slow but steady loss of hav-
anything in common. The couples get involved in different
rests, and they spend less and less time doing anything together,
the result that they drift apart, and eventually wake up one
to realize they are strangers.

The only way to avoid that is to develop some common inter-
. That may seem hard to do if you're a T or R married to an I or
You'd just as soon read the *Economist,* while your spouse wants
lay tennis. The easy thing to do at that point is to say, "We're
mpatible." But that's a cop-out. That's not commitment.

Commitment means trying lots of different activities together
l you find one that you both can enjoy. You don't have to enjoy
r the same reasons. A husband may enjoy fly fishing because it
him outdoors, there's a definite technique that he likes to
ter, and there are many details to consider in order to catch
fish. Meanwhile, his wife may enjoy the same activity because
ts her to spend time with her husband, she likes the different
rs and craftwork that goes into tying flies, and she loves to
a lunch when they go fly fishing. Who cares that they gain dif-
t satisfactions out of the day? They're doing something *to-
er,* something positive that is building their relationship and
commitment to each other.

Of all the patterns, M's probably have the most n
to honor their commitment to marriage because M's a
the day is long. As I said earlier, it's unlikely that a tr
ever file for divorce. They certainly would have to go
attitude to do so, and it would probably require sever
ate circumstances to motivate them to do so.

Barges, on the other hand, have less trouble filin
To them, it's a logical way to resolve a troubled rela
they tend to go about divorce in a fairly methodical,
way. That's a shame, because the very thing Barges g
vorce—namely, their independence—is the very opp
they most need, which is intimacy and relationship.

Barges by nature are actually well equipped to fo
on their commitments. By nature, they tend to be p
word. But the part of commitment that they don't unc
emotional and relational side of being in a marriage v
They don't realize that in addition to providing for t
remaining faithful and showing up on time and havi
the other "Barge things" at which they are so good,
requires a commitment to affection and romance an
and self-revelation and celebration and expressions
apologies. If a Barge can learn to offer things like
saying it will ever feel *natural* to do so), they would
how richer their own life, as well as their marriage,

So what are some ways that a couple can work
mitment to each other? Here are some suggestions:

1. *Keep the lines of communication open*. Communi
more than just the "content" of whatever you and yo
about. Every conversation says something about th
itself. That's why it's particularly important for a
down and listen to his wife, and really pay atten

3. *Learn the art of negotiation.* If you want to let your spouse know that you are committed to the relationship, you'll learn to give and take in order to accommodate your partner's needs and desires. For example, it's quite common for many wives whose husbands are hunters to feel like widows during the hunting season, especially on the weekends. Now a wife could put her foot down and insist that she's far more important than any deer or duck or dove or any other dumb animal, and of course she'd be right. Except that she could win the battle and lose the war. She could force her husband to stay home. But what sort of husband would she end up with? Would he be happier to be around? If he's a true hunter at heart, probably not.

A better approach would be a strategy of negotiation. Admittedly, negotiation is more an art than a science. But she might say, for instance, "Okay, honey, during deer season, you get to go hunting twelve weekends of the thirteen. I'll live with that. I won't like it, but I won't put up a fuss about it. Twelve weekends out of thirteen are yours. But in exchange, I'm asking for you to make all the other weekends of the year available to me and the family, in case we decide to do something together."

Negotiation means you give a little in order to gain what you need. It's a way of demonstrating commitment, because it says, "This isn't all about me. I recognize that you have needs, too. I want to make sure that your needs get met, so that I can legitimately make demands to get my needs met, too."

How do the three boats tend to work this step?

- Barges tend to procrastinate in making relationship commitments. But once they do commit, their accountability and responsibility to their commitment can be rather strong.
- Tugboats are quick to commit initially, and they often overcommit to too many people. That means they can end up

dropping the ball on details, which causes no end of frustration for Barges and Sailboats.

- Sailboats are quite capable of committing to the relationships they enter into, but Sailboats who lead with an I or a M tend to be like Tugboats, with poor follow-through that at times can make them look uncommitted.

4. *Conflict management.* Managing conflict is largely a subset of step 1, Communication. If you work on your communication, you will have a lot less trouble dealing with conflict. If you neglect communication, you will end up in nothing but conflict.

By now it should be obvious that a whole lot of the conflicts you experience in your relationships are, at root, a collision of *attitudes.* In fact, I'm going to suggest that almost all relational conflicts are rooted somewhere in our attitudes—in the fact that each of us sees life a bit differently. That's not to say that emotional issues and psychological factors and character issues and other things don't produce conflicts. They do. But at heart, each of us is trying to be who we are. Which means we are trying to live our lives the way we were hardwired to live them. As we do, we inevitably behave in ways that are different from someone else's hardwiring. When that happens, we've got a conflict.

That's actually good news! It means that when Shirley, who is a Tugboat, gets preoccupied with some heart-wrenching story on *Oprah* and, as a result, neglects to make out the checks she was supposed to write to pay the bills, she is not a bad person. An overinvolved person, maybe. An easily distracted person, perhaps. But not a person of flawed character.

That's important to stress, because her husband, who is a Barge, is liable to see things otherwise. "You're irresponsible!" he tells her. "Lazy! A ne'er-do-well! Good for nothing! Unreliable! Disorganized! A slacker! Worthless!" Can you think of some other put-downs?

My point is that all of us have a way of assuming the worst about other people when we find ourselves in conflict with them. We may even verbalize our conclusion and shame them by questioning their character. But if we would just back off for a minute, we might notice that what's really going on is not a lapse of character, at least not fundamentally. At root, the person is just being who they are. That may create problems for us, and if left unchecked their habits may lead to problems with their character. But let's not throw gasoline on the fire by impugning someone's character, when all they are trying to do is be who they are.

I want to point out a couple of extremes in the way that attitudes factor into conflict. The one is that Barges want to win. Barges aren't primarily concerned about relationships, least of all in a conflict. They just want to triumph. To that end, they will lay down a blistering barrage of facts, logic, and persuasion, as if to overwhelm the other person, so much so that surrender becomes the only option.

If marriage or parenting were like a court of law, that might be a satisfactory approach. But of course a family is above all a set of relationships. And guess what? Brute force *never* fosters relationships. It may win an argument, but it will never win someone's heart. Barges may think that winning an argument is all that matters in a conflict, but they're wrong. Conflict is not about getting your way, it's about finding a way to make the relationship work.

At the other extreme from the Barge is the Tugboat who seeks to appease. A moment ago I encouraged readers to demonstrate commitment by learning the art of negotiation. Unfortunately, some Tugboats will take that advice to an extreme and end up compromising about everything instead of negotiating. Every time a conflict comes up, they will diminish their own needs and give way to the other party. They may justify that behavior as "keeping the peace," but it's an extremely unhealthy way to "resolve" disagreements.

If you're a Tugboat, the first thing you need to do when you find yourself in a conflict is to pay attention to what *your* needs are in the situation. That goes completely against your attitude, I know. But that's exactly what you're going to have to do—go against your attitude—because your attitude is working against you when it comes to conflict.

Your instinct as a Tugboat is to immediately worry about the other person's needs and concerns. Well, that person's needs and concerns are legitimate. But so are yours. So when your needs and concerns collide with someone else's, don't just assume that the other person's needs and concerns are all that matter. Yours matter just as much and deserve to be noticed—most especially by you. So pay attention to yourself! It's the first step in creating *boundaries*.

And once you're clear on what your own needs and concerns are, make sure that you express those needs to the other person. Don't hide them with the thought, "My needs are so insignificant compared to theirs that it's not even worth bringing them up." And don't assume that the other person already knows what they are. Chances are they do not, as we saw in the story earlier about Tom and Lucinda.

As you and your spouse work on this step of conflict management, sooner or later you will come to a point where you recognize what every seasoned marriage counselor, arbitrator, diplomat, and negotiator knows: both parties to a conflict have to have a desire to work out the conflict in order for the conflict to be resolved. In other words, it takes two to tango. You and your spouse may see your conflicts very differently; that's to be expected. But the real question is: do you want to work things out? If you do, you can. It'll take a lot of talking, a lot of listening, a lot of honesty, a lot of humility, and a whole lot of give and take. But you can do it if you decide to do it.

Is there ever a time when you should seek a professional's help? Yes. If your conflicts escalate to violence and physical or emotional abuse, you should definitely turn to a professional. The same holds true for threats ("Maybe I should just leave"; "If something doesn't change around here, I'm going to file for divorce"; "I'm so mad I could kill myself"). Also, if the same conflicts keep coming up again and again, without resolution, it's probably a good idea to consult a trained counselor, who can provide objectivity and insight.

How do the three boats tend to work this step?

- Barges tend to have a blunt style, and that not only can create conflict, but also may make it difficult to deal with them when there's a conflict to resolve.
- Tugboats do not do well at conflict management. They avoid conflict if at all possible. And when they can't avoid it they will dodge honest, open communication. As a result, they oftentimes don't get resolution and closure to the issues involved.
- Sailboats who lead with a combination of IR, RI, IT, or TI, tend to seek control, which can create conflicts. Sailboats who lead with MT or TM more naturally seek conflict resolution.

5. *Fun and relaxation.* This is the one area of the Relationship Fitness Plan that everyone loves. Except that in our society, many of us have become too busy to have fun with one another. So maybe that should be our primary goal for this step: to free up some time each day and each week to spend with people we like and care about, and certainly with our loved ones. Otherwise we're liable to just drift apart.

But of course, when I say "free up some time," I realize that I am tinkering with some people's Fort Knox. Especially the Barges and the Sailboats who lead with T and R. To them, time is money, so taking time away from money-making activities to devote to fun seems frivolous and irresponsible.

May I suggest something to anyone who feels that way? Go ahead and be a little bit "frivolous and irresponsible" sometimes! I know you're facing severe pressure to devote even more time to your work from the other lawyers in the firm, from the other executives in the office, from the other salespeople with triple-platinum travel miles, from the senior managers in your company. As one person put it, "I'm running so fast that I don't have time to think, let alone worry about my family. I live with this haunting fear that if I stop to rest for even a second, the stampede behind me will run me down and never even look back."

At some point, you have to decide what matters. Bill knows a couple that has two kids. Both parents have professions, to which they each devote about eighty hours a week. They spend most of their evenings at social events. The kids do not see their parents except for a few hours on Sundays and on holidays. A nanny takes the kids to and from school and oversees their activities in the evening. In the summer, the kids go to camps and spend time with tutors.

Now every family has to decide what works for them. But it seems to me that a family like that begs the definition of what it means to be a family. I mean, why have kids if you're never going to see them? Why have kids if you're going to hire someone else to raise them? What's the point?

You know, my father died recently. He was 76. His passing caused me to reflect a lot on what matters in life. I realized that when all is said and done, relationships matter more than just about anything else you can think of: things, titles, status, power, money, fame, where you live. I've never been to a funeral where people stood at the casket and said, "You know, I sure wish Dad had had a bigger boat," or "I sure wish Dad had spent more time at the office." On the other hand, I've met a whole lot of people—men in particular—who have said, "I wish I had known my Dad better. I

wish he hadn't been so busy when I was a kid. And I wish I hadn't been so busy myself when he got older."

If you ask people why they work so hard, they'll often say, "So that I can give my kids a better life than I had growing up." Well, what is that life? Are people who say that saying they would have turned out to be a better person if they had lived in a big house with all kinds of computers and iPods and Game Boys and Xboxes in it, and a sporty SUV in the driveway? I think not.

At heart, don't most of us want something deeper—namely, affection, respect, and admiration from our spouse and children, and from our friends and co-workers? We can't buy those. We can only earn them through *time* spent with those people, doing stuff that builds a relationship.

How do the three boats tend to work this step?

- Barges by nature struggle the most with this step. Their careers get in the way of fun and relaxation. They tend to be driven overachievers.
- Tugboats by nature excel at this step because they love to have a good time with other people.
- Sailboats often struggle with relaxation. They think it's a great idea, but they tend to have too much going on to stop and have some fun.

6. *Career management.* I haven't spent a whole lot of time in this book on how attitude affects work. But the connection is enormous. Your attitude fits you to certain kinds of work more than others. If you pursue work that really fits you, you'll be a much more satisfied person, and a whole lot easier to live with. Conversely, if you work at something that doesn't fit your attitude, you're just asking for trouble. Your heart won't be in your work, and at best you'll be bored and stressed, at worst, incompetent and

miserable. And guess who has to deal with you when you come home from a job like that?

My co-author Bill Hendricks has devoted considerable study and research to this issue of job fit. He points out that given the ways that people end up in jobs in this country, it's amazing that anyone finds satisfying work. But the saddest thing is that so many people who really know they are in jobs that don't fit them are willing to stay in them, rather than seek out a better fit. Oftentimes they feel financial pressure to stay put, or they fear losing certain job-related benefits, such as health insurance. Whatever the reason, they feel "stuck." And people who feel "stuck" in a job or career are pretty miserable people, and usually difficult to live with. As Bill puts it, next to a bad marriage, there's nothing worse than a bad job fit. (This is one reason why so many people look for ways to start a sideline business of their own as a way of generating backup or replacement income.)

That's a pretty strong statement, but I think Bill is right. For a whole lot of marriages, the fastest and most effective way of improving the relational climate at home would be for one or both of the spouses to transition into work that fits them. That's a dramatic, and sometimes traumatic, step to take. But in many cases, it could well save the marriage.

So how do you find work or a business that fits you? Well, whether you already know you're in a terrible job fit, or whether you're in an "okay" fit—not great, not awful, "it's a job"—the place to start is with your 3-Minute Survey scoring pattern. That pattern holds a lot of clues for what fits you. For instance:

- If you lead with a T, you are most naturally suited for jobs that deal with a lot of factual information, as well as schedules, deadlines, planning, organization, and policy. T's tend to be very responsible when it comes to money, so jobs pertaining to money management also hold promise.

- If you lead with an R, you are most naturally suited for jobs that require you to think. They may be jobs that focus on ideas or issues, or on decisions that have to be made based on a lot of information. R's tend to be analytical, so fields like research, strategic planning, and financial analysis might be possibilities.
- If you lead with an I, you are most naturally suited for jobs that put you in front of people, where you can influence them and gain a response. I's tend to be creative, energetic, innovative, and "in the moment," so jobs in sales, business development, teaching, and the performing arts might make a good fit.
- If you lead with an M, you are most naturally suited for jobs in which you can serve people and meet their needs. Customer service, counseling, nursing, and hospitality would be examples of that kind of work. M's tend to have a tremendous awareness of the emotional and relational dynamics of a situation, so jobs in social work, pastoral ministry, senior centers, and youth work might be worth exploring.

These are just suggestions to get your mind going. The first letter in your scoring pattern is the starting point, but you also need to pay attention to the second and third letters, because they modify and direct how and where that first letter is best used. For instance, M's with an I in the second position definitely needs to be with and in front of people in their work most of the time, perhaps as a teacher or an entertainer. But M's with a T in the second position brings an interest in planning and structure, so they may be more inclined toward something like program coordination or event planning (e.g., a wedding planner).

The objective is to identify jobs or businesses that make the best use of how you naturally behave. The more of your attitude is called for by the job or business enterprise, the better the fit.

You'll notice that I don't just assign occupational titles to the various attitudes and scoring patterns. That's because attitudes are not "occupation-specific." There's not a one-to-one correspondence between attitudes and jobs in the workplace. That's because every job is unique, just as every person is unique. You can have two jobs that have the same occupational title—say, "accountant"—but are done in very different ways. They call for very different kinds of people to do those jobs well.

For that reason, you'll find people with all kinds of different scoring patterns in virtually every occupation or business you can name. That's right! Believe it or not there are Tugboats out there who are accountants and loving it. And there are Barges who are waitresses and loving it. It all depends on the specifics of what is called for in a given job or business venture.

Are you in a good job fit for your scoring pattern? If not, see what you can do to find ways to improve that fit without changing jobs. Perhaps you can negotiate with your supervisor to improve the fit, or perhaps you can seek out particular assignments or projects that make better use of what you have to offer. Another option is to move to another position within your employer's enterprise, one that fits you better than your current assignment. Yet another possibility is to start a "cottage" business without making a career change.

A fourth option, of course, is to change jobs or careers. But you should see that as a last resort. Changing jobs always puts a degree of stress and trauma on a family. Sometimes that short-term pressure is worth it, especially if it means getting out from under a bad job fit. But be very careful how you make that transition. You want to improve your career in order to improve things at home—not make a difficult situation even worse by making a big mistake.[2]

How do the three boats tend to work this step?

- Barges tend to be great at making money, filling leadership roles, and getting the job done. However, they don't set boundaries on their time in order to have much of a family life.
- Tugboats tend not to be ambitious or driven, and for that reason they often end up "underemployed." That is, they have more talent and capacity than their job uses.
- Sailboats whose lead letters are IR or RI tend to be workaholics. Sailboats who lead with an M tend to be torn between obligations to their family and the demands of their work.

7. *Finances.* I devoted the entire previous chapter to my 10-Point Plan for Financial Fitness, so I won't go into detail on that issue here. If you haven't read chapter 7, I encourage you to do so now.

The thing I would stress is that money is the number one source of conflict in marriage and family relationships today. I think that says everything about the importance of money to relationships. If the finances are out of control, I can guarantee you've got troubles in your relationships at home and at work. So going to work on your financial health will do wonders for your marriage. Obviously, working on issues like communication, trust, and commitment (steps 1–3) will help a lot as you work through the issues related to your finances. But making progress in your financial life will in turn do wonders to enhance these other aspects of your relationship.

How do the three boats tend to work this step?

- Barges tend to excel at making money and managing money. They avoid debt. However, they can also be stingy with their family and others.
- Tugboats do not enjoy financial matters and tend to find them very confusing. They shy away from budgets and fi-

nancial information. However, they like to spend money, usually on other people and on special causes.

- Sailboats tend to do pretty well in financial matters, unless their lead letters are I or M. I's are notorious spenders, and M's are notorious givers.

8. *Extended family.* Only in America would we need to put a special step in the Plan for Relationship Fitness that includes our "extended" family—that is, our parents, grandparents, aunts, uncles, cousins, nieces, nephews, in-laws, and so forth. Throughout history, and in most cultures around the world today, "family" includes everyone you're related to. "Family" is about the tribe, the clan, not just the "immediate" family.

In America, though, we've gone the other way and reduced the notion of "family" to the so-called "nuclear" family—Mom, Dad, and the kids. This step in the plan is intended to make sure we don't forget all those other people we're related to.

It's especially easy to forget them nowadays because families have gotten so fractured and splintered and divvied up by divorce and remarriage and blended families and so on. In fact, for a lot of young people, family is totally mixed up. There are just too many "relatives" to keep track of—stepparents and stepgrandparents, halfbrothers and half-sisters, second wives, third husbands, and so forth. Many of these players have come into the picture late in the game. So it's no surprise that many young people have decided that they'll just look out for themselves. They can't keep track anymore of who is who, so they limit their concern to their own self-interest and one or two other relatives with whom they feel especially close.

I can't change all that, but I can emphasize at least one set of relatives that every reader needs to pay attention to, and that's your parents. Whatever your relationship happens to be with them today, there's no denying the fact that they gave you life, and in most cases they've had a major influence on how you deal with life. So wisdom says it's a good thing to pay attention to your relationship with your mom and dad.

This reality is becoming especially pronounced as baby boomers are beginning to take care of their parents in their old age. I mentioned that my dad passed away recently. His final years brought home to me two areas that especially need attention as we think about our parents: financial planning and communication.

In the Financial Fitness Plan, step 9 asks you to work on your Retirement Planning. I suggest you do some of that for your folks as well, because their sunset years may well affect your own financial picture, both while they're alive and after they're gone. You know, fifty or sixty years ago when our parents were starting out, financial planning was much less sophisticated than it has become today. Also the times were different then. As a result, many parents had little or no help in thinking through their long-term financial affairs. So if you were to come alongside them now and help them think through the issues they need to face (the previous chapter spells out what those issues are), it would be an act of prudence as well as kindness. Even if you don't have financial savvy yourself, you could guide them toward someone who does, and that would be an invaluable service.

The second issue with our parents is communication. Some readers have already ruled out helping their parents get financial advice because the relationship is so strained and distant. Communication has broken down, perhaps over stuff that happened thirty, forty, or fifty years ago. I wonder: is it worth letting the relationship just drift away?

I know in my own life, my father and I had issues that had been sitting there unresolved for twenty or twenty-five years. I was fortunate in that I could see his health declining and realized that he wouldn't be around much longer. So I took the initiative and talked with him, and we were able to clear the air on a lot of our disagreements. It didn't change the past, but it restored the relationship. I'll be forever thankful that we did that. Because when a parent dies, some experts believe it's the most impactful event of one's life. Whatever is unresolved at that point will remain unresolved for the rest of the child's life.

What unresolved issues do you have with your parents, siblings, children, or extended family? What things do you need to take care of before it's too late? You won't be surprised if I tell you that one of the main things standing in your way is your attitude. Now that you know your scoring pattern, look inside and see whether your attitude isn't causing you to see things in ways that deny your family members a resolution. If so, do the mature thing and rise above your natural inclination. Go and be reconciled to them, to the extent you can be. You may be surprised that age has changed their perspective, as well.

How do the three boats tend to work this step?

- Barges tend to struggle with relationships, so they are not naturally inclined to pay much attention to extended family. On the other hand, they tend to feel financial responsibility for their family, although they can be very tightfisted with them.
- Tugboats are the most natural of the boats to reach out to extended family. However, they have trouble setting boundaries with family members, which can lead to overcommitment, conflicts, and disappointments.
- Sailboats can be quite good at helping extended family members feel accepted and cared for. However, Sailboats who lead with an R or a T tend to draw more boundaries around their money and time. Sailboats who lead with an I or M tend to try too hard to please everyone.

9. *Romance and sexuality.* You know, there's a certain irony as I come to this portion of the book. I mean, who would have ever

guessed that Wayne Nance would be writing advice to people about their sex life? I can name a whole bunch of folks who would never have believed it in a million billion years!

Of course, I'm not pretending to be an expert in romance and sexuality. But I do list this area among the steps of the 10-Point Plan for Relationship Fitness because you can't ignore romance and sexuality. They are certainly crucial to building a healthy marriage. Having said that, I freely admit that there are many ways in which couples express their affection, and there are many complexities to this subject that go far beyond the purposes of this book.

So what do I have to add to the conversation? Just two things. The first is that romance is one of the areas where Tugboats have a decided advantage and Barges are at a definite disadvantage. By now you can probably see why. Tugboats, especially those who lead with an M, are by nature sensitive and responsive. They pay a lot of attention to the emotional atmosphere in a situation, and they are attuned to other people's needs. All of that adds up to an inborn instinct for being romantic. Because romance is a matter of the heart.

Barges, of course, are wired just the opposite. They excel in matters of the head. This means they often struggle with feelings, nonverbal communication, affection, and all those other "soft" elements that make for romance. So I have a word of advice for Barges at this point: if you are married to a Tugboat or a Sailboat who leads with an I or M, allow your spouse to teach you the art of intimacy. It will probably feel a bit scary at first. It may never feel totally comfortable. But you will be serving your mate by doing that—and the value of that is priceless.

The second point I want to make is that your children will learn far more about sex from the way you treat your spouse than from any class, book, or course they take on human sexuality. That's a promise. Those formal resources may be helpful in explaining the "technology" of sexual organs and sexual reproduction. But anyone who has been married for any length of time knows that sex is about a lot more than the "hardware." It's the "software" that counts. What is the meaning of sex? How does it fit into a marriage and a family? What is its value? How does it add—or detract from—the relationship of the partners? What does it communicate about the value the persons involved. What is intimacy really all about?

These and a thousand other "soft" messages will be communicated by the subtleties of how you treat your spouse: what you say, how you say it, what you don't say, the way your actions back up or contradict your verbal statements, and many more. Children watch their parents *all* the time. *All* the time! Sometimes consciously, sometimes unconsciously, but all the time nonetheless. They are picking up clues about men and women and how they relate, about their own sexuality, and about the opposite sex—all by observing the interaction between you and your mate. So what are you communicating to your kids? Maybe the place to begin answering that question is to ask your spouse: what am I communicating about my romantic feelings toward you?

How do the three boats tend to work this step?

- Barges don't create enough margin in their schedule to accommodate the softer, more compassionate side of a relationship with their spouse.
- Tugboats tend to long for connection and physical intimacy. They certainly have a natural bent toward fostering that intimacy. But they may be frustrated if they married a Barge who does not understand their needs, or if their low self-esteem keeps them from opening up in romantic ways.
- Sailboats who lead with a T or an R will tend to be more reserved, and feel that there is a time and a place for intimacy—after all one's work is done and all one's goals are met. Sailboats who lead with an I or an M will be much more spontaneous and free-spirited when it comes to romance and sex.

10. *Spirituality*. The final step in the 10-Point Plan is the step I'm calling spirituality. Most readers will connect this step to God, or religion, or the meaning of life—those larger, transcendent realities that go beyond the day-to-day and connect us with eternity. This is the crowning step in the plan, and in many ways the most important.

For that reason, a lot of readers probably think that I should have put this step first. A lot of preachers, for instance, will say that the ideal way to structure one's life is to put God first, family second, church third, and then work and community life. I think there's probably some merit in that. Nevertheless, I put spirituality as the final step in my 10-Point Plan because it's the most important, but also the most difficult, especially for men.

I don't know why that is, exactly. I just know that a lot of men, for instance, have a hard time praying. A lot of men don't like going to church. A lot of men fumble around when it comes to talking about "spiritual" things like God, the meaning of life, the beauty of nature, or life after death.

However, difficult or not, I believe that building a strong marriage requires that some attention be given to building the relationship on a solid spiritual foundation. I and my co-authors come at this issue from a Christian perspective. But you don't have to be a Christian to share our point of view. Almost all faith traditions place a strong emphasis on marriage and family life. The family is an expression of the beliefs and ideals of each tradition. Certainly in Judaism, Christianity, and Islam, there's a strong conviction that God needs to be at the center of marriage and family life.

So how can that happen? Well, you'll need to consult the teachings of your particular faith for specific practices and guidelines. If you don't have any particular faith tradition, let me suggest that you and your spouse just begin praying together. Among your prayers, ask that you would come to know which path is right for you.

As you and your spouse pursue a spiritual relationship with each other and with God, you'll discover that your scoring patterns explain a lot about how you both approach the issue of spirituality. For instance, I's and M's will tend to prefer more expressive forms of spirituality, activities they can participate in and events they can experience. By contrast, T's and R's will likely prefer a more "cerebral" approach, one that offers reasonable, logical arguments for its beliefs and practices. As always, neither of these styles is better or worse, just different. Perhaps the wisest approach is to settle on practices of faith and spirituality that allow for both of the unique styles that make up your relationship.

How do the three boats tend to work this step?

- Barges tend to overanalyze spiritual issues. For that reason they often struggle in this area because spirituality also involves the heart and matters of faith. Barges don't like going on faith!
- Tugboats by nature tend to be rather spiritual. They certainly have a bent toward serving others. They tend to express their faith through practical acts of altruism and philanthropy, and in that way serve as an example to the other boats.
- Sailboats are capable of a deeply loving and spiritual foundation. Those who lead with an I or a T will tend to question matters of faith and want to know the facts and structure behind those convictions. Sailboats who lead with a T, R, or I tend to have the most problems with the spiritual discipline of forgiveness.

Well, that brings us to the end of the 10-Point Plan for Relationship Fitness. Obviously, each of these steps could be developed a great deal more. But if you've been diligent to work your way through all ten of the steps, I want to congratulate you! You have done something that very few people do, which is to get *intentional* about building strong relationships at home and at work.

And as we bring this section to a close, let me again point out that working on your relationships will have positive benefits to the other two lifestyle areas we have focused on, health and fitness, and financial fitness. In turn, working on either of those areas creates positive benefits for the other areas. All three lifestyle areas are connected, because all three are affected by our inborn attitudes. So as we make progress in one area, we give ourselves an advantage in the other two areas.

For instance, if we quit smoking (a health and fitness issue), we save money because we're not buying expensive cigarettes anymore (a boost to our financial fitness), and we make it easier for others to be around us, because we no longer offend them with secondhand smoke (a boost to our relationship fitness). If we get our cash flow in line so that we're able save up for a down payment on a house (a financial fitness issue), we'll eventually get that house, which will provide our family with a place to live and grow together (a boost to our relationship fitness), and hopefully provide a haven to go home to and find relief from our stress-filled job (a boost to our health and fitness).

This is the cycle of real life management. By taking positive steps in any area of our lifestyle, we benefit every other area of our lifestyle.

CHAPTER 9

91 Days to ALTERing Your Lifestyle

Here in Texas, where Bill and Keet and I live, folks often throw the word "fixin'" into a statement to tell you that something is getting ready to happen. "It's fixin' to storm," they'll say, meaning that the weather looks like rain. "I'm fixin' to go to the mall," meaning they are thinking about going shopping. "He's fixin' to bust him one," meaning a fight is about to break out.

Keep in mind that "fixin'" doesn't mean that the thing indicated is a certainty, just a possibility. For instance, "I'm fixin' to marry her" doesn't mean an engagement is forthcoming, just that the speaker plans to marry her at some point. "Fixin'" is a way of stating an intention without making any commitment. It leaves you an out.

A lot of readers have gotten this far in the book, and they are "fixin'" to make some changes in their lifestyle. Some are "fixin'" to lose weight. Others are "fixin'" to get out of debt. Others are "fixin'" to show more affection to their spouse or improve other specific relationships. If you asked them, they'd tell you straight out, "Yeah, I'm fixin' to do this or that" (at least, that's how they'd say it if they were Texans).

So will they do it? Maybe, and maybe not. See, that's the tricky thing about "fixin'." It gives you a way of delaying action. It means, "I'm preparing to do something. I'm getting ready to do something. I'm thinking about doing something. I'm intending to do something." But that doesn't mean you'll do it. You didn't promise you'd do it; you just said you were "fixin'" to do it.

And that's where a lot of folks get stuck when it comes to life-style issues. They are "fixin'" to work on their lifestyle. Meaning they are commencing to begin to start. They are getting ready to plan to think about. They are preparing to look forward to pray about. In short, their hearts are overflowing with good intentions. But where's the action? Where's the follow-through. Where's the execution?

It's time, my friends! It's time for *Execution*. That's what the fourth letter in the ALTER model stands for. It means to actually do something. Not to talk about it. Not to make plans for it. Not to be "fixin'" to do it. But to actually do it.

Remember the Nike slogan? "Just do it." It's a great line. Stop talking about what you're going to do and just do it. Stop thinking up reasons why you can't do it and just do it. Stop worrying about what might go wrong and just do it. In the ALTER model, *Execution* is the time to just do it. Because doing it is the magic formula that turns good intentions into great results. Execution produces real outcomes that literally ALTER your lifestyle.

I know that's what you want—real, live results. You wouldn't have stayed with me this far if you didn't. You believed me back in the Introduction when I told you that I could help you turn your life around. Well, this is the chapter where you actually start making the turn. Not a radical, 180-degree U-turn. That's unrealistic, and frankly unhealthy. But how about a more modest 5- or 10-degree course correction? That's doable. And that's what you need most of all—to actually do something that's actually doable. You need success.

Here's what you're going to do to achieve that success:

1   Set a realistic goal.
2   Do an activity for accomplishing that goal for 91 days.
3   Record your activity and key emotions in a daily journal.

Let's take those in turn.

Setting a Realistic Goal

I have given you three 10-step plans, one for health, one for finances, and one for relationships. Each of those plans provides a complete and comprehensive path for working on that lifestyle area. But the only way you'll be able to work those plans is to create some specific, doable goals for the various steps of each plan.

Let me give you an example. Step 4 in the health and wellness plan is Nutrition. The point of that step is that you can't have good health without paying attention to what you eat. Okay, but what does it mean to "pay attention to what you eat"? That's a great intention, but it's too broad. The only way to make that intention a reality is to translate it into a measurable goal, something you can actually do.

Let's say that you have a sweet tooth, and for as long as you can remember it's been your habit to end lunch everyday with something chockful of sugar: a double-fudge brownie, a big piece of chocolate cake, a generous slice of lemon meringue pie, or a fistful of Oreo cookies. You know those treats are adding needless calories to your diet. But they taste so darn good that you just can't help yourself.

But now you've decided to work step 4 of the health and wellness plan and start "paying attention to what you eat." One way to do that is to cut back on those sugary desserts. So how could you formulate a goal to accomplish that? Some people might say, "Just quit eating dessert." But I wonder if those folks have ever tried to make a 180-degree turnaround in some deeply ingrained habit in their own life. If they have, they probably would realize that "just saying no" isn't a realistic answer.

A more doable goal might be to see if you can eat a dessert at lunch just four days a week instead of seven. That would cut your intake of sugary desserts by 43 percent—a very respectable improvement. Another goal might be to go ahead and eat dessert every day, but cut down on the portions—say, half the portions you are used to eating. That would cut your intake in half—again, a very positive move. Yet another goal might be to start substituting desserts that are sweet but have more nutritional value than your customary favorites. So maybe one day you have an apple instead of pie, another day you have grapes instead of brownies, a third day you have a six-ounce serving of lemon meringue yogurt instead of lemon meringue pie. That way you still get your "sweetness fix," but the sugars come in a more natural state, accompanied by other nutrients that will serve you well. In short, good nutrition instead of bad nutrition.

Let's take another example, this time from the financial checklist. Let's say that you complete step 1, the Cash Flow Analysis, to see where your money is going. And one thing you notice is that you spend a lot of money on "good buys," meaning you get a discount for buying in volume. Megastores have made a lot of money off of "good buys." I love them, by the way, and I spend a lot of time there, especially on Saturdays when they hand out the free food. But megastores know that a lot of people (especially Tugboats and heart-led Sailboats) will buy stuff if it's priced well, there's a lot of it, and it won't be available for long. That's what people call a "good buy."

So, for example, maybe you see a pair of flip-flops that you like, and they have them in your size. And by golly you can buy six pairs for $19.95. That's a deal! Especially since you'd normally have to pay $9.99 a pair (or so the sign says). Wow, that's like getting four pairs for free! But you'd better act now, because the sign says, "Today only!" So you buy them. You take them home and tell your spouse, "Look what a good buy I got on these flip-flops."

Question: did you *need* flip-flops? Were you planning to buy flip-flops when you went to the store? Were you planning to spend $19.95 plus tax buying flip-flops? Can you really use six pairs of flip-flops? What are you planning to do with the other five pairs? By the way, I already know the answer to that: you're going to store them in the closet or the attic or the garage or wherever you've got all the other "good buys" you purchased on stuff you may use someday, but don't actually need today. You know, the six-dozen cases of Pepsi, the five 250-count stacks of paper plates, the variety pack of 10,000 buttons, the wooden skid of 36-dozen rolls of toilet paper. Those were really "good buys," weren't they?

Now let's say your common sense wakes up as a result of doing your Cash Flow Analysis. And you realize that buying stuff just because it's a "good buy" is not good for your cash flow. It ties up your money in stuff that is just going to sit around forever, and may never be used. So you're ready to say goodbye to "good buys."

What's a goal to accomplish that? One idea is that for the next 91 days you're going to sit down before you go shopping and make a list of the things you actually need. And your rule is going to be, "If it's not on the list, I must resist." And maybe you even go one step further and go over your list with your spouse, to make sure you're only planning to buy stuff that your family actually needs. In addition, when you get home, you go over what you actually bought with your spouse, just to make sure that something didn't wind up in the car that wasn't supposed to.

"But what happens if I see a true deal?" Well let me forewarn you: you will *always* see what to you looks like a "deal." Every retailer in America knows what the megastores know. They all put things in front of the customer that appear to be a deal. But don't go to the store and let the store tell you what to buy. Go to the store planning to buy what *you* need to buy. If what you need is on "sale," great. Otherwise, "If it's not on the list, I must resist."

Still, I know how life works, and I know there will be times when the store really surprises you with an incredibly good deal. Two suggestions when that happens: (1) rather than just add the purchase to your list, consider dropping something off the list that you didn't need as much in order to accommodate the special; and (2) consider calling your spouse and asking his/her opinion on whether or not to buy the special. The point is to stay in control of your purchases and resist the HADs of the retailer.

Can you see what it means to translate the broad objectives of the lifestyle plans into goals you can act on? My advice is to pick out one or two steps of a given checklist at a time and develop a couple of goals for those steps and act on them. Don't try to develop thirty goals for all 10 steps of three different plans. That's too much. You'll never follow through with such a scheme. I'd rather you succeeded at one or two modest goals, so that you see some positive benefits in your life. That will motivate you to create new goals later on, and lead to something you can follow the rest of your life.

91 Days of Doing

Throughout this book I've railed against quick-fix solutions. Quick fixes don't help you create healthy habits in your lifestyle. If anything, they may create unhealthy habits. By a *habit* I mean a routine way of behaving that has become so natural you don't even think about it. It's just the way you do life.

Obviously there are good habits and bad habits. A "bad" habit is a behavior that will cause trouble for you. For instance, perhaps you have a habit of showing up late for everything you do. You always apologize, and everyone laughs about your tendency to be tardy. But it's no laughing matter. Sooner or later that habit will cost you. It may cost you a job, a promotion, a client, a big sale, a relationship, or maybe just respect. Trust me, chronic tardiness is a bad habit that will eventually cause you trouble.

Conversely, a "good" habit is a behavior that brings you benefit. A long time ago I discovered the habit of learning people's names, and then using their name often in conversation. By repeating their name, I communicate a number of positive messages, such as: (1) I respect you enough to remember your name; (2) I am acknowledging your presence and telling you that you "belong"; (3) I'm interested in you as a person; (4) I keep you interested in me and what I'm saying; (5) I am personalizing my conversation to you; and (6) I am unlikely to forget you in the future because I have used your name so much. So what do you suppose are the benefits to me of communicating in that way? Probably more than I can imagine, because if you feel that I genuinely care about you, you are far more likely to give me what I need or want. For me, using someone's name has become a good habit that has brought me tremendous benefits.

So how long does it take to form a habit? Well, in the main it seems to take less time to establish a bad habit than a good one. For example, did you know that for many people it only takes seven days to get addicted to sugar? I mean, think of what happens after Valentine's Day every year. A lot of husbands will bring home one of those big boxes of candy for their sweetheart. They know their wives just love chocolate, so it's a big hit. Well, that first night she samples a couple of pieces of candy, probably her favorites. They taste great! So then the next afternoon she picks out a couple more. So it goes the third day. And then the fourth, and the fifth, and the sixth. By day seven she's pretty much hooked on those candies.

From then on, every afternoon at five o'clock a little voice inside her head says, "Where's the candy?" So it's no surprise that the first time she goes to the grocery store after Valentine's Day, she buys a couple of bags of Hershey's Kisses or whatever. Of course, if you asked her about it she'd say, "Oh, I'm just buying this because it's on sale after the holiday." But her body ain't fooled. It is now programmed to operate on a well-entrenched habit for sugar in the afternoon.

Now the good news about that story is that if it's possible to form bad habits, it's equally possible to form good habits. It just takes a little longer. Bad habits are easy to form because they usually follow the path of least resistance. Good habits take more effort and more intentionality. But they can be formed if a person will work at them long enough to start realizing the benefits. Remember what I said earlier about people who join health clubs in January? They usually quit within three or four weeks, which is a shame because that's just about the time when the real benefits of working out begin to appear. By quitting, those people never get to see those benefits. As a result, working out never becomes a habit.

When it comes to forming good lifestyle habits, I've settled on the magic number of 91. That figure comes from about fifteen years of helping people ALTER their lifestyles. If I can get you to follow a positive, healthy behavior for 91 days, you will turn that behavior into a permanent habit. Which means that after 91 days, you won't have to think about it much anymore; the behavior will just become part of your lifestyle. Like taking a shower or brushing your teeth. It will be a habit.

Now some readers are thinking, "Wayne, there's no way I can do something for 91 days. I've never had that kind of discipline in my entire life. I'll never make it!"

Oh, yes you will! If you stick with me and do as I tell you, you'll make it. I know full well that you've struggled in your life to follow through on your good intentions. But I'm also willing to bet that you didn't have a coach. You didn't have a plan. You didn't have doable goals. You didn't keep a journal. And you for sure didn't know your inborn attitude and how it affects your decisions. So I'm not surprised if you've fallen short in redirecting your lifestyle. But things are different now. You've got some key pieces in place that you simply didn't have before.

"But Wayne, you don't understand. Ninety-one days is too long. I've got ADD!" I hear that one a lot. I tell someone they need to do something for 91 days, and they tell me it can't happen because they've got ADD (attention deficit disorder). Well, ADD is a legitimate condition, and if you've been diagnosed with that I don't want to disparage it. But it's amazing to me how many people pull out the excuse of ADD when they're asked to do something they don't want to do. Ask them to read a book or listen to a tape, and they'll say they can't because they've got ADD. Ask them to volunteer for something, and they can't because they've got ADD. Ask them to carry on a conversation with their teenager, and they can't because they have ADD. But it's funny—they never have ADD when they go to the movies. They never have ADD when they're cheering for their favorite basketball team. They never have ADD when they're making love to their wife. Isn't it strange how that ADD seems to come and go, depending on how much they want to do something?

Execution doesn't bother with why you "can't" do something. Execution says, "Just do it!" You might like it, you might not. It might be hard, it might not. You might do it perfectly, you might not. Execution doesn't care about any of that. Execution just does it. For 91 days.

So, if your goal is to eat desserts four days instead of seven, then you do the best you can to eat desserts four days instead of seven for 91 days. Maybe you do okay for the first seven days. Then in the next seven you slip up and eat desserts on five days. Not a problem! The next seven days you just go back to working your plan: four days of dessert, three without. And so on for 91 days. As best you can.

Half the battle is to keep going. Especially after you've had a bad week. Maybe in week three you have a lot of stress coming down on you, and you just give in to the sugar craving. You eat dessert all seven days of that week. And by the end of that week you feel so guilty. So what do you do? Why, you start out the next seven days with the same goal: four days of desserts, three without. You don't shame yourself over what didn't happen the week before. And you don't give up. You take every day, and frankly every week, as a new day to work your plan. As best you can. For 91 days.

Barges and Tugboats struggle the most in keeping the 91-day tracking log for different reasons. Barges struggle because they do not want to write down their dominant emotions because they are not emotional by nature, so they resist. The Tugboats struggle because they are not good at details and record keeping and tracking what they've spent or what they've eaten, so they will not be good at tracking this. However, the Tugboats will write down their dominant emotions, as they tend to be more touchy-feely. Sailboats are open to the process; however, depending on their first two lead letters, they too could tend to struggle like a Barge or Tugboat.

Now you may need to play some little games with yourself, to help you get through those 91 days. In fact, let me tell you about some of the games I used to play when I was working to establish good habits for eating. These may sound a little crazy at first, but bear with me. The key thing was that I had to decide if I was really serious about losing the weight I needed to lose. I was, and so I got to the point where I would sit down at a meal and pick up my fork and say, "You're my enemy! You are not going to whip me today."

You see, what is a fork's job? To shovel in food, of course. For that reason I decided that my fork was not my best friend. If anything, it had become my worst enemy. So before every meal I would grab that fork and look at it and say, "It's me against you, buddy. And you're not going to get me." See, every time I used that fork I was trying to make myself conscious that it was not my best friend. It was not my momma, and it didn't love me. I was playing a head game with myself. And it worked.

I'd do something similar with french fries. I'd look at those fries and say, "Guys, you know what? You are not my friends! You don't give a you-know-what about what happens to me." And that would help me pass on the fries. Not always. Sometimes I'd give in and chow down on them. But I got to the point where I really did swear off fries most of the time because I came right out and fingered them as my sworn enemies. It was a game, pure and simple. But it worked.

People who've never struggled with 100 or 200 extra pounds can't imagine playing those games with themselves. It sounds silly. Likewise, people who've never had $10,000 or $20,000 or $50,000 or $150,000 in credit card debt can't imagine holding a ceremony in which they cut up their credit cards into tiny little pieces and toss them into a recycling bin. People who've never been desperate to regain their wife's trust can't imagine phoning in every hour on the hour to report where they are and what they are doing. But when you're serious about ALTERing your lifestyle, you'll do whatever it takes to put yourself in a frame of mind to actually carry out your goal for 91 days. The benefits mean that much to you.

Alcoholics Anonymous coined the phrase "one day at a time" for people who are trying to beat the addiction of alcoholism. There's a lot of wisdom in that. Don't worry about what's going to happen 91 days from now, or 31 days from now, or even tomorrow. Worry about what's right in front of you today. Do the best you can to follow through on your goal today. If you do that, you'll never need to worry about tomorrow. There is no tomorrow. There's only today. And one day, that today will be day 91. By that point, your behavior will be ingrained enough to be a habit. And you'll have won!

A Daily Journal

"Wayne, I sure wish I could hire you to be my personal coach. You just have a way of being so encouraging. I feel certain I could turn my life around if I could have you alongside me every day, to keep me going on my path of self-improvement."

Well, I'd love to do that, too. So would Bill and Keet. In fact, I'll tell you what. If you'll come up with $500,000 plus expenses, one of us will move to your town for six months and devote ourselves full-time to helping you work your ALTER plan. Would you like that? What's that you say? Oh, that arrangement is a bit steep for your pocketbook? Well, in that case, let me suggest a Plan B: for just $1,000 a call (prepaid), you can talk with one of us every day for an hour, and we'll coach you through your ALTER plan. How about that?

Still too much? Well then let me offer a real bargain-basement solution: keep a daily journal. That won't cost you a dime. But I promise you it's almost as good as having a personal coach. In fact, even if Bill or Keet or I were working with you in person, we'd still have you keep a daily journal. Because in the fifteen years I've been working with people on the ALTER model, the one factor that separates the successful from the unsuccessful is that the successful keep a daily journal. Not just a daily narrative but a specific customized and proven journal or tracking log. It's that simple.

Why is keeping a journal so powerful? I think there are three primary reasons:

1   *A journal provides built-in accountability.* In my plan, I ask you to fill out your journal at the end of the day, before you retire. That bedtime ritual enforces a moment of truth. It causes you to ask yourself, "What did I do to work on my lifestyle issue today?" Just by taking a couple of minutes to answer that question, you're holding yourself accountable. You're keeping your good intentions from slipping your memory.

You see, one reason people never make progress in their lifestyle habits is because it's human nature to forget. We are, as I've been trying to emphasize, creatures of habit. We'll just keep on living and behaving

the way we always have *unless* something interrupts
our habits and agitates our memory and brings us
back to an awareness of some new habit we are trying
to form. Two minutes a day keeping a journal will accomplish that.

2   *A journal provides a way to mark your progress.* Just
as an airliner carries a "black box" that records data
from every moment of a flight, so your daily journal
will provide a contemporaneous record of everything
you actually do as you pursue your goals for 91 days.
That's valuable because, as I just said, it's human nature to forget. I promise you, 31 days into the journey
you will not remember what you ate on day 7. You
will not remember how long you exercised on day 16.
You will not remember how you felt on day 23.

And if you can't remember those things, you have
no way of paying attention to how you are coming
along with your 91-day plan. You have no way to
know whether you are gaining ground, losing ground,
or just standing still. In other words, you'll be lost.
And what do you suppose are your odds for success-
fully completing a 91-day journey if you're lost?

3   *A journal provides a means of evaluation.* In the next
section, we're going to consider the "R" of the ALTER
model, *Re-evaluation.* The daily journal forms the basis of the re-evaluation process. It provides an overall
picture of where you've come from, so that you can
analyze what happened. In some cases you'll be
amazed at your progress, and the log will give you
tangible evidence of how far you've come. In other
cases you'll wonder why things didn't go so well, and
the log will provide clues about the source of the
problem.

REAL LIFE ◉ MANAGEMENT™ | 91 DAY PERSONAL LOG

Date: _____
Personal 91 Day Game Plan For: _____
My 91 Day Goal Is: _____

The Issue I am Working On For 91 Days

Circle One ▶ Health • Money • Relationships

91 Days	Month:				Water	Fruits / Veg	Vitamins	Yes / No	
Day Counter	Day Mon – Sun	Date	Log ▶ What I ate or bought or did to build the relationship	Log ▶ What I did for exercise today	How Much?	Yes / No	Yes / No	Yes / No	My emotions at the end of the day
									Example: Tired, Depressed, Happy, Encouraged
		1							
		2							
		3							
		4							
		5							
		6							
		7							
		8							
		9							
		10							
		11							
		12							
		13							
		14							
		15							
		16							
		17							
		18							
		19							
		20							
		21							
		22							
		23							
		24							
		25							
		26							
		27							
		28							
		29							
		30							
		31							

COPY THIS LOG AT 120% TO FILL AN 8.5" X 11" SHEET OF PAPER

© 2007 Real Life Management, Inc.

So exactly how do you go about keeping a daily journal? I've printed a sample journal on the opposite page, or you can download the form from our Web site: www.RealLifeManagement.com. Notice it has several date-related columns, and then there are three critical columns. The first shows the issue I am working on and what I did with respect to that issue today. For example if my issue is weight, what did I eat today? Or if my issue is my marriage, what did I do with my wife today? The second column asks: What did I do for exercise today? This is important regardless of the lifestyle issue you are working on. The last column is at the far right: What was the dominant emotion I felt today?

You can see that there are other columns that focus on basic nutrition (water, fruits and vegetables, vitamin supplements), and I strongly suggest that you track those areas as well. There is also a blank column for you to add something that is important to your unique program. The point is to keep track every day of the lifestyle issue that you are working on: health and wellness, money and finances, and relationships, as well as your exercise and emotions.

That last column is key: your emotions. That's the most important part of the journal. Yet that's the column some people have the hardest time filling in. You know who struggles with it the most? Barges. Barges tend to be very rational, very collected, very much under control. They don't like admitting to their feelings, especially negative feelings. So they have a tendency to skip that step. But it's a mistake—just as it's a mistake for the Tugboats to record their emotions, but skip the columns for what they ate or how they exercised or how they spent their money. That's the Tugboats' tendency.

Make sure you fill in the whole log because when it comes time for Re-evaluation, you'll discover a tremendous correlation between how you behave and how you feel. For instance, Tugboats and heart-led Sailboats will notice that on the days when they felt sad or depressed or guilty, they were more likely to eat that second helping of pie, or the double-meat cheeseburger with the super-size fries. They were more likely to charge the two extra blouses and skirt ("Because they were on sale, you know"), even though they didn't need new blouses or a skirt. Meanwhile, Barges and head-led Sailboats may notice that on the days when the relationship column records entries like "Argued with wife," or "Forgot to pick up daughter from soccer practice," the dominant emotions will be things like anger, or frustration, or disgust.

The log helps you pay attention to your feelings, which most people don't do very well. As a result, their feelings get the best of them. This is because you can't deal with your feelings if you're not even aware of them. As Bill is fond of saying, you either have your feelings or your feelings will have you. And that's what the log reveals. It shows how much your feelings influence your lifestyle: what you eat, how you spend your money, and how you treat those around you. By becoming aware of that correlation, you stand a better chance of interrupting unhealthy, hurtful, and damaging habits, and replacing them with healthy, positive, beneficial habits instead.

Are You Being Loved to Death?

Now I can't talk about Execution without coming right out and telling you what your biggest challenge is going to be. And to be honest, I wish I didn't have to write this part of the book, because what I'm going to say is hard to talk about. But by now you know I'm a straight shooter. So here it is: your biggest challenge to following through with the ALTER model, and especially Execution, will be your family, friends, co-workers, and all the other people who care about you. I hate to say it, but that's a fact.

Hear me out on this. I'm not saying your family and the others don't love you, or that they don't have your best interests at heart.

They do (at least, I hope they do). But that's the problem. They love you so much that they actually don't want to see you change. Oh, they may not like the fact that you're so overweight they have to give you a special chair at the dining room table because the normal ones can't hold you. Or that you practically bankrupt the family every year when buying Christmas presents. Or that your sarcastic manner has become completely insufferable. Believe me, they can't stand those things and would give anything to see them go away.

But what if making your bad habits go away and replacing them with good habits meant that you started behaving and thinking differently? What if it meant that you began to set some boundaries that those other people were not allowed to cross? What if your newfound ways placed demands on them? What if it meant that you began relating to them differently? What if the "new you" began to make the people closest to you feel a bit uncomfortable about their own habits?

All of that and more will happen when you ALTER your life. This is why the people closest to you will put up the greatest opposition to your efforts at change. Yeah, they'd like to see some surface changes, for sure: drop a few pounds, spend a little less, be a little more polite. But when it comes to living your life in a fundamentally different way, they have a vested interest in keeping you the way you are.

Especially your momma. Make no mistake, no one will ever love you like your momma. Her love is so great, she'll love you to death. I mean it! If you're not careful, she'll kill you with kindness.

That's how it was with my momma. She loved to see us put that food away because it tasted so incredibly good. By the late 1970s I had gotten up to 315 pounds and my doctor said I wouldn't live to see forty. So I made up my mind to change my ways. And guess who I told about my plan? That's right. I said, "Momma, I'm going to lose one hundred pounds."

"No you're not, honey," she said. "Why, everybody in our family has been fat for as long as I can remember. It's just the way we are. And you know we can't help that because we've got slow metabolism, and we're big-boned, and several of us had a big thyroid. It's the same for you, and you just can't help it. You're stuck."

Momma loved me so much. She didn't want me trying something that was certain to fail. Which is why she was utterly shocked when I actually lost the weight. Actually, I think she was kind of angry about it.

So then I decided to do something I'd always thought about doing, but never thought I could do until I lost the weight. "Momma," I told her, "I'm going to run a marathon."

Again, Momma loved me so much. She didn't want me trying something that was bound to fail. So guess what she said? "I knew a guy that did that, and he died."

You see the point? Even the people who love us most, like our parents or spouse or best friend, will resist our efforts to do life differently. Sometimes it's because they are like my momma and just have a negative way of looking at things. Other times it's because they have a hard time respecting boundaries.

For example, say you decide to eat half as many desserts as you're used to eating. That way you'll cut your sugar intake in half. It's a challenging goal, but you've decided it's a doable goal. So what happens when you go to your Aunt Mabel's for Sunday dinner? Why, she brings a warm cherry pie into the dining room after dinner, and everyone oohs and ahhs over the smell of it. Then she plops a big gallon of vanilla ice cream on the table and starts dishing out dessert. And everyone begins passing plates.

So here comes a heaping serving of cherry pie à la mode your way. In your mind you're thinking, "Uh-oh, today's one of the days when I'm supposed to skip dessert." So you pass the plate to your brother. But then here comes another one. This time, you're going to have to take a stand.

Now let me just say that right there, in that moment, is where a lot of folks lose the battle. Especially if they are a Tugboat or Sailboat who leads with an M. They don't want to offend anybody, and they assume that saying no will offend. A Barge doesn't have that illusion. A Barge will just say, "I don't like cherry pie," and be done with it. But those lovable Tugboats and M Sailboats know that their Aunt Mabel loves them almost as much as their momma. So how are they going to say no to that special someone who stayed up late the night before to make that cherry pie—and did it especially for them?

One way the people-pleasers will try to justify what they are about to do is to think, "It won't hurt to give in just this one time." Notice that they are willing to compromise their own interests, but unwilling to risk offending someone else's interests. Another way they'll justify giving in is to play a game of Next Time: "I'll go ahead and have this pie today, then I'll skip dessert tomorrow and the next day, and that will catch me up." In other words, they'll be weak now but somehow doubly stronger the next time and the next time. What are the odds they'll follow through on that "plan"?

Look, when you establish a 91-day goal for yourself, realize that no one can execute the 91-day plan for you. Only you can do that. So you're going to have to be kind of selfish if you expect to pull it off. Because lots of people around you are going to come up with all kinds of reasons why you don't need to follow through on your goal. They will not have to live with the consequences even though they may dismiss your attempt as trivial and not worth pursuing. They'll call it unrealistic. They'll ridicule it by joking about how *they* are not trying to live that way. They'll even make excuses for you if you can't think up any of your own. They may even try to impose their way of doing such a plan. But you must resist the temptation or pressure to comply, as this is *your* customized plan, and it will work if you stay true to it. As I say, you've got to be a bit selfish. You've got to draw a line in the sand and say, in effect, "No! This is my boundary. I'm sticking to it." I'm not saying to be mean or rude about it. But go ahead and do something for *you* for a change. Because it's your life and your well-being at stake.

If you don't, Aunt Mabel will kill you with kindness. Because if you take that pie, you know what's going to happen next? Everyone's going to wolf it down and tell Aunt Mabel that that was just the best pie ever. And you especially are going to tell her that, because you feel guilty for almost saying no to that pie, and because, once you did accept it, it tasted so darn good! And when Aunt Mabel hears your compliments and sees your smile, guess what she's going to say? "Well, dear, let me cut you another piece. Oh, I insist! No, no, I've actually made two pies, so there's plenty. Look, your brother's going to have some more, too. I'll just cut a little piece for you. And there—there's a little smidgen of ice cream to top it off. Would you like a little more coffee to go with that?" Bye-bye good intentions!

If we allow them to, the people who love us most will love us to death. That is why the ultimate key to ALTERing your lifestyle is to stand up for yourself. Your *self*: what do *you* want? How do *you* want to live? What is in *your* best interest? You've got to love *yourself,* even more than your momma and Aunt Mabel love you. In fact, sometimes loving yourself means saying no to Momma or Aunt Mabel or your spouse or your parents or your children or your teammate or even your best friend. When you do that, you're really not saying no to them, you're saying yes to yourself. You're saying, "Yes, I want to lose that sixty pounds I need to lose. And my goal for doing that is to eat half as many desserts. So when Aunt Mabel offers me cherry pie, I'm going to say yes to my goal, because I'm not going to deny my own needs just to keep Aunt Mabel happy."

By the way, there are ways to say yes to your goal without offending Aunt Mabel. For instance, you might just tell her straight out what's going on: "Oh, Aunt Mabel, this pie really does look delicious. You always do make the best pies. And I know you made it because you know it's my favorite. But I'll tell you what. Right now I'm on a plan to eat dessert every other day, and of all the luck today's the day I'm supposed to pass on dessert. Could I ask you to wrap me up a piece so that I can enjoy it tomorrow?"

I know, I know. If you say something like that, ten faces will be looking at you as if you are crazy. Heads will be shaking. Eyes will be rolling. And next thing you know, everyone will have a reason why you should have that pie anyway. I've seen that movie. I'm telling you, your loved ones and co-workers will be your biggest challenge to sticking with your plan as you commit to ALTERing these Real Life Management issues.

But so what if they don't understand? So what if they doubt you'll succeed in your weight-loss program, your financial plan, your new business venture, or whatever. It ain't their life! It ain't their decision. It's *your* life and *your* well-being. So stand your ground. Say yes to *you* for a change. And know that just by declaring your intentions and laying everything on the table, you are putting everyone on notice that they may be seeing some different behavior out of you from now on. That's good! It's a way of telling them to respect you and honor your boundaries. Doing that will make it easier the next time you say yes to yourself in a way that says no to them. You can mark my words: when you stand up for *you* and then later that evening fill out your journal, you will feel victorious and not guilty. I promise!

And let me just add that if you want to, you can blame everything on Wayne: "Yeah, I'm reading this book by a guy named Wayne Nance, and he says I gotta do my goal for 91 days." I like that strategy because it will get everyone talking about Real Life Management and the 3-Minute Survey and the ALTER model. In fact, you can make a copy of the 3-Minute Survey and give it to others, or send them to www.RealLifeManagement.com to take the survey online. I'm all for that. And people can deal with that. Shoot, if people didn't mind when you started eating nothing but carbohydrates, and later they didn't mind when you ate nothing but protein, and later they didn't mind when you started drinking all those meal replacements and taking good food supplements and counting fat grams and calories, why would they mind if you pass on a piece of pie because of something Wayne Nance said? They won't. They'll just figure you're on to another fad.

So what? You and I know differently. You and I know that this isn't about a quick fix. This is about ALTERing your lifestyle and developing habits you can practice for the rest of your life.

I'm with you all the way! But you've got to get going. And the time has come to get going. It's time, my friends. It's time for *Execution*. Not to talk about it anymore. Not to make plans for it anymore. Not to be "fixin'" to do it anymore. But to actually *do* it.

So let's go!

CHAPTER 10   **The Lifestyle Ladder**

We've come to the last letter in the ALTER model, "R," which stands for *Re-evaluation*. Re-evaluation means looking back in order to look ahead. You look back at what's happened in your 91-day plan in order to look ahead and make a new plan for the next 91 days.

"Oh, I never look back," someone will say. "I only look ahead. The past is the past, and there's nothing I can do about it. Best to take whatever comes today and start preparing for tomorrow."

Well, now, that's just dumb, if you'll pardon my saying so. I mean, I'm all for not getting stuck in the past. And I certainly think it's wise to live life today, as well as to prepare for tomorrow. But the problem is, you can't prepare for tomorrow without evaluating your past because your past holds a lot of clues about what's going to happen tomorrow. People who never look back to find those clues keep doing the same dumb things over and over. They're like Bill Murray's character in the movie *Groundhog Day*. They never actually get to the future, they just keep repeating the past. And so they never make progress in their life. Which is ironic, because that's the very thing they are trying to avoid—getting stuck in the past! But they *are* stuck.

I'll tell you what someone who skips this step of Re-evaluation looks like. My co-author Bill Hendricks has three daughters. Over the years, his girls have enjoyed keeping pet rats. I know that may sound repulsive to some readers. So I have to assure you that Bill's family doesn't live in some shack with a dirt floor where rats come and play. No, these rats have always been kept in a cage, with clean bedding and fresh water and wholesome rat food. Bill says rats actually make great pets. They are very friendly and quite smart, and will actually come when they are called. And, unlike hamsters or hedgehogs, which are boring because they just sit around and sleep all day, rats are very active and playful.

One of the activities rats love the most is to run inside an exercise wheel made of wire mesh. They'll get in that wheel and run for hours. Really fast, too. Their little legs will just grab those wire bars and spin that wheel like there's no tomorrow.

Now people who skip Re-evaluation are just like those rats running their wheel. They may be running really quickly, *but they're not going anywhere.* That wheel just spins. There is no forward motion. It just goes around and around. And people who never re-evaluate their 91-day plan never move ahead in ALTERing their lifestyle because they just keep making the same dumb mistakes over and over. I know, because I kept doing that for years—making the same dumb mistakes over and over.

The crazy thing is, people who keep making those mistakes will get all frustrated about not getting anywhere and tell you, "See! It's not working! I'm doing this stupid 91-day thing that Wayne Nance told to me to do, and nothing's changing! Nothing's happening! I've tried it, and it hasn't worked!"

Well, let me tell you what works. We know that if the rat runs around and around inside the wheel, that wheel is not going anywhere, and neither will the rat. But if you take a pair of wire cutters and snip the wheel on either side and flatten it, you now have a ladder instead of a wheel. And if you place that ladder up against a shelf, the rat can climb up the ladder onto the shelf.

That's what Re-evaluation does. It snips the wheel you've been running in and creates a ladder for you to climb and actually make progress. You move up. And if you keep extending that ladder by Re-evaluating your efforts every 91 days, you can move a long way up. All the way, in fact, to a whole new you. I promise that you can.

That's how it has worked for me. That's how it has worked for lots and lots of people I've been privileged to help over the years.

I call it the Lifestyle Ladder, because it's just like climbing up a ladder. With each step you make incremental progress toward exercising control over your lifestyle.

"But Wayne, I don't want to climb a ladder. That's a lot of work. Isn't there some way I can just take an elevator to the top? I mean, I know someone who had that LAP-band surgery, and he lost 220 pounds overnight. He didn't climb any ladder, and now he looks great!" Well, goody for him, but I don't care what he looks like *now*. I want to know what he's going to look like in twenty years. Because I'll say it again: the only plan worth pursuing when it comes to your lifestyle is a plan you can follow for the rest of your life. LAP-band surgery is a quick fix. It's dramatic, so people think it "works." But no quick fix works if it doesn't address the real issues that got you fat in the first place—namely, your attitude and emotions. So even if you carve off 100 pounds today, you'll put 110 pounds or more back on unless and until you change the way you make decisions about food and exercise and the other areas of health and wellness. The same principle holds true for your finances and relationships.

The key to Re-evaluation is the log you've been keeping during your 91-day plan. I hope you've been keeping it. Recall that in the last chapter I said that the people who keep that log make progress in ALTERing their lifestyle. Those who don't go nowhere. In fact, they usually drop out. As a result, nothing changes for them.

The log holds clues for four vital steps of Re-evaluation:

1   *Celebration:* notice where you succeeded and cheer yourself on.
2   *Examination:* evaluate what's working and why, as well as what's not working and why.

3   *Introspection:* become aware of the connection be-
      tween your feelings and your behavior.

4   *Revision:* set a new 91-day plan on the same issue or
      on another lifestyle management issue.

Let's take these in turn.

1. Celebration

I mentioned a moment ago that Bill has three daughters. His
youngest daughter plays the violin. She started when she was about
four years old, and she was fortunate enough to begin on what's
called the Suzuki Method. Suzuki gives students a step-by-step ladder for learning the violin or piano. Suzuki was developed in the
1940s by Dr. Shinichi Suzuki, a Japanese music professor, and today it has a worldwide following.

The very first thing a Suzuki teacher will teach a little child is
simply how to stand. That's all! I mean, the smallest ones don't
even hold their violins at first. They just learn the proper way to
stand, so that they'll be ready when they do start holding their in-
struments. To do that, their teacher creates a little chart with the
student's footprints on it, so the child can practice placing her feet
properly. There's even a little song that the child learns to reinforce
the proper stance. That one behavior may take up two or three lessons. But it's the first thing the student learns. Very, very basic.

So then along comes a recital, at which there may be twenty-
five or thirty students who are scheduled to perform. The very first
students on the program are the youngest ones who have only
learned to stand. They come up and place their little footprint chart
in the floor, and they take a bow, and they stand the right way, and
they sing their little song, and when they are finished they take a
bow. And guess what happens? The audience goes nuts! Lots of
applause and cheering. The parents absolutely love watching their

little ones do their thing. Not a big, complex thing. Just a simple, basic thing. The very first step in the Suzuki Method.

Now there's a lesson in the Suzuki Method for you and me as we work our 91-day plans. It's the lesson of Celebration. We've got to make a big deal out of the things we've done right in our plan, the things that worked. No matter how simple or basic. We've got to give ourselves a big cheer and a round of applause for accomplishing those steps.

"Oh, Wayne, that's silly. The things I did right in my plan are so small and so few that they're not really worth mentioning, let alone celebrating. Okay, so big deal, I made a goal of having fruit instead of ice cream for dessert two nights a week. Guess what? I did that for two whole weeks out of the thirteen in the plan. Whoop-ti-do! Find a way to celebrate *that*, okay?"

If that's what you're thinking, can I point something out? You, friend, are defeated before you're even started. You're skipping to the next step, Examination, and focusing immediately on what *didn't* happen, and letting that discourage you. Do you think the Suzuki Method would help kids learn to play an instrument if it focused on all the things the kid is doing wrong? I mean, imagine if that little child got up there in front of everybody and did her little curtsy, and planted her feet on those footprints, and sang her song, and took a bow, and when she was finished everyone started booing and shouting and telling her, "What a lousy performance! Is that all you can do? Why, you didn't even hold your violin. You didn't play a note. In fact, you didn't even stand straight. And your feet weren't exactly inside the outline of the footprints. You're terrible! You're never going to play an instrument. You might as well quit now."

What do you suppose would happen if the Suzuki audience did that? Well, I would hope the authorities would step in and arrest the whole lot of them and charge them with child abuse. Because that's what it would be. If children heard their teacher and parents doing that, they would never, ever take another violin lesson in their life. They'd be crushed. They'd be defeated.

Yet that's exactly what you're doing to yourself when you disparage your success in eating fruit a couple of nights for two of the thirteen weeks in your 91-day plan. You're abusing yourself emotionally, every bit as much as that fictitious audience I just described. And in fact, I'll tell you plainly that a lot of people struggling with obesity, with money problems, and with their relationships grew up in abusive situations. They had parents telling them, "You're no good! You're never going to make it! You're never going to amount to anything!" They were kids who brought home report cards that had mostly A's and B's and C's, but what did the parents dwell on? Yeah, the D's and F's. The focus was on the failures. They were kids who played nine innings on their Little League team, thereby helping their team to a win. But instead of cheering the win and celebrating their kid's great effort, what did the parents dwell on all the way home? Yeah, the one catch that the kid dropped, or the one strikeout he had out of the five times he was at bat. The focus was on the failures.

Let me tell you something about the Lifestyle Ladder: when you first get going, you don't climb very fast. That's because you're like the little kid who's never played a violin before. She doesn't know how to hold it. She doesn't even know how to stand in order to hold it. She's got to learn some new habits. And if she's like me, she's not going to learn them overnight.

So who says she has to learn them overnight? Who says you have to unlearn all the bad habits you've accumulated in your life, and substitute good ones for them, overnight? You don't! That's the great thing about the Lifestyle Ladder. Nobody says how fast you have to climb it—except you. *You* get to decide that. So if it's four nights of fruit out of 91, that's great! Celebrate that!

Oh, oh, what's that? What did you say? You think you ought to be having fruit more than just four days out of 91? Because you think that would benefit you more? Wow, terrific! That's great! If that's where you'd like to get to, I can help you with that. I'll do that when we get to step 4, Revision. But don't let the thought that maybe you should be shooting for higher goals cause you to disparage the more modest goals you've succeeded at in your previous 91 days.

In fact, here's what I want you to do. Get out your journal. Go through it with a pencil and circle or underline or in some way highlight all the things you did that you consider a success. Indicate everything that you think worked for you in the previous 91 days. If your goal was to work out on a given day, and you worked out, highlight that. If your goal was to hug your kids every morning and tell them you love them before you head out the door for work, highlight all the days on which that happened. Wherever you achieved a goal, in whole or in part, indicate 'that in the journal. And don't forget the emotions column!

Now step back and look at everything that you've highlighted. You're going to find yourself somewhere between two extremes:

(a)   *You did every goal you set out to do, or at least most
       of them.* In that case, congratulations! Well done!
       That's quite a feat, and here's what I want you to do. I
       want you to show your journal to someone you regard
       as a generally positive, upbeat person, someone who
       makes you feel good when you're around them (they
       might well lead with an I or an M). I want you tell
       them about what you've accomplished, so that you
       can hear them say, "Hey, that's great! Way to go!" It's
       very important that you hear their voice congratulating
       you and celebrating your success with you. Don't just
       rely on your own internal voice. Find an encourager
       and celebrate.[1]
              I'd also encourage you to come up with some

other tangible way to celebrate your accomplishment. I don't suggest going out to eat or buying yourself an expensive present! But maybe it's something simple like you and your spouse going to see a movie you've been intending to see. Or inviting some friends over for breakfast on Saturday. Or leaving work an hour early. Or playing a round of golf. Anything that to you feels like a reward for a job well done. Whatever you do, keep it simple. But whatever you do, make it intentional. Consciously, deliberately reward yourself for doing something positive for yourself. We don't celebrate our personal successes nearly enough in our culture, and it's one reason why we have a hard time staying the course when it comes to personal improvement. I mean, who wants to keep on setting and meeting goals if one's best efforts are met with a "so what"? So don't fall into the self-pity trap. Just keep on keeping on. As long as there is progress, celebrate, reset, and restart.

By the way, congratulations especially if you are a Tugboat. I say that because of all the scoring patterns, Tugboats have the hardest time sticking to a plan. So if you're a Tugboat and you accomplished most all of your 91-day plan, then you've done something especially noteworthy, because you've managed to overcome your natural tendency to *not* follow a plan. Why, you've ALTERed your lifestyle!

At the other end of the spectrum . . .

(b) *You didn't do any of the goals you set out to do, or at least very few of them.* If you didn't accomplish a single one of the goals you set out to accomplish, my bet is that you're feeling one or more of the following emotions: discouragement, fear, anger, frustration, depression, guilt, or shame. It's hard to celebrate much of anything if you're feeling stuff like that, isn't it? I'm not going to try and talk you out of your feelings. But I will say this: something mighty powerful must be keeping you from carrying out your good intentions. If you made an honest effort to work your 91-day plan and you didn't manage to accomplish a single goal, then I submit that there's something blocking you inside. In fact, whatever negative feelings you're experiencing may not be a result of not accomplishing your goals, but the other way around: maybe you didn't accomplish your goals because those negative feelings have got a stranglehold on you, perhaps rooted in stuff that has happened to you earlier in life. Don't you think it's worth consulting with a professional counselor to find out what that something is? Maybe that should be your main goal for the next 91 days.

Having said that, let me suggest another possibility, which is that if you can't find a single success among your intended goals, maybe you're being too hard on yourself as you look over your journal. Remember, I told you to highlight *any* goal you achieved, whether in whole *or in part*. Maybe you only accomplished part of a goal, but be sure you mark that as a success.

Let me give you a case in point. I know a man who had a goal of working out three days a week. He tried to do that for 91 days. He didn't work out a single day. But here's what his log showed: he took his gym bag with him in his car every workday, intending to work out in the afternoons. The log also showed that on the first day, he actually signed in at his health club, but realized he had no lock for his locker, so he left and bought a lock on his way home. Another day he signed in, but the pool was closed, and he had intended to swim. The log showed that on most of the other days, situations at work cropped up late in the day that kept him from leaving work to go work out.

Now technically speaking, that man didn't succeed at his goal on a single day of his plan. And yet, the log showed something important: he made the effort to work out on every single day by taking his gym bag and workout clothes. And on two or three days he actually went to his health club prepared to work out, even though he was prevented by circumstances from doing so. So how should he "score" himself? Well, while he didn't actually accomplish his goal, I would applaud him for taking steps in the right direction. (I'd also encourage him to do some Examination of what went wrong, as you and I will do in a moment.) Just by taking a gym bag, that man was doing something positive that he hadn't done for years. That counts for something. He should celebrate that, frustrating as it may be that he didn't follow all the way through on working out three days a week for 91 days. His success was partial and minimal, but it was success nonetheless.

Be careful at labeling yourself a failure. If you made an honest effort to work your plan, I'd be surprised if you didn't follow through on at least some of your goals, even just once or twice. And even if you succeeded just once or twice, or just partially, celebrate that success! How? By doing the same things I said above to the readers who accomplished all or most of their goals (go back and reread that section if you need to). Tell your successes to someone who can celebrate them with you. Make sure that person is really an encourager, not someone who will point out everything you didn't accomplish. And find a way to reward yourself for the handful of positive things that did happen in your plan. Just something simple: Ask for a hug from your spouse. Give yourself an extra hour of sleep. Take a bubble bath, or, if you're a guy, listen to the theme from *Rocky* or *Chariots of Fire*. Say a prayer of thanks. Whatever affirms you and marks your effort.

Remember the little child taking her first steps in the Suzuki Method. Her success is paltry compared to the kid who can play concertos by Bach and Mozart and Vivaldi. But why make such a comparison? They're both on the ladder. One just happens to be a few rungs higher up than the other. But you know what? That child who is higher up started at the exact same place on the ladder: learning to stand in the proper position. And when she was just starting out, and she did her little performance and took a bow at the recital, everyone cheered for her. Because she succeeded at a small thing—which was a big thing for her.

So who is cheering for you?

2. Examination

No matter how many or how few goals you accomplished in your 91-day plan, you need to figure out what happened. The place to start is with your successes, not your failures, because you first need to figure out what went right. And the first question to ask is: did you have a lot of successes, or just a few?

Let's say you succeeded at meeting all or almost all of your goals. Why do you suppose that happened? Now if you're a Barge or a head-led Sailboat, you're liable to say, "Because I'm such a naturally disciplined and responsible person. My motto is, 'plan your work, work your plan,' and that's what I did." Well, great. I would agree. Barges, as well as Sailboats who lead with a T, have a natural advantage in working a 91-day plan because people with those patterns just instinctively follow a plan. Life makes the most sense that way.

But now let me ask you a question. Whether you're a Barge or a Tugboat or a Sailboat, if you met almost all of your goals, is it possible that your goals were too easy? I'm not going back on all the things I've said about taking simple, tiny steps and shooting for small, incremental successes. Maybe that's what you planned for, and your plan worked brilliantly. But ask yourself: did your goals *stretch* you in any way? I mean, if your "goal" was to hug your kids every morning, and you've been hugging your kids every morning since the time they were born, how is that advancing you up the Lifestyle Ladder? I applaud you for practicing such a good habit, but I certainly wouldn't say you've made progress.

Making progress requires that you reach beyond your normal routines. Which means that sometimes you won't succeed. But guess what? It's not only okay, it's to be expected that you won't follow your 91-day plan perfectly. That's because you're trying to learn new habits. How many people trying to learn something new do it right the first time? I don't care whether it's learning to walk, learning to ride a bike, learning to drive a car, learning to have sex—everyone makes mistakes when they're first getting started. So if you're not making any mistakes as you pursue your lifestyle goals, you're probably not learning anything. In that case, try to set more ambitious goals that fit better with where you are on the Lifestyle Ladder.

Now what if you didn't achieve very many goals at all? Well, look at the ones where you did succeed. Are there any clues in the journal as to why success happened on those days, and not on the others? Go back to that example I gave earlier of the person who ate fruit instead of ice cream for dessert four days out of 91. His goal, remember, was to have fruit two nights a week, which comes out to 26 nights over 13 weeks (91 days). He managed four out of 26. The first question he needs to ask is not, "Why did I mess up on 22 of the 26 nights?" but rather, "How did I manage to meet my goal on those four nights?" Or, put another way, "What was different about those four nights?"

There are all kinds of possibilities. Maybe his family was out of ice cream on those nights. Maybe he and his wife went to their local farmer's market on those four days and bought a bunch of fresh fruit and vegetables, and that put him in the mood for fruit. Maybe he's a traveling salesman and spends a lot of time on the road, but those four nights he was home and had a lot more control over what he was eating. Maybe something good happened to him on all four of those days, and his mood was brighter and more hopeful than usual. Maybe those were the only four dinners of the past three months when he didn't get into an argument with his wife. Maybe those were the four dinners when he did what I suggested in chapter 9—to play a mental game with himself to help him follow through on his good intentions. And so on those four nights he picked up a banana or an apple, and he opened the freezer and said to the ice cream, "Look what I got here, pal! Sorry, but you ain't getting to me tonight. I'll be back. But for now you just stay cool in there."

Something *always* accounts for success—especially success in the 91-day plan. It's almost never just luck. Because when you're trying to develop new habits, it takes more than luck. It takes intentionality. It takes decision. So when you do succeed at following through on your goals, there's a reason for that. It may be a very practical reason. It may be a more subtle reason having to do with something inside you (we're going to talk about the emotional connection next). It may be a combination of reasons. But see if you can't put your finger on what was working *for* you when you succeeded at meeting your goals. (By the way, this will be especially helpful as you teach others lifestyle management skills.)

You know why I want you to do that? So you can seek out those factors in the future. That way, you stand a better chance of practicing the new habit you are trying to develop. For instance, if you discover that you're more likely to stay within your grocery budget when you don't have your five-year-old with you, then by all means find a way to shop without your five-year-old. A babysitter might even be cheaper! Or say you discover that not arguing with your wife at dinner correlates with your goal of eating fruit instead of ice cream. Then by all means find a way to not argue with your wife at dinner. It'll be the best diet you ever followed.

Okay, so once you've examined your successes, it's finally time to examine what didn't work and try to figure out why. Actually, you already know some of the reasons why, because the factors that account for your successes will invariably be missing when it comes to your lack of success. You will see that by the blank areas of your 91-day journal. Still, see if there are other reasons that account for not following through.

One of the most common is setting goals that are too ambitious. In a way, biting off more than we can chew is just another form of a quick fix. Many of us want to remedy our problems overnight, and so we create these impossibly difficult goals that require effort that, if we're honest, we've never in our life managed to expend.

For example, say you're tired of carrying that $8,300 in credit card debt. You've been making minimum payments on it, but not attacking the principal. So you decide you're going to start paying that sucker down. And to do that, you set a goal of paying $1,000 a month for eight months or so until the debt is gone. But when the first 91 days are up and you examine your log, you already know what you're going to find: you paid $1,000 during that first month, but by the second month your payments had fallen to $250, and by the third month you were down to just $95.

Now you could feel defeated and say, "It's not going to work." But a better approach would be to examine your credit card payments in light of your other financial obligations. If you've done step 1, Cash Flow Analysis, in the Plan for Financial Fitness (chapter 7), you should know how much money you have to work with in making monthly credit card payments. Let's say that analysis showed that realistically you can only afford to pay $185 at most toward credit card debt every month, over and above the interest payments. Well, then, make that your goal. The $1,000 goal is simply unrealistic, given your financial situation. You may not think that $185 is making much progress toward your larger objective of paying down your debt, but it's $185 more than you've been paying, and that *is* progress.

Bobb Biehl, an organizational consultant on the West Coast, says that people overestimate what they can accomplish in three days, but they underestimate what they can accomplish in three years. There's a lot of wisdom in that. It highlights the truth that there are no elevators by which to bypass the Lifestyle Ladder. You're either going to climb, step by step, up that ladder, or your lifestyle will remain unchanged. So if the process is step by step, then it only makes sense to pick steps that are manageable. Otherwise, you'll never make progress. You'll just get frustrated.

If you get frustrated enough, you'll get defeated, and then you'll probably drop off the ladder. That happens sometimes. Especially for folks who have lived their whole life with disappointment. Like I described earlier, they've had negative messages thrown at them, and they've had defeats. And so when they slip up and don't work their plan, they get into that mind-set that says, "See, I'm failing again. This won't work for me." And they just give up.

If that describes you, I challenge you to give yourself some grace and forgiveness, and say, "You know what? Today I struck out. Today I didn't play the game so well. But the good news is that I can go to sleep tonight and know that tomorrow morning the sun is going to come up, and I get a whole new chance at living my life." And so the next morning you get back on that ladder and you make some different decisions about how you're going to spend your day, what you're going to eat, how you're going to spend your money, how you're going to relate to the other people in your life. The key is coming back. The key is not giving up and letting disappointment defeat you.

Oftentimes whether or not people succeed at their goals boils down to some very practical realities. We saw an example of that earlier in the case of the man who kept taking his gym bag with him to work, but never managed to work out. Workplace commitments late in the afternoon kept sabotaging his efforts to get to the health club. He felt very frustrated, but in truth the problem was not with him, the problem was that his plan for working out in the afternoon was impractical. Given his work situation, it just wasn't going to happen.

So if you're seeing a lot of days in your 91-day journal when you lapsed in following your plan, consider whether your goal is practical enough. You're not going to swim laps on your business trip if you stay at a hotel with no pool. You're not going to set up a savings account for your child's college education if you have zero dollars left in your cash flow after meeting your current expenses. You're not going to have a "date" night with your daughter every week if she has commitments with school and homework every night of the week. The point is, be realistic, and don't be afraid that you might fail. You might. But if that happens, just get up and start again.

3. Introspection

It's easy to see the practical realities that keep you from succeeding at your goals. The more difficult factor to pinpoint is the connection between your feelings and your behavior. That's why I have you write down your dominant emotion for the day in your daily journal. If you've been faithful at logging that information, you've got a valuable set of data there by which to evaluate your emotional life.

The first thing to ask is, what emotions showed up the most during the 91 days? If on 63 of the 91 days the dominant emotion was anger, or sadness, or guilt, or depression, or whatever, what does that say about you? That's right, it means you're an angry person, or a sad person, or a depressed person, or whatever. Not a bad person. It doesn't make you bad to feel negative feelings. But it does mean you're a person who's got some negative feelings percolating away somewhere inside you. Were you aware of that?

Another key thing to pay attention to is this: what were the dominant emotions on the days when you lapsed in following your plan? For Barges and Sailboats who lead with a head letter, that dominant emotion will tend to be anger or fear (not always, but often). For Tugboats and Sailboats who lead with a heart letter, it will tend to be guilt (not always, but often). The point is that this analysis provides a very clear picture of how certain feelings will keep you from carrying out your goals. Were you aware that those feelings were blocking your progress?

But let's turn that around and ask, what were the dominant emotions on the days when you *succeeded* in following your plan? For example were you happy? Confident? Determined? Hopeful? Respected? This analysis may be even more helpful, because it provides hope. It shows that when you're feeling confident, or secure, or loved, or some other positive emotion, you can accomplish quite a bit.

That provides a strong incentive to seek out ways to bring those positive feelings into your life more often—perhaps by being more careful about whom you spend time with, or what activities you engage in, or the places you go, or the things you read, or whatever accounts for why you normally feel negative feelings. Feelings are a subjective response to what is happening to you.[2] So if you are feeling poorly, don't just say, "So-and-So is causing me to feel this way." That gives So-and-So way too much power. Instead, say, "I'm noticing that I am not feeling the way I want to feel when I am with So-and-So. What can I do differently to avoid feeling that way?"

This brings me to the issue of boundaries. I know I bring up boundaries a lot, but setting boundaries—both for ourselves and for others—is vital to carrying out the 91-day plan. In fact, a lack of boundaries is the main reason why Tugboats and Sailboats who lead with a heart letter (I or M) struggle the most with the 91-day plan. They love to please, they love to play, they're impulsive, they're impressionable. All of that adds up to a hard time saying "No!"

But the issue of setting boundaries isn't just about having a strong will, it's about emotions, as well. You see, the fact that a Tugboat or a heart-led Sailboat loves to please is not a bad thing. It's a great thing if they're in sales or customer service or some other line of work in which customer satisfaction is Job One. But what lies at the heart of that need and motivation to please? Their inborn attitude, for sure, but also some deeply rooted *feelings* that may or may not be serving the person well. For example, feelings of low self-esteem, or feelings of guilt, or feelings of worthlessness. Negative feelings like that are like acid on a person's will. No matter what their good intentions, they can be manipulated into going against their own best interests in order to satisfy someone else whose affection and approval they need.

That's one reason why I talk about boundaries so much. Boundaries are crucial because sometimes your friends and family are "negative encouragers," meaning they push or pull you in a negative direction. Unless you erect some boundaries and enforce them, those "negative encouragers" will lead you away from what is in your best interest—especially if you've got some negative emotions that are also contributing to the situation. For example, after you set a goal to work out three days a week, your friend will try to get you to not work out. "Oh, you work out all the time," they'll say. "Why don't you skip today and go with me to the movies?" That forces you to make a decision: are you going to follow through with your plan to work out, or is your desire to please your friend going to cause you to capitulate and go to the movies?

I'm not going to tell you which way to go. But I will tell you to look at your journal and see whether you have been enforcing your boundaries. What happened on the days when you didn't work out (if working out was your goal)? Did you get in your own way, meaning your own negative feelings sabotaged your efforts? Did your attitude get in the way, meaning you allowed yourself to be manipulated by outside influences?

There are times when you've got to be "selfish" for yourself. You've got to say yes for yourself, even if it means saying no to others. When I was on my weight-loss program to lose one hundred pounds, I decided I had to be ruthlessly faithful to my program. It was something I was doing for *me* for a change. Sometimes that meant disappointing other people. Leading with an "I," I didn't want to do that. So it was hard at first. But since then I've discovered that people were not nearly as disappointed as I thought they might be. In other words, my fear of disappointing others was worse than the actual disappointment they felt when I told them no.

4. Revision

There's only one reason to carry out the step of Re-evaluation in the ALTER model, and that's to move up a step on the Lifestyle Ladder. You take that step by formulating a new 91-day plan that takes advantage of what you've learned in the Re-evaluation process.

To this point, you've only looked back at what happened in the past. Now you're ready to look ahead and make plans for the future: "What new goals do I want to set for the next 91 days?"

Notice that you've got a lot of information and perspective by which to set those goals. You know a lot more than you knew 91 days ago about what works and why, and what doesn't work and why. You know a lot more about what you're capable of. You've seen how practical realities can either help or hinder you from reaching your objectives. You've seen how your emotions affect your performance, and vice versa. And you've seen how critical it is to establish and keep boundaries for yourself and others, in order to follow through.

In light of all that, your goals this time around should be that much more doable. Not that you won't have some lapses. You inevitably will. But hopefully you've learned a few things that will translate into fewer lapses and more successes.

Here are some questions to ask yourself as you formulate a new set of goals for the next 91 days:

- Is this goal challenging enough for me? Is it something that's going to stretch me toward developing a new positive habit? Is it a step beyond where I've been previously?
- Is this goal too ambitious for me? Do I need to make it a bit easier to accomplish, so that I'm more likely to have success?
- Do I need to set a completely different goal in this particular lifestyle area? Do I need some variety? Have I been doing the same basic activity over and over, to the point where it's become boring?
- Are there some practical realities I need to factor into this goal, in order to make it more achievable?

Once you've formulated your goals, step back and ask yourself, "Do these look like something I can realistically accomplish over the next 91 days?" Keep revising them until you can answer yes to that question. Then you're ready to get going on your next 91-day plan!

Now I can hear someone saying, "Wayne, this sounds like a lot of work." Well, maybe it does when we lay it all out in a book like this. But in real life, the Re-evaluation step is not much work at all. I mean, how much work does it take to think over your lifestyle for a half hour or so every three months? And you don't have to make it a chore. If anything, I suggest that you make it fun. Do it with a friend. Laugh a little bit together. Crack a few jokes.

You see, that's another thing Dr. Suzuki figured out about learning to play an instrument. If a kid hates the process, what are the odds she's going to stick with it? But if she's having fun, she'll improve every time. And over time, she'll be like Bill's daughter, who now loves to perform and will gladly play these very complicated violin pieces for anyone who asks. In about five or six years she went from learning to stand and learning to hold her violin to playing the Bach Double Concerto in D-Minor. She no longer has to think about how to stand, or how to hold the bow, or how to do the fingerings, or any of those other basics. There was a time when she did. But now they've become habits. They've just become part of what it means to play the violin.

That's exactly what happens on the Lifestyle Ladder. You take incremental steps over time that build positive habits that become part of your lifestyle. And your lifestyle starts to ALTER.

Look, I know that right now today a lot of readers are looking at people around them who are trim and healthy, and they're thinking, "I could never look like that." A lot of readers are looking at people who are debt-free and thinking, "That could never happen for me." A lot of readers are looking at families with happy relationships and thinking, "I could never have that."

Could I make a suggestion? Would you try to look at things through the eyes of a child? When Bill's daughter was just starting out on the violin, she wasn't thinking about playing the Bach Double. She just concentrated on getting her feet in the right position. That's all anyone asked of her. And when she got that part right, everyone celebrated wildly. Then she went to work on holding the instrument. That took a little bit of time and effort. But when she got that part right, everyone celebrated wildly. And so it went: she learned a new step, everyone celebrated wildly. On and on, up the ladder, until one day she was asked to learn the Bach Double. And she did. And when she was all ready and played it at her recital, everyone celebrated wildly.

There's not one bit of difference between you and Bill's daughter. You *can* regain control of your lifestyle. You just can't take an elevator there. You've got to climb a ladder. The best way to climb that ladder is the way a child does—one step at a time. No matter how tiny or basic those early steps might seem, you take them. And every time you take a step upward, you celebrate that. You celebrate wildly! And by that process you keep climbing and celebrating all the way to a whole new you. That's where the Lifestyle Ladder takes you.

One piece of advice, though: don't climb that ladder alone. Get a coach. I'll tell you how to do that in the next chapter.

CHAPTER 11

The Value of a Coach

Jack Nicklaus. Lance Armstrong. Jackie Joyner-Kersee. Michael Jordan. Joe Montana. Jerry Rice. Muhammad Ali. Chris Evert. Nolan Ryan. Ted Williams. Olga Korbut. Mark Spitz. Names like these practically define the term "world-class." These athletes were the best of the best in their game. To watch them compete was to see a work of art in the making.

What's interesting is that every single one of them had a coach. In fact, some of them had multiple coaches. Which is kind of odd, don't you think? I mean, here's an athlete who does something better than anyone else in the world. So how is it that he or she needs a coach? The coach can't play the sport anywhere near as well as the athlete. So what business does the coach have telling the athlete what to do?

The answer is: it's exactly the coach's business to tell the athlete what to do, because it takes proper coaching to produce a world-class athlete. No one's ever ended up at the top without one.

Now I'd pay attention to that. Because if the people with the greatest talent recognize that they can't win without a coach, certainly us lesser mortals will never win without a coach. Not that we're trying to hit a ninety-mile-an-hour baseball. Or win seven NBA championships. Or seven Tour de France races. No, we've got more modest prizes in mind. Like trying to quit spending as if there's no tomorrow. Or learning how to get along with the person we married. Or eating more of the food that God created and less of the junk that the fast-food industry creates.

Those objectives would seem to be a lot easier than strapping on boxing gloves and climbing into the ring with Joe Frazier, right?

Yet, my, how we struggle to reach them! Well, here's a piece of advice: we'll do better if we find ourselves a coach.

A coach is someone who wants us to win, and helps us find a way to win. Isn't it obvious that that's whom we need? We keep making the same dumb mistakes over and over because we don't, in fact, know what we're doing. We can't even see what we're doing half the time, because we live inside our skin. We need someone from the outside to point out what we're doing right, and to show us a better way when we're doing something wrong. That's what a coach provides—objectivity, along with the determination that one way or the other, we *are* going to win.

Let me tell you about the guy who jump-started my efforts to ALTER my lifestyle. I've told you the story about how I lost a hundred pounds. What I haven't told you is that it took a coach to get me there. You see, when I decided I wanted to lose 100 of the 315 pounds I was carrying, I did what most everyone does. I went on a diet and I started working out. And by golly I lost fifty pounds! And gained it right back, and then some.

After doing that a few times, the thought occurred to me: "Maybe there's something here that I don't understand." Isn't that a brilliant insight? So I went to a health club and found an exercise physiologist with a Ph.D. I don't know why a Ph.D. was running a health club, but he was, and he was very busy. I had heard that he did fitness coaching on the side. So I told him I wanted to lose about sixty pounds. He looked at me and said, "Mr. Nance, I don't know that I can help you. I've talked to a lot of people like you before, and to be honest, I really don't have time."

I was in shock! I couldn't believe he didn't want to help me. I guess most people would have just walked away at that point. But, you know, I have that "I" as the first letter in my scoring pattern, so I at least had to try again. "No, no, I'm serious," I said. "I need someone to help me lose some weight."

Well, of course, he had a scoring pattern, too. And even though I didn't have the 3-Minute Survey back then, I think you can guess what sort of pattern he probably had: he was a big old Barge. So he didn't have any problem telling me point-blank, "Look, I really can't help you. I mean, it would require you to do exactly as I tell you to do, and you'd have to stick with it for a long time. And I've been doing this for thirty years, and most of the people who come in and say they want to lose weight never do. So by now I'm just tired of people not listening to me, so I really don't make time for that anymore."

Well, I could see that he didn't have a knack for sales. But I do, and by now he'd activated every motivation inside of me to get him to say yes. So I stood there at the counter looking at him, and I asked a third time. I said, "Sir, you don't understand. I drove forty-five minutes to come up here to ask you for help, because I heard you're the man who can help me. I know you've given me all the reasons why most people fail, but I'm not most people. I'll work your program. I'll do exactly as you say. I got a lot of problems, but not keeping my word ain't one of them."

Can you see what he wanted to find out? He wanted to know whether I was serious. He didn't want to waste his time on someone who didn't want to win. Who wasn't *willing* to win. You see, when it comes to taking control of a lifestyle area, like weight, there's four kinds of people in this world: Thinkers, Talkers, Stalkers, and Walkers.

A Thinker says, "You know, I've been *thinkin'* about being thinner for years." But that's all he does, is think about it. He doesn't do anything about it. A similar type of person is the Talker, who says, "Wayne, just the other day my spouse and I were *talkin'* about going on a diet." But that's all it is—talk. No action. And then you've got the Stalkers, the people who are always "lookin'" for that perfect solution to their lifestyle issue. "If I ever *find* that program, that diet, that exercise equipment, or whatever it is that's going to solve my problem, I'm sure going to get it." But what they don't tell you is, "The reason I haven't done a blessed thing about my problem is that I haven't found that perfect solution yet." And they never will, because of course it doesn't exist.

The only people who make progress in their lifestyle problems are the Walkers. They don't just talk about their problem, or just think about it, or keep wandering around "lookin'" for the perfect solution. No, they walk the walk. They get after it. They gain Awareness of their attitude, they Learn about the lifestyle area they're trying to fix, they get a practical and Tactical plan of action, they Execute that plan, and they regularly Re-evaluate how they're doing in order to improve their efforts and move up the Lifestyle Ladder.

That Barge who was an exercise physiologist with a Ph.D. wanted to know whether Wayne Nance was a Walker. It's a fair question to ask. You see, when you ask people to devote time and energy into helping you develop different habits, you're asking a lot! Because there are going to be days when you don't want to be there in their program, and you're asking them to put up with you anyway. There are days when you're going to complain and say, "This is too hard!" and you're asking them to push back and keep you on task. There are days when nothing seems to be working and you just want to give up, and you're asking them to pick you up and somehow find a way to win.

Walkers are the only kind of people that a coach wants to work with. And so that exercise physiologist asked me what my goal was. I told him I wanted to lose weight. I told him I needed someone to help me do that because I didn't understand nutrition or exercise or any of the other stuff involved, and that was because I hadn't done anything physically since football in college, and that was twenty years earlier.

He heard me out. He thought about it for a minute. Finally he said, "Here's what I'm going to do. I'll take you on for three weeks and see whether you're for real. I want you to come back next Monday, and I'll have an index card waiting for you at the front desk. I'm going to write on that card all of the exercises that I want you to do, and how many reps, and how many days a week. I'm also going to write on another card what I want you to stop eating and what I want you to start eating. You have to do exactly what I tell you. And between now and Monday, I want you to read a book called *Fit or Fat*, by a guy named Covert Bailey."

So that's how I got started with a coach. He wasn't the most inspirational coach, that's for sure. But that was okay, given my scoring pattern. I didn't need inspiration. I needed boundaries. He was great at setting boundaries. In effect, he was telling me up front, "Wayne, you won't be in control of this program. I'm in control of this program. You're in charge of doing it." That's what I needed to win in my lifestyle "game"—someone to set the boundaries and point me in the right direction.

If you're a Tugboat, or if you're a Sailboat who leads with an I (like me) or M, then you especially need a coach, and especially one who will set boundaries. Remember what I said in the last chapter, that people like us love to please and love to play and we're impulsive? That means we have a hard time setting boundaries. So we need another person—a coach—to help us create proper boundaries and give us that extra determination we need to stick to them.

Now when I talk about a "coach," I don't necessarily mean a paid professional who makes a living by coaching people using a formal program or process. That Ph.D. was a professional coach, and sometimes a professional coach is just what you need.

For instance, in the health and wellness area, there are fitness trainers, nutritionists, weight-lifting coaches, swimming coaches, running coaches, sports psychologists, yoga instructors, and many more. Your doctor is also a type of professional coach. In the area of money and finance, you can find financial planners, insurance agents, debt counselors, estate and family lawyers, accountants, investment advisors, consultants, business mentors, stockbrokers, bankers, real estate agents, and others. As for relationships, many couples and families turn to counselors, psychologists, pastors, and ministers. Some companies have relationship coaches, as well, who coach business leaders in areas of leadership, teamwork, mentorship, and sales development. In fact, an entire industry has grown up around the idea of Customer Relationship Management (CRM).

All of these are examples of professional coaches who get paid for their services. But there are also informal coaches. And in many ways an informal coach is more valuable than a paid coach, because if they help you, they're doing it for more than money. They're probably doing it because they care.

That's good news if you don't have any money. Just because you can't pay someone to coach you doesn't mean you can't find a coach. Why, there are potential coaches all around you. So let's say you're like I was when I weighed 315 pounds, only you can't afford to join a health club and hire an exercise physiologist like I did. That's okay. What about your niece who works out all the time and is in great shape? Do you think she'd be willing to show you a few things and go over your 91-day plan with you? (By the way, a coach doesn't have to be older than you; they can be younger.)

Or say your finances are a mess, and you really don't have a clue as to how to even get started on a cash flow analysis. Well, how about your uncle, the lawyer who handles all of your family's business matters? I'll bet he'd be willing to sit down with you and show you a few basics. He'd probably be thrilled to walk with you as you work your 91-day plan.

Or what about in your marriage? You already spend hours on the phone every week talking with your best friend about the troubles in your relationship with your husband. Is it possible to make those conversations more productive by asking your friend to coach you as you work on some of your goals?

By the way, you don't have to call any of these people a "coach." That's just a term I use to explain the role they play. But you can call them whatever you want to: coach, guide, mentor, trainer, teacher, friend, buddy, accountability partner, or taskmaster. Whatever you call them, just make sure that they fit the definition of a coach: someone who wants you to win, and helps you find a way to win.

You can significantly increase the odds of that happening by finding a coach who complements your scoring pattern. So how do you know whether coaches' scoring patterns are compatible with yours? By having them go through the 3-Minute Survey. Ask them to fill out a copy of the survey printed in this book, just as the instructions explain. When you have their pattern, you'll know a lot about how you and that person would interact if they started coaching you.

For instance, if you're a Barge and your prospective coach turns out to be a Tugboat, you'll probably get frustrated with him (if you aren't already), because you won't feel that he brings enough structure and discipline to the process. If you're a Tugboat and your prospective coach turns out to be a Tugboat, too, you'll become fast friends with her (if you aren't already), and you'll love being with her, but you probably won't make as much progress as you need to because she won't push you hard enough.

In the main, the people who make the best coaches are Sailboats, because Sailboats are the most adaptable. If they're a Sailboat who leads with a T, they'll bring a lot of structure to the process. If they're a Sailboat who leads with an R, they'll probably bring a lot of wisdom and insight to your efforts. If they're a Sailboat who leads with an I, they'll make the process fun and keep you pumped up. And if they're a Sailboat who leads with an M, they'll pay a lot of attention to your needs and how things are working for you.

One combination to definitely avoid is a coach whose scoring pattern is identical to yours. Oh, you'll understand each other perfectly. But when you're working on a lifestyle issue, you need someone who supplies motivational strengths that you don't possess.

Hence the Tugboat who is trying to get recovery from her addiction to chocolate needs someone besides her Aunt Jane, who is also a Tugboat and makes the best brownies in town. Likewise, the Barge who is trying to re-establish communication with his teenage son needs someone besides the fellow executive at his company who is even more of a Barge, and is also in the middle of a very nasty divorce. Identical scoring patterns can empathize, but they can't catalyze change because they're prone to make the same mistakes that you keep making. That's why you get along so well!

Now I can't talk about this matter of coaching without throwing down a challenge to every reader: just as you need to find a coach, you need to become a coach yourself. Maybe not a formal, professional coach. But at least an informal coach to someone who needs what you have to offer.

"Me?! I don't have anything to offer," I can hear someone snickering. Hold on. Take another look at your scoring pattern. Whatever it is, it reveals a contribution that you have to make to someone else. If you're a T, someone in your life could benefit from your ability to plan. If you're an R, someone needs help thinking through an issue they are struggling with. If you're an I, someone is waiting for a playful person like you to come along and brighten his day and set his mind in a more positive direction. And if you're an M, someone could use your compassionate insight into people and their needs.

Every pattern has a contribution to make. So, conceivably, every pattern could be useful in coaching someone somewhere about something. You just have to open your eyes to see who that someone might be, and make yourself available to be useful to them.

Several years ago, my co-author Bill Hendricks and his dad, Howard Hendricks, wrote a book on mentoring (which is another word for coaching) titled, *As Iron Sharpens Iron: Building Character in a Mentoring Relationship*. In the research they did for their book, they talked with men who were forty and younger and found that almost all of them were eager to find an older mentor. But when they talked to men over forty and asked them if they would be willing to serve as a mentor, a majority of them felt that they were not qualified to be a mentor. They said they didn't think they had anything to offer. How interesting, that the younger men had more faith in the older men than the older men had in themselves!

My other co-author, Keet Lewis, is also an expert in this area of mentoring and coaching. He has years of experience working with leaders in a wide variety of industries and organizations as a life coach. In fact, Keet's network is so extensive that I think he could parachute into any place in the United States, and probably even around the world, and it would take him all of about two hours to find someone who is a friend of someone he has poured his life into. He has literally touched thousands of people in this special way.

It just goes to show that you don't have to have a Ph.D. to be someone's coach. What you mostly have to have is a desire for someone to win, and a willingness to help them find a way to win. So I want to challenge you that if you'll invest a little time in someone who wants your help, walking with them as they try to establish some habit that for them is hard but for you seems easy, you'll be amazed at how much impact you can have.

You may think that you have nothing to offer because your own life is out of control in some area, and so what business do you have giving advice to somebody else? But that misses the point.

Your hardwiring endows you with some degree of strength in some way, and if you come alongside somebody else and offer that strength to them, you will be amazed at how much you gain out of that relationship, not just how much you give.

I'm very serious about this challenge, because in truth all of us are already in the role of a coach with someone somewhere, whether we realize it or not. I'm a father with a wife and three daughters. Don't you think I have a role in my family to help the four women in my life succeed? I attend a church in my community. Don't you think there are men there whom I could be influencing in a positive way, especially as they work on their lifestyles? I'm the founder and president of Real Life Management. Don't you think I have some responsibility to find ways for all the people associated with RLM to win?

The same is true for you. In your family, your workplace, your neighborhood and community, all around you are people who need to benefit from what you have to offer. They're waiting for you to act like a coach. Not so much to give them advice as to point out what they're doing right, and to show them a better way when they're doing something wrong.

And you know what? When you're helping someone else succeed, it causes you to think differently about your own life. Imagine people looking to you—yes, *you*—as they work on some area of their life. Wouldn't that inspire you? Wouldn't that be a boost to your confidence and self-esteem? To know that you *matter* to someone, that they are gaining strength because you've invested in that person?

Friends, I guarantee there's someone in your world who is struggling with something that seems impossibly out of their reach. There's the person at your office who lies awake at night wondering how she's going to pay off her credit cards. There's the guy in your church who won't live to be forty because he can't get his weight under control. There's the partner you play golf with who'd give anything to regain the respect and affection of his wife and kids.

For countless people, the one thing that will spell the difference between tragedy and victory is a coach. So why couldn't that coach be *you?*

A Word About Real Life Management Coaches

Real Life Management (RLM) formally trains and certifies individuals to use the 3-Minute Survey and other tools of the RLM system to do professional coaching in fields such as financial planning, fitness training, nutrition, business development, education, and relationship counseling, to name a few. Visit www.RealLife Management.com for more information about finding a certified RLM coach or to be trained as an RLM coach.

CHAPTER 12 Navigating Your Real Life Journey

I ended the previous chapter by encouraging you to serve as a coach to someone you know. Coaching is a form of leadership. So let me turn my attention to readers who are in formal positions of leadership.

By "leaders" I mean parents, teachers, school administrators, business owners, managers, supervisors, consultants, public servants, community officials, ministers, preachers, rabbis—anyone who is in a position of leadership anywhere in our society. If someone is following you or looking to you for any kind of leadership, then you qualify as a "leader."

To you I have this to say: whatever it is that you are trying to accomplish, the lifestyle issues I've raised in this book dramatically affect that objective. This means that you have a vested interest in helping your followers take responsibility for their lives and gain control of their lifestyles.

I have described three kinds of boats in this book, and given steps for how each of the boats can ALTER their lifestyles. However, the most exciting and interesting part of anyone's life journey is navigating Real Life. Real Life is much like the sea. It comes at us in many different ways during a twenty-four-hour period, and sometimes it hits us without warning. There are storms, high winds, and rolling waves, as well as calm waters and beautiful days when it's pure bliss to navigate the ocean.

The key for you as a leader is to learn to use your own attitude in a positive way as you lead other boats in maneuvering on life's waters. The last thing you need is a storm brewing in your life, or a collision with other boats.

You may be self-employed, a corporate executive, a minister, a college professor, a financial planner, a trade specialist, an administrative assistant, or a stay-at-home mom. Ultimately, your position doesn't matter. What matters is, can you use the skills, attitude awareness, and reality check that you have encountered in this book? The good news is, yes you can. The journey has just begun for you.

Attitudes and beliefs have a dramatic impact on our homes, our schools, our churches, our corporations, and our organizations on a daily basis. We take our attitude and the way we live life into every place we go.

That's why it's so important that we start thinking about ourselves as our number one customer, and everyone else in our life as a secondary customer. If we don't manage or ALTER our own attitude first, we can't help or serve others in our daily life. Of course, when I say "number one customer," I'm not telling you to place yourself above God. I'm just making the point that you can't help others until you first ALTER your own attitude to find the proper balance between your head and your heart.

Assuming you are doing that, let's look at the importance of your attitude in several arenas of Real Life. (By the way, Bill Keet and I have developed an educational CD program entitled *How to ALTER Your Life Without Changing Who You Are*. This program and our online reports will reinforce what you have learned in this book and allow you to connect it to the following areas.)

At Home

I believe a great way to have an abundant home life is to have all of your family go through the 3-Minute Survey. Then talk as a group about what your patterns reveal—what your individual needs are, and how your head and your heart combine to make you who you are. I believe you will discover a new appreciation for each other's wiring, and as a result new insight into the way each of you looks at money, at food and health matters, and at relationships. Each of you is different, not wrong. It is so important to recognize and serve each family member's needs. And to be a great leader, you must first learn to be a great servant. If you give more, you will get back more.

At Work

People take their weight issues, their health issues, their financial issues, and their relational issues to work every day. Many organizations and corporations ask me to talk to their groups on topics such as leadership, management, team building, time management, and sales and service. Whenever they do, they always ask me for a list of topics for my talks. I always tell them, it's the same for every topic: "Who is Your Number One Customer?"

The irony of those issues in corporate America is that the struggle people face in all of those areas results from their underlying attitudes. Your job as a leader is to take your attitude to work and impact in a positive way all of those people who are under your authority. First become the best leader you can be, whether in sales, service, team building, or whatever. Then help others around you.

You may be saying at this point, "Wayne I am not a leader or a salesperson." My response is, "There goes your attitude again!" We are *all* in sales—selling ourselves—and we can all be leaders and set examples for those at work, because our co-workers are all our customers. If you want to find the best way to improve your company and its performance in the areas we've discussed, give the 3-Minute Survey to your boss, your co-workers, your employees, and even your customers, clients and vendors. Doing so will give you—and them—substantial insight into their needs and their unique wiring. You may find that you have not been working with these people in the most effective ways. Remember, to be a great leader or a great team player you must be a great servant first.

At Your Place of Worship

I frequently visit with ministry leaders, Sunday school teachers, and executives of many religious organizations. They ask, "What does this stuff about attitudes have to do with the things our churches teach?" My answer is, everything! In a church, just as in a business, it is important that leaders understand their inborn attitudes, as well as the inborn attitudes of their ministry leaders. Frequently churches discover that they have placed someone with the wrong wiring in a given job—for example, a Tugboat handling the church's books, or a Barge trying to teach K–5 children (which requires much patience), rather than working on the endowment or the building fund.

If you are a leader in a church, give the 3-Minute Survey to your church staff and ministry leaders, and train them in turn to give the survey to their Sunday school classes or Bible study groups. Doing so will help you learn to appreciate people's strengths, and also see some of their challenges. It will help everyone learn to interact with one another and maximize each other's strengths and minimize each other's weaknesses.

If you have responsibility as a church counselor in the areas of marriage, parenting, or financial stewardship, use the 3-Minute Survey as a tool to help people understand themselves better. If you are working with children who are at least thirteen years old, they are old enough to take the survey and will respond to it in a positive way. Remember, Tugboats and some Sailboats who lead with an I or an M tend to struggle with financial stewardship. Barges usually do not. By using the survey, you'll be able to see how the stress of money and lifestyle issues is impacting Tugboats, Barges, and Sailboats alike, along with their families.

Schools and Universities

I frequently have opportunities to teach about attitudes and the boats in high schools and universities. Unfortunately, many high school seniors and college graduates are leaving schools today a little fatter than when they enrolled, due to fast food. They're also in debt, due to credit cards. (Remember that the Hidden Agenda Drivers [HADs] I spoke of in chapter 5 are financially rewarded for these negative consequences.)

I encourage both faculty and students to take the 3-Minute Survey, because what's being taught about lifestyle management in American schools does not go nearly far enough. We need to start educating young people about the real life issues of health, money, and relationships, because we are turning out graduates who are more obese, more in debt, and more troubled in their relationships than any previous generation in America.

Organizations

Civic, corporate, sports, and nonprofit organizations might ask, "How does this stuff about attitudes impact our group?" The answer is that you are recruiting individuals from all walks of life to get involved in your organization. Every one of them brings a unique attitude to the situation. It's no secret that quarreling, unrest, and problems recruiting people plague many an organization. From my perspective, those problems are sourced in having the wrong people in the wrong slots. For example, you'll have Barges trying to do recruiting, which is not their long suit, rather using Tugboats and Sailboats to do that job. Or you'll have Barges trying to control everything and run the organization as if it were their own company, which is tough when you have a lot of volunteers. Meanwhile you'll have Tugboats overcommitting to everyone and not controlling their stress or time management.

If your organization wants to maximize what you have learned in this book, take the time to have every leader, committee chairperson, board member, and volunteer go through the 3-Minute Survey. Then use people's patterns to make sure they are in the correct job for their wiring. Once everyone is in their correct job, start appreciating everyone's strengths. We should avoid setting people up to fail by asking them to perform tasks that are not a good fit with their God-given wiring.

In the Financial Industry

I have thirty-four years of experience in and around the financial industry. I've concluded that the reason Americans struggle in managing their money is because they don't understand their attitude about money, they lack education about money, and they are dealing with a financial industry that they fundamentally don't trust.

During the past seventeen years, I have trained or surveyed more than five thousand financial planners, stockbrokers, and insurance agents. More than 50 percent of them were Barges. That's significant, because of the people who buy financial services and products that I have been able to survey nationwide (that's more than 40,000 people), 65 percent were Sailboats and Tugboats. Can you see the problem? Representatives from the financial industry use terms like "trust," "risk tolerance," and "customer-friendly," when in fact they don't understand the attitude of the buyers and how it disconnects with the attitude of the financial advisor and/or salesperson. Our research at RLM suggests that the financial industry is losing between 35 percent and 50 percent of its potential sales because of "attitude mismatch" between advisor/salesperson and consumer.

If you are in the financial industry, or if you are a financial consumer, I encourage you to give the 3-Minute Survey to your staff or management, or to family, so that you understand their financial attitude. Then refer them to the 10-Step Plan for Financial Fitness in chapter 7. If 85 percent of Americans are essentially retiring broke in a country that has abundant wealth and financial products at its disposal, we'd better start looking closely at the attitudes of both the financial industry and the consumer.

In the Health and Fitness Industry

Many health care professionals who treat stress, cancer, heart disease, diabetes, and other lifestyle-related conditions are reading this book. However, we are all consumers when it comes to protecting our health. RLM's research shows that Tugboats and Sailboats who lead with an I are the most at risk for obesity, which is a major contributor to diabetes, heart disease, cancer, and other conditions. Those people are asking themselves at this point, "What do I do? I've tried all the diets and failed, and no one at home, at work, or anywhere else seems to understand the way I feel."

Well, now you've got good news for them. You can show them your 3-Minute Survey results, then give them the 3-Minute Survey. When you do, you will understand clearly why they don't understand and relate to you. This will not only allow you to be accountable to yourself, but will create a bridge of communication on the topic. Then go to the 10-Step Plan for Health and Fitness (chapter 6) and use it as a daily checklist.

If you are a health care professional, or a personal trainer, or some other professional who works with people to help them lose weight, you should know that approximately 50 percent of the public are estimated to be Tugboats and Sailboats who lead with a heart letter, I or M. Those people don't respond to rigid rules and diets. They simply will not follow them. Give your patients and your clients the 3-Minute Survey, and you will quickly see why they resist your efforts and fall off the wagon again and again.

It is time that we all come together to understand the consumers' attitudes in health care. Everyone already knows they should do things like exercise, eat a healthy diet, and minimize stress. But we are not doing those things as a society. I think I know why: the health industry is not paying attention to the attitudes of its clients. Or of the health care professionals themselves, I might add.

In the Counseling Industry

If you are a counseling professional or the client of a counselor, I want you to know that I saved this topic for last. As someone who has been through years of counseling myself, has in turn counseled with many individuals, and has also trained many counselors and psychologists to use the 3-Minute Survey, I have learned how critical it is to start understanding very early in the counseling process what the inborn attitudes of a person are. Doing so saves time and money, and it gives the counselor a direction for working with the client most effectively. Properly using the 3-Minute Survey will allow for quicker connecting and decrease the client drop-off rate.

From Crisis to Control

The reason leaders need to lead is because there's a crisis in America. That's the first thing I said in this book. I pointed out that we've got a crisis in our health: 67 percent of us are overweight. We've got a crisis in our finances: 85 percent of us will retire broke. We've got a crisis in our relationships: over half of us are divorced, or, if still married, "psychologically divorced." In short, too many of us are fat, broke, and unhappy. Clearly, there's a crisis in America!

But I insist that things don't have to stay that way. At least, they don't have to stay that way for anyone who doesn't want to live that way. Anyone can regain control over their lifestyle. The key is to start paying attention to their attitude.

In doing that, they'll need to redefine success. I'm tired of— no, I'm flat-out angry at—all the "magic" solutions that I see advertised on TV and in the media! All those quick fix gimmicks for losing weight and making money and transforming our love life. We need a new definition of success when it comes to lifestyle management. All those "magic" solutions make it sound as if we can have the heart and body of a twenty-four-year-old Marine. We can have the bank account of a Bill Gates. We can have a marriage and family like *The Sound of Music*.

But that's not realistic for most people. Most of the folks I've encountered through my RLM workshops over the past seventeen years are working with some tremendous disadvantages because of poor decisions they've been making throughout their life. Those poor decisions don't make them bad people, just people who've made bad decisions. So what does success look like for them? Well, it means now, having started to pay attention to their attitudes, they are developing a habit of, say, eating fresh fruit instead of ice cream or cake. A habit of eating grilled chicken instead of fried. A habit of paying cash instead of charging it. A habit of paying themselves first. A habit of paying attention to the boundaries in their relationships. A habit of asking for their spouse's input before making major decisions.

Things like those are *successes*. They may not sound like much. But they're actually a big deal, because they pay off in spades over time, and because a person can do them for the rest of his or her life. Success is not how many pounds you lose, it's the way you take control of your lifestyle. Success is the way you *decide* to live your life. It's all about living on purpose and being in control of your lifestyle.

Let me leave you with a basic truth: Today's Choices are tomorrow's Reality. That means that if you keep making little decisions day by day that are not in your best interest, then you pretty much determine your tomorrow. Tomorrow you'll have that bypass surgery. Tomorrow you'll have diabetes. Tomorrow you'll have that heart attack. Tomorrow you'll lose that house. Tomorrow you'll wish you could afford the elder care you need. Tomorrow you'll miss the companionship of marriage. Tomorrow you'll wish you had a decent relationship with your kids.

See, there's really no big mystery about what tomorrow is going to bring. All you have to do is look at how you're living today, and the choices you are making today. Yes, today's Choices are tomorrow's Reality.

But of course, it works the other way, too. By making small decisions today that *are* in your best interest, you basically are investing in a brighter future. Those little, positive steps add up to a whole new lifestyle—an ALTERed lifestyle.

One word of caution though: you can just assume that you're going to have setbacks as you walk that ALTER path. You can just count on making mistakes and having days when you really mess up.

But now here's some good news: even though you may not follow the ALTER model perfectly, that doesn't change the fact that the ALTER model works. It works! The more you work the ALTER model, the better your life gets.

Woody Allen once said that 90 percent of life is just showing up. That's definitely true in lifestyle issues. Some days I show up to my fitness center, and I don't have such a good workout. In fact, some days I don't particularly want to go to begin with. But if I do go ahead and show up and just do something, I never regret it. Never! I've never left the fitness center and thought, "Well, that was a waste of time." In fact, just the opposite: every time I've left, I've said, "Boy, that felt great! I'm glad I went." Ninety percent of life is just showing up, and the point is that staying on the wagon toward lifestyle management is not about perfection, it's about progress. *Any* progress counts for success—even if it's just learning a better way to eat a potato.

I think I would have given up a long time ago, except that a friend taught me five tips for hanging in there instead of caving in to discouragement:

1   *Be willing to take a risk.* If you're not falling off the
    wagon occasionally, it's because you're not on the
    wagon in the first place! The only people who don't
    slip up are the ones who aren't making any effort.
    You've got to risk the small likelihood of failure in
    order to pursue the great probability of success.

2   *Stand up for something you believe.* If you believe that
    you need to get your money under control, or you
    want your family to take a new direction, or you want
    to change jobs, or whatever your goal is, you've got to
    take a stand for that. Down here in Texas we've got
    the Alamo. You'll remember that before the big battle,
    Commander William Barrett Travis took his sword
    and drew a line in the dirt and said, in effect, "If you're
    with me, come across the line. If not, get out now."
    That's how you need to be about your lifestyle. You've
    got to draw a line in the sand and say, "This is what
    I'm doing. This is good for me and my life and my
    family. So either get on board with that, or leave me
    alone." Which brings us to . . .

3   *Don't associate with negative people.* That may be
    easier said than done, because a lot of us are in the
    shape we're in precisely because we've surrounded
    ourselves with negative people, people who are always
    running us down, always nay-saying, always giving us
    reasons why things won't work, why we can't do it,
    why we won't succeed. We need to find a new set of
    cheerleaders, and a new set of fans who are like those
    parents at the Suzuki recital: people who will just clap
    and cheer and go nuts with joy over every tiny step we
    take.

4   *Be willing to pay the full price.* You can't get some-
    thing for nothing. You have to pay for everything, and

that includes your lifestyle. How much you're willing to pay determines how much your lifestyle will be AL-TERed. Paying the full price means doing all the steps, not just the easy ones.

5   *Have faith in God's wiring and yourself.* You've got to believe in yourself. Sir Edmund Hillary was the first Westerner to climb Mount Everest. He tried three times and failed. His fourth try succeeded. Afterward, well-wishers praised him by saying, "You've conquered the mountain!" Hillary replied, "No, I've conquered myself."[1] Conquering yourself may be a far bigger challenge than conquering any debt or weight or relational issue. In fact, it may be the victory that makes all other victories possible, because the people who succeed are the ones who see themselves succeeding. What is it you want to accomplish in your lifestyle? Then imagine yourself doing that—and *believe* you can!

In the end, my message to you, reader, is this: you have intrinsic worth. God wired you just the way you are. You are made in His image, and there is a purpose and plan for your life. And if God thought that was good enough, then that's good enough for me, too. More than anything else, I want you to feel good about who you are.

But it's hard to feel good about yourself when your lifestyle is out of control, isn't it? I'm telling you that can change. I'm not saying you should change who you are. I'm saying you can change the way you live. You do that by joining the community of the self-controlled. You do it by ALTERing *your* lifestyle, starting with *your* Attitude. Yes, you *can* ALTER your life without changing who you are.

REAL LIFE MANAGEMENT℠

Books, Workbooks and CD/DVD's

Real Life Management (RLM) offers a wide variety of resources for ALTERing your lifestyle, as well as helping others on their Real Life journey. To find out more, visit us at: www.RealLifeManagement.com. Click on PRODUCTS.

Speaking and Corporate Training

RLM provides a variety of corporate training in the Real Life Management system and its use in areas such as:

- Sales and Marketing
- Customer Service
- Team Building
- Leadership Development
- Hiring
- Management
- Financial Planning
- Managing Change

Wayne Nance and the ABC's of Real Life Management program provide the tools necessary to understand the attitudes and beliefs of your employees and marketplace. He is a nationally recognized speaker and trainer on managing your life to its fullest potential. Wayne is a gifted communicator and will connect with your audience in a humorous style. For information on having Wayne Nance or one of his associates, Bill Hendricks or Keet Lewis speak to your group, please e-mail: Bookings@RealLifeManagement .com. To find out more, visit us at: www.RealLifeManagement .com. Click on SPEAKING & TRAINING.

Real Life Management Licensee Programs

Corporate and Organizational Licenses are available so that your entire organization may benefit from the 3-Minute Survey and the RLM system. Individual Licenses are available for those in sales, counseling, mentoring, consulting, financial planning, fitness training, or other professions who would like to become a certified RLM advisor or coach. Contact us by e-mail: Licensing@ RealLifeManagement.com. To find out more, visit us at: www .RealLifeManagement.com. Click on OPPORTUNITY.

NOTES

Introduction

1 Letter from Doug Harper, cited in Danielle DiMartino, "Reader Shares Concern About People Overloaded with Debt," *Dallas Morning News*, July 12, 2004, p. 4D.

2 "McVISA Cardholder Way Over Her Mclimit," *The Toque*, http://www.thetoque.com/020416/mcvisa.htm.

Chapter 2

1 Heavily but not exclusively. Our early experiences, especially our parents' child rearing, also have an important influence on our approach to life.

2 I am not saying that there are only 32 types of people in the world. Ultimately, every person is unique—one-of-kind. But the scoring pattern is a step toward beginning to understand a person's uniqueness. Actually, there's a great deal more about individuals that we can say from their scoring pattern. However, in this book I am only giving an introductory, "top-level" explanation.

3 To be fair, you can find all four of the lead letters represented in virtually every occupation there is. My point in spelling out specific occupations for this and the other lead letters is to show that the strengths of each letter predispose someone to do well in occupations that call for those strengths.

Chapter 5

1 Jonathan D. Klein and Steve St. Clair, "Do Candy Cigarettes Encourage Young People to Smoke?" *British Medical Journal*, August 5, 2000, pp. 321, 362–365. Also available at http://bmj.bmjjournals.com/cgi/content/full/321/7257/362.

2   Walter C. Willett, *Eat, Drink, and Be Healthy: The Harvard Medi-
    cal School Guide to Healthy Eating* (New York: Simon & Schuster,
    2001), p. xxx. Dr. Craig Lambert, deputy editor of *Harvard Maga-
    zine,* has called Willett's book "arguably the best and most scientifi-
    cally sound book on nutrition for the general public."

3   Linda Stewart Ball, "In Couple's Life, a Huge Weight Has Been
    Lifted," *Dallas Morning News,* September 26, 2005, p. 8B.

4   See "Child Abuse Can Last a Lifetime," *Facts of Life: Issue Brief-
    ings for Health Reporters,* vol. 4, no. 2 (March 1999), at http://
    www.cfah.org/factsoflife/vol4no2.cfm. This Web page features an
    interview with Dr. Vincent J. Felitti, head of preventive medicine at
    Kaiser Permanente, a managed care organization in San Diego,
    California. Felitti has tracked the effects of "adverse childhood
    experiences" including physical or sexual abuse and living with a
    violent, alcoholic, or mentally ill parent, for 20,000 patients of
    Kaiser.

5   Ball, "In Couple's Life," p. 8B.

6   Bill Clinton, "I Was a Heart Attack Waiting to Happen," *Parade
    Magazine,* September 25, 2005, p. 4.

7   Tamara Holub, "Credit Card Usage and Debt Among College and
    University Students," *ERIC Digest,* at http://www.ericdigests
    .org/2003-2/credit.html.

8   Lucy Lazarony, "Credit cards teaching students a costly lesson," at
    http://www.bankrate.com/brm/news/cc/19980605.asp.

9   A June 2001 GAO survey reported that the average undergraduate
    student loan debt upon graduation is $19,400. Cited by Tamara
    Holub at http://www.ericdigests.org/2003-2/credit.html.

10 Cited by Tamara Holub at http://www.ericdigests.org/2003-2/
    credit.html.

11 I would welcome the opportunity to partner with a researcher or
    research group to scientifically sample the population and deter-
    mine the relative distribution of the various scoring patterns yielded
    by the 3-Minute Survey, among other studies.

12   1 Corinthians 6:20.

13   The FDA has an excellent Web page explaining how to read food labels at http://www.cfsan.fda.gov/~dms/foodlab.html.

14   Laura Beil, "Pound for Pound, Top Diets Don't Differ," *Dallas Morning News,* January 5, 2005, p. 1A.

15   Source: Wikipedia.com

16   Cited by Jonathan Shaw, "The Deadliest Sin," *Harvard Magazine,* March–April, 2004 p. 36.

17   Source: BrandCameo at http://www.brandchannel.com/ brandcameo_films.asp.

18   Michael Leeson, screenplay, *The War of The Roses,* 1989.

19   Leeson, *The War of The Roses.*

Chapter 6

1   Adapted from "Stretching: Focus on flexibility," at http://www .mayoclinic.com/health/stretching/HQ01447.

Chapter 7

1   A 2002 annual survey by FindLaw.com, a legal Web site, found that 57 percent of Americans do not have a will.

Chapter 8

1   You can give the 3-Minute Survey to kids of any age. My belief is that their attitude is certainly hardwired by the time they can read and write. So they have an attitude. Obviously, the older they get, the more aware they become of that attitude, and the more accurate will be the results of their 3-Minute Survey. Hint: teens especially like the 3-Minute Survey because it's quick, it gives them insight, it's positive, and it's fun. You can find a copy of the 3-Minute Survey at the end of chapter 2, or go online to www.RealLifeManagement.com

2   If you want more information about using your 3-Minute Survey scoring pattern to identify jobs that fit you, consult our Web site at www.RealLifeManagement.com. If you are seeking in-depth career

guidance and life planning, contact the Giftedness Center at www
.thegiftednesscenter.com.

Chapter 10

1 I wouldn't mind hearing about your success myself. You can e-mail
   me at Success@RealLifeManagement.com. I'll be glad to cheer for
   you!
2 I don't want to discount the fact that some feelings arise from phys-
   iochemical processes in your body and brain. For example, depression is known to have a chemical basis associated with it.

Chapter 12

1 Steve Young, *Great Failures of the Extremely Successful* (Los Ange-
   les: Tallfellow Press, 2002), p. ii.

ACKNOWLEDGMENTS

The first two people I want to acknowledge and thank for their help with this project are my co-authors, Bill Hendricks and Keet Lewis. Bill is a successful author in his own right and president of The Giftedness Center of Dallas. He has worked tirelessly to word-smith, edit, and produce the manuscript. Without his talent and degrees from Harvard University and Boston University, the book would not be the quality that it is.

Meanwhile, Keet Lewis has become a valued friend over the past several years, as well as a big fan of the 3-Minute Survey. Keet has made countless special contributions to the book and to Real Life Management (RLM). He has tested our concept extensively and counseled me on rolling it out nationally. He has helped me develop our Web site and licensing system, spent untold hours revising the manuscript for the book and played the key role in taking the RLM message to both the corporate and Christian (church and parachurch) markets.

Way to go, guys! You're the best. I will be indebted to you for a lifetime.

Closer to home, there's no question that this book could never have become a reality without the love and loyalty of my wife, Shannon. She unselfishly allowed me to spend seventeen years traveling the country researching and speaking on the RLM topics. Likewise, my daughters Christel, Melissa, and Kara missed a lot of their dad's attention because of my absence, but they have loved and supported me anyway. I am the luckiest man in the world to have these four women in my life.

Special thanks go to my business manager, Clyde Bright, in Nashville, Tennessee. Clyde believed in me when many others did not and has given me more than ten long years of support on this journey.

Thanks, too, to my stockholders who believed in me and put their money behind this project, to do the research and publishing.

Thanks to Mel Berger, my agent at William Morris, for believing in me, in my writing team, and in our message.

Finally, I want to thank Nancy Hancock and Cherise Davis, my editors at Simon & Schuster, for being such vital champions for this book. Your belief in this project has meant so much.

Wayne E. Nance

INDEX

ABOUT THE AUTHORS

Twenty-nine years ago **WAYNE NANCE**'s life was completely out of control. He weighed 315 pounds and smoked two packs of cigarettes a day. His marriage was dissolving, and his finances were bottoming out. Wayne reached inside himself and discovered that there was a correlation between his obesity, poor money management, and unhappiness.

Today, Wayne is a trimmed-down success story. He is a sought-after speaker and author on managing your life to its fullest potential. It's a power he says is within us all, and one that we all can harness, starting with a 3-minute commitment.

Wayne was a financial advisor for more than 25 years, but his passion was researching this link between obesity, financial strain, and relationship meltdown. This brought him to the creation of Real Life Management, a company dedicated to providing the education that isn't taught in school, at church, or at home on weight, money, and relationships, and how these three main components of life are connected. He's carried out the company's mission through his acclaimed books, *Mind Over Money* and *Liten up for Life,* his Real Life Management CD/DVD Educational Series, national seminars, and media appearances.

"For seven years, I studied with stress psychologists, sports nutritionists, and a personal therapist developing and researching these findings," says Nance. "What we learned is that lifestyle issues stem from inborn attitudes and beliefs that account for eighty percent of our personal choices—attitudes and beliefs most of us don't even realize we have. To really make a difference, we don't need to change who we are, only alter our attitudes."

Wayne soon left his successful career in the financial industry to follow his passion of educating businesses and families on the way attitude impacts obesity, financial management, marriages, and parenting.

Born and raised in Texas, Wayne still resides in the Lone Star State with his wife, and daughters Christel, Melissa, and Kara. His "ABC's of

Real Life Management" program is currently utilized by top corporations, organizations, institutions, and church groups throughout the United States. There isn't a topic his Real Life Management program can't address.

WILLIAM HENDRICKS is president of The Giftedness Center, a Dallas-based consulting firm specializing in organizational effectiveness and strategic people management. Bill and his colleagues are able to identify not just what people *can* do, but what they *love* to do and will instinctively do by virtue of their natural, inborn motivational bent, or *giftedness*. Bill is the author or co-author of seventeen books, and his writings have appeared in the *Wall Street Journal,* the *Dallas Morning News,* and numerous other publications. He holds an undergraduate degree in English from Harvard University, a master of science in mass communications from Boston University and a master of arts in biblical studies from Dallas Theological Seminary. He is the proud father of three amazing daughters, Brittany, Kristin, and Amy, by his late wife Nancy.

J. KEET LEWIS is an inventor, entrepreneur, international management and marketing consultant, CEO coach, speaker, and trainer. As a CPA and consultant, Keet spent eight years in the financial services, real estate, and investment banking industries and then for more than ten years he served as the president and CEO of a manufacturing company. Keet is the managing partner of Lewis Group International, as well as an executive officer and/or director of several diversified companies, Christian ministries, and public policy organizations. He has served on the staff of Campus Crusade for Christ and as Chairman of the Deacons at Prestonwood Baptist Church. He is an active Southern Baptist layman serving on several Southern Baptist Convention and Southern Baptist of Texas Convention committees. He is a graduate of the University of Texas. He lives in Dallas with his wife, Margaret, and daughters Caroline and Cannon, and Cannon's husband Gavin Todd McClintock.